The International Coffee Agreement

Bart S. Fisher
foreword by
Isaiah Frank

The Praeger Special Studies program—
utilizing the most modern and efficient book
production techniques and a selective
worldwide distribution network—makes
available to the academic, government, and
business communities significant, timely
research in U.S. and international economic, social, and political development.

The International Coffee Agreement
A Study in Coffee Diplomacy

Praeger Publishers   New York   Washington   London

PRAEGER SPECIAL STUDIES IN INTERNATIONAL ECONOMICS AND DEVELOPMENT

PRAEGER PUBLISHERS
111 Fourth Avenue, New York, N.Y. 10003, U.S.A.
5, Cromwell Place, London S.W.7, England

Published in the United States of America in 1972
by Praeger Publishers, Inc.

© 1972 by Praeger Publishers, Inc.

Library of Congress Catalog Card Number: 73-170270

Printed in the United States of America

For Margaret

International commodity arrangements have a long history, much of it a tale of failure and frustration. A notable exception is the International Coffee Agreement, which, despite the storminess of its ten-year life, must be declared an impressive achievement.

The checkered experience of most efforts to regulate commodity markets on a world scale can be largely explained by the diversity of objectives they are intended to fulfill and by the conflicting stakes of the parties at interest.

In the case of coffee, the avoidance of sharp short-term price fluctuations is a goal upon which both producing and consuming countries could readily agree. Not so noncontroversial, however, has been the question of the longer-term trend in coffee prices. Although the rich consuming countries have tacitly accepted the goal of assisting the producing countries by improving their terms of trade, sharp conflict has arisen over the extent to which the coffee agreement should be used as a vehicle for transferring resources from rich to poor countries. And closely related to the latter issue is the question of how the agreement should be employed to encourage diversification in the producing countries as a long-term solution to the problems caused by their heavy dependence on coffee exports.

As difficult to cope with as the diverse goals of the coffee agreement have been the conflicts among the producers themselves over market shares. Here, one of the major problems has been to construct a mechanism for the control of coffee exports that, at the same time, would afford scope for changes in quotas, to reflect underlying shifts in national supply capabilities, as well as in shifts in demand, e.g., among particular types of coffee.

Bart Fisher's study is a pioneering effort to illuminate these and other issues in both the original negotiation of the International Coffee Agreement and in its subsequent administration and renegotiation. In exploring how the various conflicts were resolved, Fisher employs an interdisciplinary approach, skillfully blending economic and political analysis. In addition, he provides the reader with a lively sense of the numerous practical problems that had to be surmounted in administering and enforcing the Agreement. The work constitutes an important contribution to our understanding, not only of the International Coffee Agreement but, also, of the more general problems encountered in international efforts to regulate commodity markets.

Isaiah Frank
William L. Clayton Professor of
International Economics
Johns Hopkins University

A commodity agreement is an implausible construct in which producers and consumers cooperatively regulate a market.

Two sets of tensions inevitably arise in a commodity agreement: conflicts among producers over market shares and conflicts between producers and consumers over price levels. It is, then, not surprising that such agreements have rarely been very successful.

An exception is the International Coffee Agreement (ICA), the subject of this study. The rich and the poor countries alike frequently allude to the ICA as a "prototype" for future commodity support arrangements, and the renewal of the accord in 1968 was strongly supported by both producing and consuming members. These two facts are solid evidence of its success.

How can the success of the ICA be explained? That is the question that forms the central thread in this study.

The answer has economic and political aspects. Coffee is economically "right" for a commodity agreement, as it is the subject of an inelastic demand, is produced largely in the developing countries, and has no close substitutes. Equally important, however, was the willingness of the participants in the ICA to agree at crucial moments.

This study focuses on the latter point—the politics of the International Coffee Organization (ICO). How and why did the members of the ICO resolve their differences? What were the swaps, concessions, deals, packages, and negotiating gambits used as Band-Aids to hold the ICA together?

Three chapters are presented as a prelude to consideration of the Agreement. Some economic aspects of the coffee problem are discussed in Chapter 1 to provide a background for the problems of the regulated market. A brief description of earlier attempts to regulate the coffee market is given in Chapter 2. An attempt is made in Chapter 3 to explain the economic and political problems faced by export quota arrangements.

The last seven chapters explore problem areas of the ICA in depth.

Chapter 4 discusses the 1962 United Nations Coffee Conference (UNCC) which set up the ICA.

Chapter 5 examines the politics of price regulation. It analyzes the conflicts between the exporting and importing members of the Agreement by focusing on their response to the 1963/64 price rise, caused by weather conditions in Brazil.

Chapter 6 explores enforcement, which is always a bugbear for commodity agreements. The sources of "tourist coffee," an intriguing name for coffee shipped outside of the quotas of the ICA, are traced back to the company level.

The politics of quota revision are treated in Chapter 7. The quota reallocation crisis was resolved by an ingenuity unmatched in the history of commodity agreements, which saved the accord for the remaining two years of its duration.

The 1968 ICA, the treaty that currently regulates world trade in coffee, is described in Chapter 8.

Chapter 9 is addressed to the soluble coffee controversy between the United States and Brazil.

The last chapter evaluates the effectiveness of the ICA in the areas of price-maintenance and stabilization, enforcement, and structural reforms and suggests ways in which the Agreement can be improved. This problem is particularly timely, as the ICA may be renewed in 1973.

This study covers only a part of the "politics of coffee." National internal coffee policies have been discussed only as they relate to the ICA.

Certain aspects of the 1962 ICA have not been dealt with as completely as I might have wished. Promotional activities under ICA auspices have not been discussed. Nor has the relationship between the ICA and the diversification programs in Brazil and elsewhere been dealt with explicitly.

The study covers events in the ICO through the summer of 1971.

Portions of this book have appeared in an article, "Enforcing Export Quota Commodity Agreements: The Case of Coffee," Harvard International Law Journal, XII (Summer, 1971), 401, and are reprinted with permission of the publisher.

There are many debts to be acknowledged. The ICO kindly allowed me to interview delegates to the Organization at the plenary meeting of the International Coffee Council (ICC) in September, 1968. Numerous documents were also made available by the ICO.

Completion of this study was made possible by financial assistance from the Brookings Institution and the Johns Hopkins School of Advanced International Studies.

A debt of gratitude is owed to those who have read sections of the manuscript, including Isaiah Frank, Charles Pearson, Edward Fried, Jerome Jacobson, Sanford V. Berg, Robert A. Lystad, Robert Keohane, Peter Knight, Charles Morrison, Jerome D. Davis, Joe Short, Harold J. Berman, Raymond Vernon, Robert Asher, Stephen F. Gates, and Steven D. Krasner.

Deepest thanks are reserved for my wife, Margaret, who has been a constant inspiration and has been used as a sounding board for many of the ideas expressed in this study.

CONTENTS

xiv

APPENDIXES

LIST OF TABLES AND FIGURES

LIST OF ABBREVIATIONS

EEC	European Economic Community
Fedecame	Coffee Federation of the Americas
FNC	National Coffee Federation of Colombia
GAO	General Accounting Office
IACO	Inter-African Coffee Organization
IBC	Brazilian Coffee Institute
ICA	International Coffee Agreement
ICC	International Coffee Council
ICCICA	Interim Coordinating Committee for International Commodity Arrangements
ICO	International Coffee Organization
LDC	Less Developed Country
NCA	National Coffee Association
OAMCAF	Organisation Africain et Malgache du Cafe
OAS	Organization of American States
PCCA	Pacific Coast Coffee Association
UNCC	United Nations Coffee Conference
WCPC	World Coffee Promotion Committee

The International Coffee Agreement

Coffee is an important commodity for the less developed countries (hereafter cited as LDC's). It ranks first among agricultural commodities in world trade and is second only to petroleum in primary commodity trade, with exports since 1962 averaging over $2 billion annually. In 1969, coffee provided over 25 percent of the total foreign exchange receipts for six Latin American countries (Brazil, Colombia, Costa Rica, El Salvador, Guatemala, and Haiti), and eight African countries (Angola, Ethiopia, Ivory Coast, Kenya, Malagasy, Rwanda, Burundi, and Uganda). And coffee is the staff of life for the estimated 20-million people in the LDC's who work in the world coffee economy. Trade in coffee is, thus, an "engine of growth" for much of the developing world—and the "coffee problem" a potential deterrent to that growth.

The "coffee problem" encompasses three separate market problems—annual price instability, seasonal marketing difficulties, and, until recently, a declining price trend.

ANNUAL PRICE INSTABILITY

The price of coffee often varies sharply from year to year, due to large variations in supplies, the short-run inelasticity of supplies, relatively inelastic demand by final consumers, and activities by speculators. *

---

*"Coffee" in this chapter refers to green coffee, which is the primary product as it leaves the producing country for export.

3

The result of these conditions is that an unusually large crop will tend to bring very low prices during the marketing year, due to the lack of a compensating increase in the amount demanded by final consumers. When there are small crops, intense speculation results, tending to push prices up further than the underlying supply and demand situation would seem to indicate. This is because middlemen and processors in the consuming countries distrust, often with good reason, the condition of stored coffee. Speculation is also frequently encouraged by the producing countries, which are primarily interested in foreign exchange maximization.

The determinants of price instability will now be explored in more detail.

Supply Variability

The frosts and droughts that strike Brazil and other coffee-producing areas from time to time are serious natural sources of supply variability. The problem of frost has been more severe in recent

---

It is important to note that "coffee" is not a homogeneous product. There are two major generic types of green coffee—Arabica and Robusta—the former mainly produced in the Western Hemisphere and the latter in Africa and Asia.

The world coffee "market" consists of the market for the primary product, green coffee, which, in turn, is composed of four submarkets for the types of green coffee. There are also two markets for the processed products of green coffee: regular coffee and instant (soluble) coffee.

The price brackets in the world coffee market, from the most expensive coffee type to the cheapest, have typically been Colombian Milds, Other Milds (mainly from Central America), Unwashed Arabicas (mainly from Brazil), and Robustas (mainly from Africa). The place of each coffee in the international market's pecking order is determined by the commercial assessment of the different varieties and the methods of preparation used in the different centers of production. Particular demand factors are also relevant; see, for example, the current crossover placing the Unwashed Arabicas above the Other Milds. See Chapter 4 for a more detailed description of the coffee submarkets.

years, due to the increase in production in the state of Parana in Brazil, much of which lies below the frost line of that country. *

Significant variations in supply may also result from attacks on coffee trees by diseases and pests. **

The yield cycle of the coffee tree itself augments the effects of Mother Nature in disturbing supply patterns. Large yields by coffee trees are typically followed by lower yields and low yields by higher yields. A heavy yield tends to deplete the yielding power of a tree, so that, even when favorable weather follows the next year, the tree fails to compensate.

The effects of supply variability are magnified by the extreme concentration of coffee production. This results in a lack of compensatory reallocation for supply variability in Brazil, which has the largest coffee industry in the world (in marketing year 1971/72, Brazil had 33 percent of total world production). The major variations in supply within Brazil occur in Parana.

Inelasticity of Demand

The demand for coffee by final consumers is relatively price inelastic, due to the habit-forming nature of the drink. The price elasticity of demand of retail prices is estimated at about -0.2 or -0.3 in the United States and between -0.4 and -0.7 in the Western European countries.[1] Thus, if retail prices for coffee in the United States dropped by 10 percent, only a 2 percent increase in demand would be expected.

---

*The increase in land used for coffee production in Parana from 1954 to 1962 was about 1.2 million hectares, or, in percentage terms, from 13 to 36 percent of the total area under coffee production in all Brazil. Peter T. Knight, "The Critical Coffee Sector in Brazil," Study Paper, U.S. AID (Washington, D.C.: By the author, 1966), p. 17.

**These usually move in tandem with other unsanitary conditions or environmental factors damaging to coffee trees, such as drought. If the coffee tree overbears on an "on" year of its off/on cycle, it is especially susceptible to diseases.

Inelasticity of Supply

Inelasticity of supplies further intensifies prices rises and declines. Arabica trees (grown mainly in the Western Hemisphere) have a gestation period of four to five years, and Robusta types (grown mainly in the Eastern Hemisphere) have a two to three-year gestation period, i.e., from planting to profitable bearing. After this gestation period, the coffee tree will then bear productively for about twenty-five to forty years. This growth pattern means that, if coffee prices start to rise due to a feared or real supply shortage, new trees can not be brought into bearing immediately. Instead, a few years' wait must take place before a new supply can enter the market to depress rising prices.

Speculative Influences

The suspicions of the coffee trade about the quality of stocked coffee, fed by the unreliability of national statistical information, add to price volatility. The presence of substantial coffee stocks might be assumed to be a counter to price instability. But the quality of the stocks is an unknown factor, and coffee buyers tend to prefer fresh crop coffee instead of "old" coffee. Storage is typically less harmful for Brazils than for Mild coffees, which bleach and become insipid.[2] The reason is that Brazilian coffees have a typically harsher flavor than the Mild coffees of Central and other Latin American countries. Mild coffees are, therefore, particularly suspect when they come out of storage, but all coffees are to a degree, and this explains why the slightest supply disturbance results in an intense scramble by speculators for "new" crop coffee.

Import, spot, and wholesale prices tend to move closely together, with, however, some time lag between them. Although retail prices generally follow the lead of these prices, they tend to lag behind them and to show less variation. The lag in retail price rise time is due to the time required for processing, packaging, and distribution before the processed coffee is placed in the hands of the consumer. As is the case with many agricultural products, coffee prices become less volatile, the closer the product moves to the consumer.

THE SEASONAL MARKETING PROBLEM

Not only do coffee prices vary substantially from year to year, but price instability often takes place within the coffee year, due to the harvesting of a large part of the world's production at about the same time (the summer and the early fall). The pressure on coffee prices is greatest in the early months of the calendar year.

The seasonal marketing problem is frequently intensified by the following complications:

1.   Coffee-producing countries, other than Brazil and Colombia, in Central America, Africa, and Asia have poor storage facilities as a rule and are, therefore, under pressure to ship out all their crop as soon as it is harvested; if the coffee is not shipped out immediately, the harmful effects of storage may seriously impair its quality.

2.   An early harvest may create pressure for immediate shipments.

3.   A declining price trend may put growers under further pressure to rush large and early crops to the market instead of holding them for marketing in an orderly manner, because of the fear that prices will worsen in the meantime.

4.   The problem of generally low prices tends to force growers who are low in capital to sell their crops hurriedly in order to obtain cash.

5.   Many small exporters lack the economic incentive to set up an efficient marketing system.

6.   Due to unsettled political conditions, exporters are often anxious to sell to foreign buyers as soon as possible.

PRICE TRENDS

Finally, pronounced price trends in either direction pose a threat to the world coffee economy.

A declining price trend, which was detrimental to the coffee-exporting countries, was the central feature of the world coffee market from the mid-1950's through the late 1960's. That trend—interrupted in July, 1969, by a frost in Brazil—was due to overproduction of coffee relative to final consumer demand.

Excesses in production in Brazil have accounted for most of the world's oversupply of coffee during this century. During the 1950's, Brazilian coffee production nearly doubled, while African production doubled from a much lower base. The key year in the spiral of oversupply was 1954, due to the frost in Brazil in July, 1953, and the resulting severe damage to a large part of Brazilian coffee production. The high prices for green coffee encouraged planters in Brazil to plant more coffee trees. In 1955/56, due to earlier plantings and more intensive harvesting, total supply jumped to 57.5 million bags

TABLE 1

Green Coffee: Production in Specified Countries, Average
1962-63/1966-67, Annual 1967-68/1971-72[1]
(In Thousands of Bags)[2]

Region and Country	Average, 1962-63/1966-67	1967-68	1968-69	1969-70	1970-71	1971-72
North America:						
Costa Rica	1, 043	1, 350	1, 260	1, 400	1, 250	1, 330
Cuba	527	450	500	500	550	550
Dominican Republic	611	635	540	640	675	625
El Salvador	1, 898	2, 400	1, 900	2, 500	2, 000	2, 200
Guadeloupe	7	5	5	1	1	1
Guatemala	1, 808	1, 850	1, 740	1, 750	1, 800	1, 800
Haiti	542	500	480	440	480	450
Honduras	411	480	450	550	550	580
Jamaica and Dependents	24	21	17	20	20	20
Martinique	5	4	4	1	1	1
Mexico	2, 671	2, 900	2, 850	3, 075	3, 000	3, 000
Nicaragua	495	550	540	565	580	560
Panama	76	86	75	83	75	80
Trinidad-Tobago	61	72	65	43	69	80
United States-Hawaii	55	39	36	28	31	30
United States-Puerto Rico	254	325	280	300	300	300
Total	10, 488	11, 667	10, 742	11, 896	11, 382	11, 607
South America:						
Bolivia	65	150	160	165	105	105
Brazil	24, 580	23, 000	16, 500	19, 000	9, 750	23, 600
Colombia	7, 820	8, 000	7, 900	8, 450	7, 500	1, 800
Ecuador[3]	833	1, 175	1, 000	660	1, 200	1, 200
Guyana	12	19	20	18	18	18
Paraguay	53	40	65	50	33	37
Peru	835	880	860	940	990	1, 030
Surinam	11	7	7	6	5	6
Venezuela	809	750	860	900	900	920
Total	35, 017	34, 021	27, 372	30, 189	20, 501	34, 716
Africa:						
Angola	3, 017	3, 400	3, 100	3, 300	3, 300	3, 400
Burundi	200	315	275	240	350	325
Cameroon	939	1, 100	1, 100	1, 200	1, 250	1, 250
Cape Verde Islands	2	2	2	2	2	2
Central African Republic	155	175	160	200	150	160
Comoro Islands	3	3	3	3	3	3
Congo-Brazzaville	14	10	20	15	15	15
Congo-Kinshasa	1, 005	1, 000	1, 000	1, 100	1, 200	1, 250

Region and Country	1962-63/1966-67	1967-68	1968-69	1969-70	1970-71	1971-72
Dahomey	28	15	18	15	15	15
Ethiopia	1,603	1,750	2,045	2,000	2,100	2,150
Gabon	17	15	20	20	15	15
Ghana	56	94	83	95	75	85
Guinea	164	170	180	200	250	250
Ivory Coast	3,565	4,500	3,400	4,600	4,000	4,000
Kenya	769	650	800	1,000	935	915
Liberia	58	58	65	75	95	75
Malagasy Republic	915	1,100	900	830	900	850
Nigeria	34	51	53	50	65	65
Rwanda	147	190	200	145	235	200
Sao Tome-Principe	6	6	6	4	4	4
Sierra Leone	90	80	95	90	125	100
Spanish Africa Nec	125	145	125	120	120	120
Tanzania	653	740	950	775	900	900
Togo	184	175	280	230	225	225
Uganda	2,669	2,700	3,335	2,900	3,200	3,000
Total	16,419	18,444	18,215	19,209	19,529	19,374
Asia:						
India	1,181	1,050	1,300	1,150	1,600	1,325
Indonesia	2,016	2,150	2,000	2,200	2,350	2,250
Malaysia	111	135	135	100	100	100
Philippines	679	700	735	785	750	750
Portuguese Timop	38	48	55	50	55	50
Vietnam South	57	55	55	50	50	50
Yemen	77	60	70	60	60	60
Total	4,159	4,198	4,350	4,395	4,965	4,585
Oceania:						
New Caledonia	35	35	30	30	30	25
New Guinea	118	243	355	408	470	490
New Hebrides	4	4	4	3	3	3
Total	157	282	389	441	503	518
Grand Total	66,240	68,612	61,068	66,130	56,880	70,800

[1] Coffee marketing year begins about July in some countries and in others about October.
[2] Of 60 kilograms each.
[3] As indicated in footnote 1, the coffee-marketing year begins in some countries as early as July. Ecuador is one of these countries. Hence, the crop harvested principally during June-October, 1971, in that country is shown as production for the 1971-72 marketing year. In Ecuador, however, this is referred to as the 1970-71 crop.

Note: Production estimates for some countries include cross-border movements.

Source: Foreign Agricultural Service. Prepared or estimated on the basis of official statistics of foreign governments, other foreign source materials, reports of U. S. Agricultural Attaches and Foreign Service Officers, results of office research, and related information.

of green coffee, more than 12 million bags in excess of the total
supply in any single year in the early 1950's. When the ICA was
negotiated in 1962, a surplus of 80 million bags of green coffee—or
enough for world consumption for two years—was looming. [3]

The overproduction of coffee between 1954 and the mid-1960's
was due to the following factors:

1. The price paid by governments to their producers in local
currency for green coffee induced overproduction; the LDC's—like
the developed countries—have a "farm problem," as producers of
coffee have demonstrated; they can often exert political pressure to
influence the government to give them a high price, which, in turn,
calls forth oversupply. [4]

2. The large exporting countries found it to their advantage to
overproduce in order to have stocks as bargaining weapons; in Brazil,
for example, the sanctioning of overproduction permitted a stock
buildup in 1962, which gave it "control" over the world coffee market. [5]

3. The low cost of coffee production encouraged easy entry
into the coffee market. *

---

*Within this low-cost overall framework, fixed costs for coffee
production are much greater per unit of product than are variable
costs. This is due to the perennial character of coffee production.
The main costs of cultivation for the grower are the cost of purchasing
land (about 25 percent of total amount invested per hectare of planting
in São Paulo, Brazil) and planting coffee trees (about 50 percent)
rather than harvesting per se. On cost figures, see "The Coffee
Industry in São Paulo," Economic Bulletin for Latin America, Vol
V (October, 1960), 68. The figures relate only to the specific conditions
of São Paulo, but they give a general idea of the costs in coffee
planting.

The importance of the first fixed cost—land—is that when world
prices or producer prices are rising, the presence of relatively cheap
land will encourage a rush to till that soil. In Brazil, for example,
land was available at almost zero cost in the state of Parana in the
late 1950's and early 1960's, causing production to rise sharply. The
presence of cheap land in Africa also encouraged overproduction
there.

The importance of the second fixed cost—planting trees—is that,
once the trees have been planted, coffee production tends to take place,
regardless of what the producer price is. The result is a slow exit
by producers from the coffee market.

Since the mid-1960's, a major shift in the world supply and demand equation has taken place. There has been a series of annual supply deficits of varying significance. The result is that, in the early 1970's, after many years of almost universal preoccupation with excessive production, world coffee production is in current overall approximate balance with world demand. Somewhat higher price levels than prevailed in the mid-1960's thus appear likely in the next few years.

The dimensions of the decline in coffee production can be appreciated when it is realized that, in the last four years of the 1960's, world exportable production—which averaged 46 million bags—was about 5 million bags below average production for the coffee years 1960-64. (See Table 1.)

The decrease in available supplies for export during the latter 1960's was due: (1) to the declining world price level for coffee (which, translated by producer governments into a lower local price, provided little incentive to maintain farms in optimum condition); (2) to the fact that yields had improved to the point where heavy capitalization would have been required for any further increases in production; (3) to increases in wages and other operating expenses; (4) to a frost of staggering dimensions in Brazil in July, 1969; (5) to the development in many areas of alternative farm commodities; and (6) to a steady increase in local consumption of coffee in the producing countries. The 1962 ICA, by fixing basic and annual export quotas, also provided an incentive for members to eliminate surplus production.

Accompanying the decline in coffee production has been a stagnation in coffee consumption in the importing countries at about 52.5 million bags (1965-68 figures), still somewhat above exportable production. These figures augur a reduction in world coffee stocks, now only at 38 million bags, or 73 percent of world consumption requirements. [6]

The recent dramatic price and supply shifts illustrate the complexity of the coffee problem. To ameliorate the difficulties of marketing coffee under the conditions described in this chapter, the coffee-exporting countries have, from time to time, sought international regulation of the world coffee market.

NOTES

1. Gertrude Lovasy, "The International Coffee Market: A Note," IMF Staff Papers, IX (July, 1962), 233.

2. Vernon D. Wickizer, Coffee, Tea, and Cocoa, An Economic and Political Analysis (Stanford, Calif.: Food Research Institute, Stanford University, 1943), p. 58.

3. Estimate by Vernon D. Wickizer, "International Collaboration in the World Coffee Market," Stanford Food Research Institute Studies, IV, No. 3 (1964), 282.

4. This problem is explored by Nathaniel H. Leff in his excellent study Economic Policy-Making and Development in Brazil, 1947-1964 (New York: John Wiley & Sons, 1968). Leff argues that a major cause of Brazil's overproduction in the late 1950's and early 1960's was the producer price policy followed by its government.

5. On the use of coffee stocks by Brazil, see J. W. F. Rowe, The World's Coffee (London: H.M. Stationery Office, 1963), p. 182.

6. Thus, even in 1971/72, with a coffee crop of 70.2 million bags, the largest since the 1965/66 year of record production, it appears doubtful that stocks will be replenished to any significant degree. See The Journal of Commerce (December 24, 1971), p. 5. For a perceptive analysis of the present world coffee situation, see John I. Kross and J. Phillip Rourk, "Story of the 1960's: Coffee in World Trade," Foreign Agriculture (January 12, 1970), p. 8.

THE BRAZILIAN EXPERIENCE, 1905-40

The earliest large-scale coffee control measures were Brazilian initiatives known as "valorizations."

The first valorization, in 1905/06, had the following elements:

1. The state of São Paulo purchased coffee from its planters.
2. São Paulo then stored the coffee.
3. São Paulo later resold the coffee on the world market at a propitious moment.
4. São Paulo placed restrictions on new planting.

The valorization pushed coffee prices from 6 cents per pound in 1907/08 to above 14 cents in 1912. This prompted the first of several U.S. Congressional investigations on the "consumer tax" aspect of valorization. *

In 1917/18, when World War I led to the closing of the vital European market, due to insecurity of the shipping lanes, the state of São Paulo again valorized.

In a third valorization, in 1921/22, the Brazilian federal government purchased 4. 5 million bags of coffee. By 1924, all the valorized coffee was successfully marketed.

---

*The 1912 investigation was led in the U. S. Senate by Senator George W. Norris of Nebraska, who argued that valorization was costing Americans over $35 million per year.

Valorization was a limited success. It did stabilize the world coffee market periodically through orderly marketing. The long-run effects were, however, unfortunate, as the higher prices created by valorization tended to encourage an extension of planting.

The second phase of Brazilian coffee control, a permanent plan known as "coffee defense," was instituted in 1925 by the state of São Paulo. Under this plan, stocks were stored in the interior of the country, and their movement to port was controlled on a permanent basis.

Unfortunately, the São Paulo Coffee Defense Institute financed coffee stocks by making loans to farmers on the basis of the current selling price of coffee rather than its prospective price. This both depleted the Institute of its resources and encouraged overproduction. The Brazilian federal government refused to replenish the Institute's resources. Prices dropped sharply as a result (from 25 cents per pound in 1925 to 8 cents in 1931*).

In 1933, the Brazilian federal government again took over coffee control policy. It prohibited new planting and began to destroy some of the existing supplies.

By 1936, the federal government had destroyed 40 million bags of coffee in an effort to hold up prices. This price defense policy allowed Brazil's Mild competitors to take away a large part of its market share (consumers favored the higher-quality Milds, which were then selling at about the same price as Brazils).

Brazil, in an effort to restrain the advance of the Milds, tried unsuccessfully at the Havana Pan American Conference of 1936 to get agreement on planting, export restriction, and the defense of coffee prices.

At this point, Brazil finally adopted a volume market strategy to win back her "rightful" market share. Price defense was abandoned, and the export tax was cut by one-quarter. Brazilian coffee exports rose sharply as a result, while Mild sales continued at about the same level.

---

*The citation used is Santos 4 grade, which is the median quality level of Brazilian coffees.

THE INTER-AMERICAN COFFEE
AGREEMENT, 1940-48

When World War II began, both the other Latin American coffee-producing countries and the United States discovered that they had a common interest with Brazil in stabilizing the coffee market. The Inter-American Coffee Agreement, signed on November 28, 1940, was, thus, a measure of Pan American solidarity among allies.[1]

The administration of the Agreement was executed by the Inter-American Coffee Board, on which the United States had twelve votes, Brazil nine, Colombia three, and the twelve other exporting countries one each. The Board's regulatory function was exercised through its annual setting of import quotas for the U.S. market, both for members and for nonmembers, and its specification of export quotas for members to other markets. American interests were protected by a provision allowing an unlimited increase in import quotas to be ordered by a one-third vote of the Board and by the requirement of a two-thirds majority vote for other important decisions.

The Agreement said nothing about prices, leaving the quota provisions alone as safeguards for American consumers.[2]

After Pearl Harbor, U.S. prices were frozen at about double the levels prevailing when the Agreement was negotiated. While some gesture of goodwill and economic support was necessary, the doubling of coffee prices was questioned at the time by critics.[3]

After 1945, the Inter-American Coffee Board did little more than serve as a forum in which Latin American producers could request the removal of the price ceilings. Quotas lost their regulatory effect after 1945, as they were allocated on the basis of year-to-year shifts in production. In 1948, the Board dissolved the Inter-American Coffee Agreement, reporting that the oversupply problem was under control and that the coffee problem could more efficiently be handled on a national basis.

RETREAT FROM REGULATION, 1945-54

The coffee market from 1945 through the early 1950's was characterized by an excess of consumption over world exportable production. The high prices of this period culminated in the sharp price rise of 1954, when the price of Brazils (Santos 4) rose to almost $1, averaged 88 cents per pound for one month, and ended the year with an average of 78.7 cents. The generally high level of prices was due to the exhaustion of Brazilian stocks, pentup demand in Europe, and the run-down condition of the Latin American agricultural sector. The result of the heavy demand relative to current supply was relatively little interest by producers in international collaboration to boost coffee prices.

INCUBATION OF REGULATION, 1955-57

In 1954, at Quitandinha, Brazil, a meeting of the Inter-American Economic and Social Council of the Organization of American States (OAS) called upon a Special OAS Committee on Coffee to study the world coffee situation and to propose solutions for the anticipated problem of declining prices.

The requested study was made in 1955. It concluded that the trend of production was leading to a large coffee surplus and recommended international cooperation to prevent a serious drop in prices.

The U.S. response to the study was given on April 27, 1956, in the form of a letter by Ambassador Harold M. Randall to the OAS. It was negative in tone and substance, stating that the United States could not take the lead in negotiating an international coffee agreement or become a participant in one.

Meanwhile, in lieu of an international accord, a series of informal marketing "ententes" provided a modicum of international cooperation in the market.

The most important entente was between Brazil and Colombia. In April, 1955, the President of the Brazilian Coffee Institute (IBC) and the President of the National Coffee Federation of Colombia (FNC) agreed to cooperate to limit price fluctuations and speculation. This policy was carried out by both countries through stock retentions and cooperation in retaining the agreed price differentials between Brazils and Colombian Milds.

The second entente in operation was the Coffee Federation of the Americas (Fedecame). This group was composed of Central American producers* and advocated, as early as 1955, a broad international plan based on stock retentions and export quotas for Latin American and African producers.

----

*Members of Fedecame included Costa Rica, El Salvador, Guatemala, Honduras, Mexico, and Nicaragua.

FIGURE 1

Movement of Coffee Prices, 1950-68
Spot New York
(Cents Per Pound)

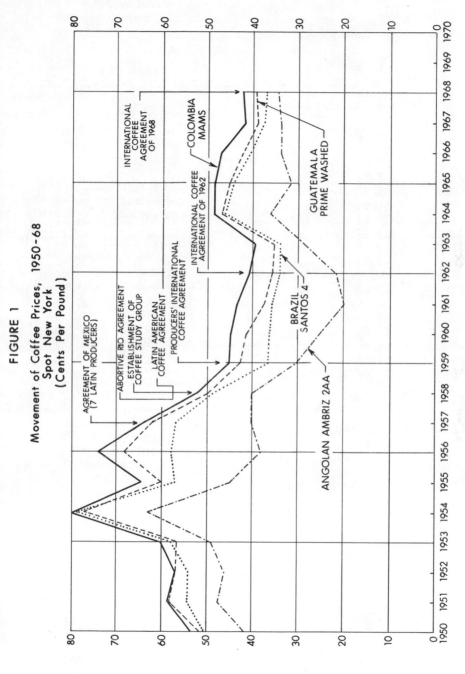

Source: International Bank for Reconstruction and Development.

17

TABLE 2

Coffee Price Movements, 1950-68
(In U.S. Cents Per Pound, Spot New York)

	Colombia Mams	Guatemala Prime Washed	Brazil Santos 4	Angolan Ambriz 2
1950	53.25	51.37[1]	50.52	41.53
1951	58.74	58.58	54.20	47.56
1952	57.01	57.05	54.04	46.17
1953	59.82	56.85	57.93	49.22
1954	80.02	77.24[2]	78.71	63.02
1955	64.57	60.28	57.09	45.23
1956	73.97	68.48	58.10	38.35
1957	63.94	62.94	56.92	40.22
1958	52.34	49.81	48.41	40.25
1959	45.22	42.62	36.97	30.60
1960	44.89	41.33	36.60	25.27
1961	43.62	37.55	36.01	19.93
1962	40.77	35.83	33.96	21.55
1963	39.55	35.40	34.11	28.73
1964	48.80	47.16	46.66	36.38
1965	48.49	45.51	44.71	31.59
1966	47.43	42.25	40.83	33.98
1967	41.94	39.23	37.82	33.83
1968[3]	42.36	39.69	37.43	34.70

1. Good Washed.
2. Mexican Prime Washed.
3. January-June.

Source: Pan American Coffee Bureau, New York.

Fedecame used informal "gentlemen's agreements" to try to maintain prices at certain weak periods of the marketing year, e.g., in the early months of the calendar year, due to seasonal marketing pressures. Price cooperation within Fedecame, however, broke down on April 12, 1957, when Mexico and the Central American countries agreed on a flexible price policy, with each country free to pursue an independent policy.

The inadequacy of the "entente" system led to two proposals by the OAS Secretarial for an international coffee agreement.

The first agreement that was drafted had price stabilization as an objective, to be obtained through a combination of export quotas and buffer stock operations.[4] It called for export quotas and floor and ceiling prices for one or more of the principal types of coffee to be set annually by an international coffee authority. The alternative plan had more modest objectives—promotion of coffee and provision of statistical information on coffee production, processing, and marketing.[5]

PRODUCER COUNTRY COOPERATION: 1957-62

The Agreement of Mexico

Neither OAS plan was adopted. Instead, an accord known as the Agreement of Mexico was signed in Mexico City on October 18, 1957, by seven Latin American Coffee producers.*

Under the Agreement, Brazil agreed to retain at least 20 percent of its estimated exports (in exportable coffee grades) from October, 1957, through September, 1958; Colombia and the other Mild-producing countries agreed to limit exports from November 1, 1957, to March 31, 1958, to 80 percent of the average in the same period of the two preceding crop years; and the Mild-producing countries of Central America agreed to a stock retention equal to 10 percent of exports between November 1, 1957, and September 30, 1958. Quarterly export quotas, based on the above formulas, limited the available supplies on the world market.[6]

Prices recovered for the first few months of 1958, but then declined for the rest of the marketing year. This decline in prices

---

*Members included Brazil, Colombia, Costa Rica, El Salvador, Guatemala, Mexico, and Nicaragua.

was a result of the growing problem of oversupply, which the Agreement of Mexico did nothing to ameliorate. A more inclusive approach in substance and in participation was needed to solve the coffee problem.

The 1958 Shift in U.S. Coffee Policy

The coffee problem finally caught the attention of the U.S. government in 1958. Administration policy toward Latin America was reshaped in large part by Douglas Dillon, who returned from Paris in 1957 to become Under Secretary of State for Economic Affairs. Although Dillon was not a Latin Americanist, he became interested in this region when he saw the paucity of new ideas in State and Treasury Department economic policy toward Latin America.[7] After the Buenos Aires conference of Western Hemisphere finance ministers in the fall of 1957, Dillon became convinced that a new policy toward development assistance and commodity agreements should be adopted. Dillon's agitation for new economic policies for Latin America was reflected in a new American attitude toward commodity agreements, replacing the former "hands off" policy of the Randall letter. On January 13, 1958, Roy R. Rubottom, Jr., the Assistant Secretary of State for Inter-American Affairs, signalled this shift: "It is in our common interest, then, and that of Latin America and the United States, to find rational solutions to coffee problems."[8]

On March 31, 1958, after an abortive attempt by fourteen Latin American countries to set up an international coffee organization for coffee promotion,* Rubottom moved further from the "hands off" policy, by stating that

I do not think that the American housewife, any more than the Government of the United States, wants to see a disastrous price decline . . . the United States is searching for the useful means of cooperating with its Latin American friends on the problem of coffee.[9]

Higher-echelon support for American cooperation with Latin America on the coffee problem came on April 14, 1958, at the Pan-American Day ceremonies in Washington, D.C., when Secretary of State John Foster Dulles said:

---

*The goal of the projected international coffee organization—promotion—was too narrow to elicit much support. Only a few countries ratified the convention setting up the organization, and, therefore, it never came into being.

The United States Government realizes the potential consequences of violent fluctuations in the prices of Latin America's exports and is daily searching for ways and means to contribute toward a solution. . . . [This policy represents] a considerable amount of new ground. [10]

Vice-President Richard M. Nixon picked up the new line by telling Colombians, on May 12, 1958, that it was necessary for the United States to adopt a more positive policy regarding the coffee problem. Although there would be opposition in the United States to any action on price fixing or coffee quotas, he said, other measures might be possible.

Openmindedness on the part of the U.S. government was still far short of commitment. This was supplied by a group of concerned coffee men in New York City as 1958 began. Arthur Ransohoff—a burly and salty-tongued green coffee broker—was the catalyst. After brooding over the position of the world coffee market, he met George V. Robbins, Director of Green Coffee Operations within the Maxwell House Division of General Foods, for lunch and explained his fears about a break in the world coffee market and its implications for U.S. security. Robbins agreed with Ransohoff on the gravity of the situation. On their urging, the National Coffee Association passed a resolution authorizing industry discussions with the State Department on the coffee problem.* The Association named Edward Aborn, Peter Folger, Fred Silence, and John F. McKiernan to accompany Robbins and Ransohoff on a trip to Washington, D.C., to explain the coffee situation to the State Department. The Department scheduled a meeting for the six coffeemen with Thomas Mann, then Assistant Secretary of State for Economic Affairs. Mann listened carefully, thanked the coffee men for their warning, and then proceeded to press within the bureaucracy for a higher U.S. profile on the coffee problem.

The motivations involved in prompting the American coffee "establishment" toward a proagreement stance in 1957/58 appear to

---

*The information on the Robbins/Ransohoff initiative was supplied by Arthur Ransohoff in an interview in New York City on June 26, 1969. The National Coffee Association (NCA) is the largest coffee trade association in the United States. In 1970, it had 235 members, including 103 roasters, 63 green coffee importers, and 69 allied firms. These firms handle 85 percent of the total coffee imported and roasted in the United States. Information from World Coffee & Tea (August, 1970), p. 82.

have been inordinately complex. The large publicly held corporations, such as General Foods, were aware of the consequences for U.S. security if the market should break and Latin America went Communist.[11] The issue, as General Foods saw it, was not whether, but how, the United States could best help to regulate the coffee market. Its sole expressed fear was that a commodity agreement might lead to "unreasonable" prices for General Foods's customers.

A collapse in the coffee market would not only have been ruinous for American diplomatic interests in the Western Hemisphere, but, many in the industry thought, might have caused enormous difficulties in obtaining supplies. John F. McKiernan, President of the NCA, stated that "If the economies of the coffee-producing nations are not stabilized, the resultant chaos would wreak havoc on our lines of supply of green coffee."[12]

Finally, many large roasters were banking on the inelasticity of final consumer demand for their product and felt that approximately the same amount of coffee would be consumed at a "reasonable," albeit somewhat higher, price.

Enthusiasm from the large green brokers in the United States for an agreement for coffee is, at first blush, harder to understand. An agreement would certainly reduce price fluctuations and, thus, reduce their profit-taking. But most large brokers—like the large roasters—were worried about the possible difficulties in obtaining supplies if the market broke. As the best-traveled of all segments of the coffee trade—and, often, its eyes and ears abroad—they feared that a market collapse might be imminent. They were also moved by unabashed sentimentality for the region they knew so well and simply were not willing to see their corner of the globe fall upon evil times if it could be prevented.

The mix of industry sentiment in the United States, then, included self-interest (assurance of supplies), ideology (an anti-Communist Latin America), and affection. It appeared to add up to a majority of the U.S. coffee "establishment" in favor of some form of international regulation of the world coffee market.

The Coffee Study Group

The result of the new interest within the Administration and the coffee trade in the United States in the coffee problem was the convening of the Coffee Study Group in Washington, D.C., on the initiative of the United States in June, 1958. The Study Group—composed of all the major producing and consuming countries—gave a central focus to the search for international collaboration in the coffee market. It also provided the "technical" work for a series of short-term agreements and, eventually, a long-term agreement. Most importantly, it meant that the active interest of the United States in the coffee problem had been secured. On the other hand, participation in a long-term international coffee agreement was still excluded "as a sin against free enterprise"[13] by the Eisenhower Administration.

Following unsuccessful negotiations with the African producers within the Coffee Study Group, fifteen Latin American countries,* on September 27, 1958, signed an agreement among themselves to support the price of coffee. The representatives of France and Portugal promised unilateral action to control exports, although they did not sign the pact.

The Latin American Coffee Agreement

The terms of the Latin American Coffee Agreement were that Brazil would withhold 40 percent of its 1958/59 exportable production, Colombia 15 percent, and other countries 5 percent of the first 300,000 bags and 10 percent of the balance. Brazil agreed to maintain its traditional price defense policy, while other countries were to limit exports to customary historical norms. The Agreement provided for orderly marketing by empowering the Board of Directors to set export quotas on a quarterly or biannual basis.

Despite the Agreement, all Arabica prices continued to decline. Robustas also fell, prompting the Africans to take a second look at an international agreement.

In September, 1959, Portugal (for its coffee-exporting territory of Angola) and the French Community, together with Cameroun and Togo, agreed to adhere to a new export quota agreement, along with the fifteen Latin American countries. The British and the Belgian delegations stated their moral support for the agreement, which they had no instructions to sign, and announced unilaterally that they would limit exports of their overseas territories in coffee year 1959/60. Consuming countries, however, were still not represented.

---

*Brazil, Colombia, Costa Rica, Cuba, Dominican Republic, Ecuador, El Salvador, Guatemala, Haiti, Honduras, Mexico, Nicaragua, Panama, Peru, and Venezuela.

THE 1959 ICA

The 1959 ICA, which was signed on September 24, 1959, contained the following provisions:

1. Export quotas: Each participant in the Agreement had export quotas specified on its choice of either: (1) "a figure of 90 percent of the exports that took place during the best calendar year of the last decade (1949-58);" of (2) "a maximum figure of 88 percent of the actual exportable production," for any country having less than 2 million bags of exportable production. [14]

2. Orderly marketing: It was agreed to distribute the total export quota "quarterly, in order to balance supply and demand." [15]

3. Promotion: The signatories bound themselves to carry out a "publicity campaign" to promote coffee consumption; contributions were fixed at 25 cent per sixty-kilo bag (about 132 pounds per bag) for the Latin American states and 15 cents per bag for France and Portugal. [16]

4. New markets: Exports to nontraditional markets in Eastern Europe, Asia, and Africa were excluded from quota allotments; this was an attempt to open up areas of low consumption and high potential for coffee marketing. [17]

5. Administration: The administration of the Agreement was carried out by a Board of Directors, which met in Washington, D.C.; one member from each signatory was on the Board; decisions were by majority vote, but no member could be bound by decisions of the Board without its consent.

Performance under the 1959 ICA was impressive. The same group of "coffee men"—Miguel Angel Cordera, Jr., Francois Gavoty, and Joao O. Santos among them—that would play such a key role in the 1962 long-term agreement guided the 1959 ICA and were largely responsible for its success in checking the coffee price decline.*

After chaotic price declines from 1958 to 1959, the prices of all Arabicas held from in 1960.

---

*Miguel Angel Cordera, Jr., was Chairman of the Board of Directors of the 1959 ICA, Francois Gavoty was Vice Chairman, and Joao O. Santos was Secretary of the Board.

There were, however, two major problems under the 1959 ICA—annual and basic quotas that were too large and export controls that did not work effectively.

Unfortunately, the global quota in the 1959 ICA was too large at 33.9 million bags. (See Table 3.) This quota exceeded actual exports by 1.6 million bags, as Brazil and Colombia—following their price defense policies—did not sell all of their quotas.

Export controls under the 1959 ICA depended largely on national control systems, which ranged from nonexistent to very good. Many countries overshipped their quarterly quotas, but only one, Guatemala, overshipped its annual quota by more than 10 percent.[18] The ICA's relatively good record on annual quota enforcement in 1959/60 was due to the fact that most of the quotas exceeded the annual exportable production of the members.

Renewal of the 1959 ICA

On July 11, 1960, the ICA was extended for another year. In terms of size, the ICA for 1959/60 was impressive, covering 94 percent of world exportable production. It added the United Kingdom (on behalf of Kenya, Tanganyika, and Uganda), and eight newly independent African countries and had twenty-eight countries as members.

Operational difficulties during 1960/61 mirrored the problems of the proceding year—again, export quotas were set and, again, they were too large.* In addition, export controls were a major problem, since three countries exceeded their basic quota by more than 9 percent and because many countries exceeded their quarterly quotas.**

———————————

*The global quota in 1960/61 was 37.8 million bags, 3.3 million bags above actual exports to quota markets. Source: International Coffee Organization, International Coffee Council, History of Recent International Coffee Agreements: Their Background, Provisions, Operations and Related Development, ICO Doc. No. ICC-1-1 (1963), p. 33.

**Honduras exceeded its 1960/61 basic quota by 26.9 percent, Nicaragua by 9.6 percent, and Peru by 41.1 percent. The countries with large quarterly quota overshipments included Ecuador, Guatemala, and Venezuela (source: data of the Coffee Study Group, Washington, D.C).

TABLE 3

Basic Export Quotas Under the 1959 International Coffee Agreement

Country	Annex of the Agreement	Adjustment for 1959/60	Adjustment for 1960/61
Brazil	17,431,000	17,431,000	17,431,000[a]
Colombia	5,969,000	5,969,000	5,969,000
Costa Rica	694,000	743,600	924,000
Cuba	312,000	312,000	312,000
Dominican Republic	398,000	440,000	440,000
Ecuador	455,000	455,000	572,000
El Salvador	1,259,000	1,355,000	1,355,000
Franc Zone	638,000	1,010,240	1,099,120[b]
Guatemala	1,085,000	1,249,600	1,249,600
Haiti	500,000	550,000	550,000
Honduras	176,000	272,800	272,800
Mexico	1,303,000	1,408,000	1,408,000
Nicaragua	344,000	344,000	352,000
Panama	10,000	22,000	22,000
Peru	251,000	404,800	404,800
Portugal	1,165,000	1,325,000	1,850,000
United Kingdom (for Kenya, Tanganyika, and Uganda	—	—	2,985,000[c]
Total	32,650,000	33,952,040	37,856,320

[a] Add 855,128 bags and 440,338 bags, respectively, to the quotas for Brazil and Colombia, which quantities were carried over or transferred from the coffee year 1959/60.

[b] Cameroun, Central Africa, Congo-Brazzaville, Dahomey, France, Gabon, Ivory Coast, Malagasy, and Togo.

[c] Includes shipments to the Commonwealth.

Source: ICO, History of Recent International Coffee Agreements: Their Background Provisions, Operations and Related Development, ICO Doc. No. ICC-1-1 (1963), p. 33.

Coffee prices reflected the increasing disarray in the world coffee market.[19] While Colombian Milds and Brazils held firm, the Other Milds and the Robustas, competing within each submarket, tumbled badly. It was becoming increasingly obvious that consumer countries would be needed to police future coffee agreements. The issue was whether the consuming countries in general, and the United States in particular, would respond to the requests of the producing countries to participate in coffee control.

CHANGES IN U.S. COFFEE POLICY

The advocates of a commodity agreement for coffee in 1961 found a sympathetic listener in the newly elected U.S. President. John F. Kennedy had an avid interest in Latin America, dating from a tour of the region taken in 1940. Kennedy—who was not at home in many areas of international economics, notably the U.S. balance of payments problems—did realize the relationship between foreign aid and foreign exchange earnings. He had, in fact, advocated commodity agreements for Latin America as early as 1958,[20] and during the 1960 campaign, had called for stabilization of the prices of the principal commodity exports in a speech in Tampa, Florida.

After the 1960 election, Kennedy called on Richard Goodwin— his man on Latin America—to set up a Latin American Task Force. Other members of the Task Force, besides Goodwin, were the Chairman, Adolph Berle, Arturo Morales-Carrion, Teodoro Moscoso, Lincoln Gordon, Robert Alexander, and Arthur Whitaker. The mission of the Task Force was to submit its report to Kennedy on a new U.S. Latin American policy early in 1961.

The reports of the Latin American Task Force were to be seminal in changing U.S. policy toward an international coffee agreement. The Task Force—concerned with the possible spread of "Castroism" to other parts of the Western Hemisphere and the immediacy of the coffee oversupply problem[21]—recommended U.S. cooperation in establishing commodity arrangements. This key recommendation was explained in a memorandum sent by Gordon to Goodwin, who was in charge of collating the various Task Force reports and writing them into Kennedy's major address on Latin America.

Gordon noted that

The dependence of Latin American export earnings on a small number of mineral and agricultural commodities is well known. For many of these commodities, prices and sales volumes have been notoriously unstable. Market instability has gravely

hampered Latin American developmental efforts and in some
cases has injected serious inflationary pressures into their
economies. It would be neither wise nor feasible to seek international stabilization for all these products. [22]

On the coffee problem, Gordon wrote:

In the especially important case of coffee, the market is overhung
by vast and still growing surpluses in storage which make it
evident that continued efforts for market stabilization must be
accompanied by strenuous measures to reduce overproduction. [23]

The operative recommendation on commodity trade policy in the
"Gordon memorandum" was paraphrased by President Kennedy on
March, 13, 1961, in his famous Alliance for Progress speech:

The United States is ready, however, to cooperate with the Latin
American and other producing country governments in a serious
case-by-case examination of the major commodities and to lend
its support to practical efforts to reduce extreme price fluctuations [Italics added.][24]

The "Gordon memorandum" was incorporated almost verbatim
in Goodwin's draft of Kennedy's Alliance for Progress" speech of
March 13, 1961, which proposed transforming "the 1960's into an
historic decade of democratic progress."[25] On commodities, the
fifth point on the Alliance for Progress outline, President Kennedy
said:

The United States is ready to cooperate in serious case-by-
case examinations of commodity market problems. Frequent
violent changes in commodity prices seriously injure the
economies of many Latin American countries, draining their
resources and stultifying their growth. Together we must
find practical methods of bringing an end to this problem.
[Italics added.][26]

In one bold stroke, President Kennedy lifted U.S. coffee policy
far beyond the rather limited beginnings of the Eisenhower Administration. The United States was now committed to consider a long-term
coffee agreement with consumer country participation. Interestingly,
however, the specific reference by Gordon to the coffee problem was
dropped in the March 13, 1961, speech. President Kennedy wanted
to keep his options open.

Implementation of the commodity agreement idea for coffee was
the next step. The Coffee Study Group, which was still meeting in

Washington, D.C., had under consideration a proposed draft agreement that called for a gradual reduction in a guaranteed price level, the internationalization of surplus stocks, and a buffer stock mechanism. Brazil found the internationalization of its surplus stocks unacceptable, and U.S. coffee trade interests disapproved violently of the buffer stock. On July 2, 1961, the NCA warned that the United States should "not become the owner of or responsible for the disposal of coffee."[27] The buffer stock concept was quietly interred by Assistant Secretary of State for Inter-American Affairs Woodward on July 27, 1961, when he told the NCA that he opposed "the idea of the U.S. becoming a party to the financing of coffee buffer stocks."[28]

If the form of a commodity agreement for coffee was in doubt, the basic commitment to one by the United States was not. At the Punta del Este Conference, on August 7, 1961, at a Special Meeting of the OAS Inter-American Economic and Social Council, the Secretary of the Treasury Douglas Dillon stated:

> [The United States is] prepared to join a workable coffee agreement, to use its good offices to urge the participation of other consuming countries, and to help in the enforcement of export quotas through the use of import controls.[29]

When Dillon returned to Washington, he said that the United States was committed to join a "proper" coffee agreement, which was to be drawn up later in the year.

PRELUDE TO THE UNCC

On December 4, 1961 the Drafting Committee of the Coffee Study Group produced a preliminary document which, although later revised, eventually became the basis of the 1962 ICA. The full Study Group concluded that the December draft offered a solid basis for the negotiation of a long-term coffee agreement.

Accordingly, the Coffee Study Group requested the Interim Coordinating Committee for International Commodity Arrangements (ICCICA) of the U.N. Economic and Social Council to call a U.N. conference for the negotiation of a long-term coffee agreement. The Secretary General then convoked the UNCC to meet on July 9, 1962, in New York City.

The end of an era was at hand. Producing countries were to be joined by consuming countries in the search for a cooperative solution to the coffee problem. Whether their cooperation in an export quota commodity agreement could better the record of the short-term arrangements remained, however, to be seen.

NOTES

1. For a full explanation of the events leading up to the Inter-American Coffee Agreement, see Paul Daniels, "The Inter-American Coffee Agreement," Law and Contemporary Problems, VIII (Autumn, 1941), 708-21.

2. The full text of the Agreement may be found in The Inter-American Coffee Agreement, in U.S., Treaty Series 970.

3. Vernon D. Wickizer, Coffee, Tea, and Cocoa, An Economic and Political Analysis (Stanford, Calif.: Food Research Institute, Stanford University, 1943), p. 103, criticized the "largesse" of U.S. diplomacy under the Agreement.

4. Proposals for an International Coffee Agreement (Washington, D.C.: Pan American Union, 1957).

5. Proposals for an International Coffee Organization (Washington, D.C.: Pan American Union, 1957).

6. ICO, ICC, History of Recent International Coffee Agreements: Their Background, Provisions, Operations and Related Development, ICO Doc. No ICC-1-1 (1963), pp. 1 and 2.

7. Arthur M. Schlesinger Jr., A Thousand Days, John F. Kennedy in the White House (Boston: Houghton Mifflin Company, 1965).

8. George Gordon Paton and Co. Coffee Annual, 1958 (1959), p. 155.

9. George Gordon Paton and Co. Coffee Annual, 1958, p. 155.

10. Ibid., p. 157.

11. See, for example, George V. Robbins, "Floor/Ceiling Coffee Prices," in George Gordon Paton and Co. Coffee Annual, 1958, p. 81.

12. John F. McKiernan, "The NCA and Free Enterprise," in George Gordon Paton and Co. Coffee Annual, 1958, p. 48.

13. Schlesinger, op. cit., p. 189.

14. International Coffee Agreement, 1959, Art. 6.

15. Ibid., Art. 7.

16. Ibid., Art. 9, Annex 3.

17. Ibid., Art. 6.

18. Source for the data is the Coffee Study Group, Washington, D.C.

19. See ICO, ICC, op. cit., for the price narrative.

20. See John F. Kennedy The Strategy of Peace, ed. Allan Nevins (New York: Harper & Brothers, 1960), pp. 135-41.

21. See the estimate by Vernon D. Wickizer, "International Collaboration in the World Coffee Market," Stanford Food Research Institute Studies, IV, No. 3 (1964), 282, that a short-term surplus of 80 million bags of green coffee was looming in 1962. The conclusion that "Castroism" dominated the thinking of several of the Task Force members emerges from a reading of all of the Latin America Task Force reports.

22. Memorandum from Lincoln Gordon, Latin American Task Force, Department of State, to Richard J. Goodwin, White House, March 6, 1961.

23. Ibid.

24. Ibid.

25. Ibid.

26. Department of State Bulletin (April 3, 1961) p. 473.

27. George Gordon Paton and Co. Coffee Annual, 1961, (1962), p. 164.

28. Ibid., p. 168.

29. Department of State Bulletin (August 28, 1961), p. 360.

3

**THE THEORY
OF EXPORT QUOTA
COMMODITY
AGREEMENTS**

Export quota agreements have been the most commonly used type of commodity agreement since World War II.* Within the agreement, market shares are allocated among its members. Price stabilization results from the annual adjustment of national export quotas.

---

*Export quota agreements have been used for coffee (1962, 1968), sugar (1954, 1959, and 1969), and in combination with a buffer stock in tin (1956, 1961, and 1966). The presence of consumer countries as members distinguishes the agreement from a straight producer cartel.

Consumer countries are also participants in the two other major types of commodity agreements—those based on the use of buffer stocks and those based on the multilateral contract. Under the buffer stock arrangement, excess stocks are used to keep prices within a predetermined range by purchases or sales from the stock. Current examples of the buffer stock form are the International Tin Agreement (1966) and the proposed International Cocoa Agreement. Under the multilateral contract, prices are also supported within a given range. At the maximum price set by the contract, producing countries must sell set quantities to consuming countries, and, at the minimum price, consuming countries must purchase set quantities from producers. Post-World War II wheat agreements (1949, 1953, 1956, 1962, and 1968) have been based on the multilateral contract.

POSSIBLE BENEFITS OF EXPORT QUOTA
COMMODITY AGREEMENTS

Terms of Trade

Export quota commodity agreements can check declining price trends—especially for products that are the subject of an inelastic demand—by limiting the offerings of the supported product on the world market.

Supporting the terms of trade of the LDC's by export quota agreements may be more politically palatable than direct foreign aid in consuming countries, assuming that the product supported is produced largely in the developing countries. Resource transfers—if made—do not show up in the government budget, and consumers may find it difficult to isolate their out-of-pocket losses. The commodity agreement mechanism may also be politically acceptable for the LDC's, reflecting the "farmers' preference for disguising the subsidy."[1] Most people, it has been noted, "prefer to receive charity in disguise."[2]

Price Stability

Export quota agreements may check price fluctuations. By setting price floors and ceilings and by adjusting export quotas to ensure that the price stays within the prescribed levels, they may permit the LDC's to carry out long-range development plans based on a stable revenue source. Consumers may also benefit occasionally by a dampening of extreme price rises.

Structural Reform

Export quota agreements may perform a sort of "holding action," during which structural reform of the market can take place. If prices remain stable at a remunerative level, the LDC's may have both time and resources to overcome their dependence on the supported commodity by diversifying into stronger sectors.

National sovereignty, however, is a formidable barrier against a supranational export quota agreement capable of overseeing effective production goals, tax, and diversification policy. In the last analysis, it is up to the producing countries to solve their own problems.

PROBLEMS WITH EXPORT QUOTA
COMMODITY AGREEMENTS

Inefficient Quota Allocation

Export quota commodity agreements may make two forms of serious resource misallocations. First, at the time national export quotas are set, the largest quotas may not go to the lowest cost producers but, instead, to those who have the most economic power and are the best bargainers.[3] Even a "technical" solution based on historical market performance may not reflect the lowest cost producers, as cost performance is always in flux. The second allocational error may occur during the course of the agreement, if quotas are not adjusted to reflect changing cost conditions.

The difficulty of renegotiation of market shares—as the experience of the ICA in 1965/66 and 1967/68 demonstrated—is that "for domestic political reasons, exporting countries may find it difficult to accept reductions in export quotas."[4]

Enforcement

Assignment of export quotas is one thing; enforcement is another. Large producers in the export quota commodity agreement—the oligopolists—will hesitate to drastically overstep their export quotas for fear of lowering the general price level, but small producers—or revisionists—aware that their impact on the general price level is likely to be slight, "have an economic incentive to avoid tight controls."[5]

The magnitude of the enforcement problem increases in proportion to the number of countries participating in the export quota agreement. This is a problem for a commodity such as coffee. Although about 50 percent of world coffee exports come from two countries—Brazil and Colombia—there are over thirty exporters of the commodity, as opposed to tin, for example, which has only a few major exporters.

Enforcement plays a dual role in an export quota commodity agreement. The first role is boundary maintenance.* Members

---

*For the Parsonian view that a key aspect of all organizational

must be kept <u>within</u> their assigned quota shares by effective legal mechanisms. Otherwise, the desired price-stabilizing effects of the agreement are less likely to be attained. Less obvious is the role of the enforcement system as an equilibrating mechanism, [6] needed to "get around" rigid export quotas. In other words, a tolerable amount of <u>overexports</u> to satisfy the legitimate grievances of dissatisfied members and new low-cost producers bound to emerge during the life of the agreement must be permitted in order to maintain the organizational equilibrium.* The enforcement paradox in export quota commodity agreements is that it is preferable to have some noncompliance with international law rather than none. The difficulty is knowing at what point to impose meaningful sanctions. [7]

Structural Difficulties

Export quota agreements, by raising prices, may call into being synthetic or other substitute products in place of the commodity being supported.

The "synthetics problem" varies from product to product, depending on market characteristics. It is technically easier to profitably make substitutes for some products (e.g., rubber) than for others (e.g., coffee). In addition, consumer standards differ from product to product. In the case of coffee, due to its habit-forming nature, consumers tend to resist substitutes.

Another structural problem is that export quota commodity agreements, by offering a guaranteed "reasonable" price for the

––––––––––––––

life is boundary maintenance, which develops under a constantly moving equilibrium, see Talcott Parsons, <u>The Social System</u> (New York: The Free Press, 1951), p. 481.

*As Kennan notes:

International political life is something organic, not something mechanical. Its essence is change; and the only systems for the regulation of international life which can be effective over long periods of time are ones sufficiently subtle, sufficiently pliable, to adjust themselves to constant change in the interests and power of the various countries involved.

George F. Kennan, <u>Memoirs</u> (New York: Bantam Books, 1967), p. 229.

supported product, may actually encourage overproduction. Opinion, however, is not unanimous that commodity agreements will call forth oversupply.[8]

A "working" export quota agreement has as its greatest check on oversupply the export quota given to each producing country. If the members know that they can only export a limited amount, the incentives for overproduction are greatly lessened.

AN IDEAL EXPORT QUOTA COMMODITY
AGREEMENT SYSTEM

There are four minimum requirements for an ideal export quota commodity agreement system:

1. Export quotas: export quotas should be based on national quotas, aimed at limiting world supply, and should be designed to keep prices at a given target level; quotas should be constantly real-located in favor of the more efficient producers.

2. Prices: a pricing system should evolve that would reflect the price movements in the various submarkets, if any, of the commodity.

3. Enforcement: an enforcement system should develop to see that export quotas are complied with—the adherence of as many countries as possible to the pact is important; otherwise, transshipments will be likely to occur.

4. Structural reform: a program of structural reform should be set up to correct the underlying market problems; this could include programs to limit or expand national output, depending on the nature of the market problem.

Political accommodation among the members of the commodity agreement is a precondition for its success. This often neglected aspect of export quota commodity agreements is analyzed next.

THE POLITICS OF EXPORT QUOTA
COMMODITY AGREEMENTS

Commodity agreements—and other international organizations—may fruitfully be conceptualized as consisting of three intersecting levels of political dynamics. The first level is between the various member governments pursuing different national policies. This is the level that is traditionally analyzed in the discipline of international politics, [9] and, indeed, it dominates the rest of this book. The second level is the political dynamics between the executive and legislative components of the commodity agreement—in the case of coffee, the Executive Board and the ICC. Finally, the interactions between governments and their constituent interests (in consuming countries, processors, brokers, and final consumers, and in producing countries, producer interests and middlemen) should be considered. A complete analysis of a commodity agreement should thus be multidimensional, moving "forward" into the international organization and "backward" into the politics of the member countries.

In terms of the conflicts between members of the commodity agreement, it would seem safe to generalize that there are two sets of pervasive conflicts that will inevitably arise: conflicts among exporting members over market shares and conflicts between exporting members and consuming members over prices.

Conflicts among exporting members over the fair division of market shares are between those exporters with export quotas that are relatively large and revisionist countries which feel they should have larger export quotas.

The experience of the 1962 ICA indicates that an export quota commodity agreement, to be successful, must develop annual equilibrating mechanisms between these two groups for flexibility in its export quota system. Limited duration and review arrangements are not enough to allow a commodity agreement to survive.

If equilibrating mechanisms do not develop, then the agreement will probably be restrictive and will serve only the interests of the entrenched oligopolists instead of the low-cost (or price) newcomers on the world market. The problem of "getting around" fixed export quotas, however, is less than overpowering in a viable agreement, as dissident members are generally unwilling to destroy an accord that is bringing them substantially higher prices than they would receive in its absence. The essentially political task of bringing market shares into a satisfactory balance with the desires of the exporting members thus tends to dominate its work.

The next six chapters explore in some detail the game of fair division among the exporting members of the 1962 ICA.

Chapter 4 describes the UNCC, which set up the 1962 ICA. Problems of methodology, statistical difficulties, and "exceptions" in the negotiating process are treated therein.

Chapter 6, on enforcement, describes implicit bargaining over export quota shares among the exporters, done by overshipping export quotas (i.e., outside the quotas negotiated in the 1962 Agreement). All commodity agreements share to a degree the problem of enforcement, with unhappy revisionists usually the worst offenders.

Chapter 7 again returns to a specific game of fair division within the ICA. The context, however, was somewhat different, as the issue was one of quota revision rather than original quota-setting. After three years, the members were to revise basic export quotas. Fortunately, they succeeded in doing so in a de facto manner, as opposed to the case of the 1958 International Sugar Agreement, which floundered on a similar three-year quota review provision.

The problems of "original" quota-setting (i.e., for a five-year period or for the duration of the agreement until revised) are revisited in Chapter 8, which describes the 1968 ICA.

The division of the soluble coffee market, and its relation to the green coffee market, is discussed in Chapter 9.

The second set of conflicts is between exporting and importing members of the commodity agreement over prices. Importing members are usually interested in doing their duty under the agreement—with a minimum of administrative obligations—to stabilize prices at levels they consider "reasonable." Exporting members, on the other hand, usually want more than that, i.e., price increases.

There was close cooperation on the whole in the ICO between consumers and producers. Differences over annual quota levels were usually equably settled. Chapter 6 explores a concrete case of conflict between the exporters and the importers over the annual quota level in the wake of the 1963/64 price rise caused by natural disasters in Brazil. The experience showed that the ICA was a two-way street, able to check sharp price rises harmful to consumers, as well as to support the price of coffee for the producers.

The experience of the 1962 ICA showed that the members were usually willing to compromise. Without compromise, no commodity agreement can succeed: that is the central lesson of the 1962 ICA.

NOTES

1. Isaiah Frank, "New Perspectives on Trade and Development," Foreign Affairs, XLV (April, 1967), 529.

2. John A. Pincus, Trade, Aid and Development (New York: McGraw-Hill Book Company, 1967), p. 277.

3. Wilson E. Schmidt, "The Case Against Commodity Agreements," Law and Contemporary Problems, XXVIII (Spring, 1963), 320.

4. John A. Pincus, "What Policy for Commodities," Foreign Affairs, XLII (January, 1964), 239.

5. Ibid.

6. The concept of the equilibrating mechanism is developed in Herbert Simon, Administrative Behavior: A Study in Decision-Making Processes in Administrative Organizations (New York: Macmillan, 1957). For an illuminating application of equilibrium analysis to international organizations, see George Liska, International Equilibrium (Cambridge, Mass.: Harvard University Press, 1957), p. 15.

7. See, in general, Bart S. Fisher, "Enforcing Export Quota Commodity Agreements," Harvard International Law Journal, XII (Summer, 1971), 401.

8. Wallich argues that commodity agreements will not lead to oversupply. See Henry C. Wallich, "Stabilization of Proceeds from Raw Material Exports," in Howard S. Ellis, ed., Economic Development for Latin America (New York: Macmillan, 1962), p. 351.

9. Chadwick F. Alger, "Research on Research: A Decade of Quantitative and Field Research on International Organizations," International Organization, XXIV (Summer, 1970), 433.

CHAPTER

4

THE
1962
INTERNATIONAL
COFFEE
AGREEMENT

The UNCC convened in New York on July 9, 1962. More than 350 delegates and observers from seventy-one countries and organizations concluded the 1962 ICA there on August 25, 1962. This chapter examines the politics of the 1962 negotiations and the system set up by the UNCC.

POLITICAL ACTION UNITS AT THE UNCC

The purpose of this section is to delineate the objectives and bargaining positions of the political action units at the 1962 UNCC. This is not an easy task, as the political action units—the principals in the UNCC negotiations—were often neither clearly defined nor spoken for by the real parties in interest.[1]

The Major Trading Countries

The major trading countries on both the producing and consuming sides wanted their importance on the world market to be translated into influence in the ICA. This showed up during the UNCC in the determination of the basic export quotas and, later, in the negotiations on voting procedures within the ICO.

The Smaller Trading Countries

The smaller trading countries were also interested in having a voice in final decisions of the UNCC and the ICO. Despite the slight importance of the small countries in terms of world output, coffee was often their major source of foreign revenue. The smaller countries, therefore, lobbied insistently for a one-man, one-vote regime, to protect their interests.

The Exporters

The exporters not only wanted to stabilize coffee prices but to raise them. Despite the common interest of the exporters in higher prices, the negotiations were characterized by divisiveness over issues of market allocation. Table 4 shows the marketing strength of the exporters in 1962.

The Latin Americans

The Latin Americans—as exporters—were interested in checking declining prices, achieving price stability, and maintaining their market position vis a vis the African producers, who had been advancing since 1950 in their share of world exports. The Latin Americans also wanted the European Common Market to drop preferential treatment for its African associate members.

Brazil

Brazil, a producer of Unwashed Arabica coffees, * hoped to obtain the following benefits from the ICA: (1) maximization of foreign

---

*The Unwashed Arabicas are the centrists of the world coffee market. They are typically sold at a lower price than are Colombian Milds or Other Milds and are usually above the Robustas. Their central price position results from preparation and consumer tastes. The bulk of Brazilian coffee is unwashed, prepared by the dry method, and, therefore, of poorer quality than the coffees of the other South and Central American Arabica-producing countries.

The dry method consists of three steps: (1) picking the ripe or unripe coffee cherry, (2) drying the cherry, and (3) hulling the dried cherry, when the parchment and the dried fruit skin are hulled away at the same time.

It is the second step that causes the harsh taste of "Brazils," as the cherries that are stripped or shaken from the tree are left in piles on the ground to dry and, then, are gathered.

TABLE 4

World Exports of Green Coffee, 1962

Countries of Origin	Thousands of Bags of 132.276 Pounds Each[a]	Percentage of Total
Western Hemisphere:		
Pan-American Coffee Bureau		
Brazil	16,377	35.4
Colombia	6,561	14.2
Guatemala	1,552	3.4
El Salvador	1,478	3.2
Mexico	1,458	3.2
Costa Rica	902	1.9
Ecuador	551	1.2
Dominican Republic	487	1.1
Nicaragua	338	0.7
Venezuela	319	0.7
Honduras	266	0.6
Cuba	139	0.3
Panama	27	0.1
Total Pan-American Coffee Bureau	30,455	66.0
Other Western Hemisphere:		
Peru	624	1.3
Haiti	514	1.1
Various[b]	250	0.5
Total Other Western Hemisphere	1,388	2.9
Total Western Hemisphere	31,843	68.9
Africa:		
Kenya, Uganda, and Tanganyika	3,232	7.0
Ivory Coast	2,670	5.8
Angola	2,620	5.7
Ethiopia	1,023	2.2
Cameroun	635	1.4
Malagasy Republic	934	2.0
Congo-Kinshasa	600	1.3
Rwanda-Burundi	383	0.8
Guinea	200	0.4
Togo	192	0.4
Central African Republic	130	0.3
Spanish Africa	110	0.2
Various[c]	200	0.4
Total Africa	12,929	27.9
Asia and Oceania:		
Indonesia	961	2.1
India	331	0.7
Yemen	67	0.1
Various[d]	125	0.3
Total Asia and Oceania	1,484	3.2
Total World	46,256	100.0

[a]132.276 pounds is equal to 60 kilos.
[b]Includes Bolivia, Guadeloupe, Hawaii, Jamaica, Martinique, Paraguay, Puerto Rico, Surinam, Trinidad, and so forth.
[c]Includes Cape Verde, Comores Islands, Congo-Brazzaville, Dahomey, Gabon, Ghana, Liberia, Mauritania, Nigeria, São Thomé and Principe, Sierra Leone, Samalia, and so forth.
[d]Includes New Caledonia, New Guinea, New Hebrides, Singapore, Timor, and so forth.

Source: Annual Coffee Statistics, 1963 (New York: Pan American Coffee Bureau, 1964), Appendix.

exchange earnings, (2) stabilization of foreign exchange earnings, and (3) minimization of the loss of market shares.

The first was closely related to the imperatives of economic development. Brazil, like the other LDC's, needed foreign exchange to import capital equipment and other essentials.

With respect to stabilization of foreign exchange earnings, Brazil also wanted stability of the proceeds from coffee exports. It was important for Brazil to be able to plan ahead for its economic development. Stability of foreign exchange from coffee exports at between $700 and $750 million per annum was, thus, a hallmark of Brazilian coffee policy.

The third benefit was concerned with minimizing the loss of market shares. The loss of Brazil's "rightful" market share — Brazil's share of world coffee exports declined from 64 percent (in volume) in 1939/40 to 35.4 percent in 1962—was seen as "necessary to keep its external coffee prices at an artificially high level.

Brazil chose not to check African market entry. To have challenged the Africans directly would have required abandoning a price defense strategy for a volume strategy.

Brazil's fear of a volume strategy to counter the African Robusta exporters was founded on several premises. The first was a technical mistake of analysis on African costs. Brazil credited the Africans with lower costs than they, in fact, had.[2] Furthermore, much of the world's high-cost obsolescent capacity was in Brazil, and a price war would have caused much economic distress and unemployment there.[3] Finally, had Brazil adopted a volume strategy, it might have suffered a substantial—if temporary—reduction in foreign exchange, because of the low price elasticity of demand for coffee. This risk was not to be taken lightly with the country's key export commodity.*

Colombia

Colombia, like Brazil, was interested in foreign exchange maximization, stability of export proceeds, and retention of its

---

*In other words, Brazil was not in a position to carry out its threats to "dump" coffee to win back its "rightful" market share. For information on the concept of "threats" in markets as viable strategies, see Martin Shubik, Strategy and Market Structure (New York: John Wiley & Sons, 1959), p. 107.

market share. Colombia, as a large oligopolist, had an interest in preserving the status quo and, therefore, favored an export-quota type of agreement.

Both Colombia and Brazil had an interest in burden-sharing. As they saw it, their price defense policies and stock retention were acts of sacrifice and self-abnegation. The other producers had an "obligation" to share the burden by cutting production down to assigned quotas.

Columbia was competing against the Central American Mild producers for the first-quality blend segment of the world coffee market.* Consequently, Colombia wanted to tie down the Central Americans into tight export quotas, much as Brazil wanted to tie down the Africans.

The Central Americans

The Central American exporters, falling into the "small" exporter group, shared with Brazil and Colombia an increase in foreign exchange maximization, stabilization of export proceeds, and retention of market shares. Like Brazil and Colombia, the Central Americans attacked to "obstacles" of the European Economic Community (EEC) as "unfair" barriers to consumption of their coffees.

---

*The Colombian Milds are the aristocrats of the world coffee market, typically selling above all other Arabicas and Robustas.

Tradition and consumer taste generally establish Colombians at a slight premium over the Other Milds bracket and at a somewhat larger premium over Robustas. As their name indicates, Colombians have a more "Mild" flavor than do Brazils and Robustas. The main reason for the flavor difference—which makes Colombians valuable for blending purposes—is the method of preparation and care used in cultivation.

Colombian coffee is prepared by the wet method, as are the Central American coffees in the Other Milds group. The wet process differs from the dry process, which is used for Brazils and most of the Robustas, in these respects: (1) in the wet method, the picked coffee does not rot in the fields after picking; (2) the coffee is pulped, repeatedly washed, whereas, by the dry method, the pulping is done without washing; and (3) the coffee is pulped, fermented, and hulled in separate steps, whereas, by the dry method, all three steps are accomplished at the same time.

The Central Americans had, since 1945, been organized into Fedecame. Unfortunately, Fedecame was an impotent organization that was consistently bypassed by its members in policy discussions on international agreements. The minimal cooperation among the Central Americans put them at a disadvantage in bargaining against Brazil and Colombia.

The Africans

The Africans wanted to continue their impressive advances on the world coffee market. African exports had grown from 21.9 percent of the world coffee market in 1957 to 27.9 percent in 1962. Meanwhile, Western Hemisphere exports had declined from 74.3 percent of the world's coffee exports in 1957 to 68.9 percent in 1962.

The reasons for the growth of the African share of the world coffee market were as follows: (1) the availability of cheap land and labor in Africa, which allowed producers to set up low-cost operations; (2) the Brazilian external strategy of price defense, which held a price umbrella over the world coffee market; (3) the African market strategy of selling coffee at the prices needed to move it out of storage, rather than stocking coffee to raise prices; (4) the suitability of Africa's mainly Robusta production for the manufacture of instant coffee, consumption of which rose sharply in the 1950's, and early 1960's;* and (5) the European Common Market preference, which increased its African associate members' exports into Europe. As African exports into the U.S. and European markets grew apace, so did Latin American interest in locking the African producers into a tight export quota agreement.

Given the continuing advance of the African exporters in world coffee trade, it is more difficult to fathom their reasons for entering an export quota agreement. The main reason for African cooperation at this point seems to have been the fear of further price declines in their Robusta exports. Robusta prices had declined steadily since

---

*Robustas differ generically from the Arabica coffees, and as might be guessed from the name, are a more durable, typically larger, tree than the more fragile Arabica varieties. Unlike Arabicas, Robustas can flourish at fairly low altitudes, tend to grow in very dense shade, and thrive on consistently hot weather. Robustas produce a largish fruit, which has a marked pungent flavor, due partially to the tree variety and to the fact that Robustas are typically unwashed and prepared by the dry method.

1954 (1954, 63.0 U.S. cents per pound; 1962, 19.9 U.S. cents per pound). (See Table 2.) Further declines might have brought African producers below their low-cost production level. An unnerving factor for the Africans was the presence of the massive Brazilian stocks. The Africans knew that Brazil could either dump their stocks on the world market or snipe at them in particular markets by dumping selectively. Finally, the Africans assumed that the 1962 ICA would be flexible in its application for the expanding Robusta submarket through waivers, a pricing system based on differentiated quota expansions by submarket (selectivity) and a porous enforcement system. Their hopes were realized during the life of the ICA, as they continued to expand their market share, despite national export quotas.

The contest over market shares explained the constant rifts between the Africans and the Latin Americans at the UNCC and, later, in the ICO. The dominant oligopolists, Brazil and Colombia, attempted to maintain the status quo, to minimize their losses, and to cut African gains. Conversely, the Africans, seeking expanding market entry, played the role of revisionists and were always trying to widen their market share at the expense of the Latin Americans.

The Inter-African Coffee Organization (IACO), formed on December 7, 1960, served as a forum for the Africans to work out a common negotiating position, as well as a device for the coordination of marketing policy. The IACO, however, represented many African interests.

The Franc Zone

The "franc zone" consisted of the former French coffee-producing territories. Bound together by a common marketing system—the Caisse de Stabilisations des Prix—these generally West African countries had a common interest in the preservation of their EEC and French preferences. The Common Market preference—viewed by the Latin Americans as an unfair obstacle—was seen by the Franc Zone as an economic necessity and a political fact of life.

The franc zone group also fought for, and won, the concept of group membership within the ICO. They later organized themselves into OAMCAF (Organization African et Malgache du Cafe) to try to counter the Latin American oligopolists.

The East Africans

The British-controlled exporting territories of Kenya, Tanganyika, and Uganda shared with the franc zone producers an interest in expanding sales. They advocated—as did the franc zone producers—a selectivity pricing system to reflect the demands of consumers.

The Other Africans

The other Africans were Portugal (speaking for Angola), Ethiopia, and Nigeria. Portugal wanted an exemption from its export quota for coffee shipped from Angola to the mother country. It also wanted, as did Ethiopia and Nigeria, export quotas that were as large as possible.

The Importers

The importers (see Table 5) wanted to do their duty at minimum cost. They wanted stable but not higher prices, with a minimum of administrative "policing" obligations. The Scandinavian countries were particularly sensitive on the latter point.

The United States

The United States hoped the ICA would achieve coffee price stability, check declining prices, buy time for structural reform of the market, and prove to be a politically palatable manner of transferring resources to the LDC's.

The economic interests for the United States under the ICA were its spin-off benefits for American exporters (who would sell more to more prosperous LDC's) and the interest of its coffee roasters in market stability and an assured source of supplies. These economic interests were arguably offset, however, by the higher coffee prices resulting from the ICA's support of the coffee market and by the fact that much of what the LDC's would be buying with their additional foreign exchange would not be from the United States.

The interests of the U.S. coffee trade in the ICA were defined by the changing shape of the domestic market. Within the U.S. market, African imports were gaining steadily on imports from Brazil and Colombia. African exports rose from 2 percent (in quantity) of the U.S. coffee import market in 1949 to 20.8 percent in 1962. Meanwhile, Brazilian coffee exports to the United States declined from 57.9 percent (in quantity) in 1949 to 37.1 percent in 1962. Colombia's share dropped from 22.4 percent (in quantity) in 1949 to 17.7 percent in 1962, and the Central American coffees held steady at about 12 percent (in quantity) of the U.S. market. The large

TABLE 5

World Imports of Green Coffee, 1962

Countries of Destination	Thousands of Bags	Percentage of Total
United States	24,549	52.1
Canada	1,230	2.6
Other Americas:		
Argentina	486	1.0
Chile	69	0.1
Uruguay	40	0.1
Various[a]	5	-
Total Other Americas	600	1.2
Europe:		
Germany (West)	3,899	8.3
France	3,472	7.4
Italy	1,865	4.0
Netherlands	1,063	2.3
Belgium-Luxembourg	923	2.0
Total EEC:	11,222	24.0
Sweden	1,397	3.0
United Kingdom	1,155	2.4
Denmark	761	1.6
Finland	654	1.4
Norway	516	1.1
Switzerland	507	1.1
Spain	481	1.0
Austria	224	0.5
Portugal	204	0.4
Yugoslavia	171	0.4
Greece	146	0.3
Various[b]	110	0.2
Total Other West Europe:	6,326	13.4
U.S.S.R.	376	0.8
Germany (East)	484	1.0
Czechoslovakia	147	0.3
Poland	120	0.2
Hungary	57	0.1
Various[c]	35	0.1
Total East Europe	1,219	2.5
Total Europe	18,767	39.9
Africa:		
Algeria	456	1.0
South Africa	206	0.4
Sudan	128	0.3
Morocco	143	0.3
Egypt	58	0.1
Tunisia	43	0.1
Various[d]	50	0.1
Total Africa	1,084	2.3
Asia and Oceania:		
Japan	256	0.5
Lebanon	58	0.1
Australia	185	0.4
Thailand	79	0.2
Israel	83	0.2
Syria	28	0.1
Various[e]	200	0.4
Total Asia and Oceania	889	1.9
Total Imports	47,119	100.0

[a]Includes Netherlands West Indies and other Caribbean Islands.
[b]Includes Cyprus, Gibraltar, Iceland, Ireland, Malta, Trieste, and Turkey.
[c]Includes Albania, Bulgaria, Roumania, and so forth.
[d]Includes Libya, Mozambique, Rhodesia and Nyasaland, Tangier, Zanzibar.
[e]Includes Ceylon, Hong Kong, Iran, Iraq, Jordan, Macao, New Zealand, Pakistan, Philippine Republic, Viet-Nam, and so forth.

Source: Annual Coffee Statistics, 1963 (New York: Pan American Coffee Bureau, 1964), Appendix.

African increases were due to an increased demand for solubles in the United States, new uses for Robustas in U.S. blends, and the Brazilian policy of price defense, which held up a price umbrella for African entry.

The result of African entry into the U.S. coffee market was a close working relationship between several large roasters in the U.S. industry, including General Foods and African Robusta-exporting countries (e.g., the Ivory Coast).

The U.S. Government, as the representative of the largest single political action unit on the importing side, was thus faced with a difficult balancing act, as it was simultaneously representing the American consumer, the American trade (which was itself split into large and small roasters and large and small coffee brokers), and the diplomatic interests of the United States.

The EEC

The second largest importing unit was the EEC. The Yaounde Convention had ended all duties and quotas on imports from associated African countries and was to confront "outsiders" with a common external tariff on coffee of 9.6 percent as of June 1, 1964. Protecting this preference from the attacks of the Latin Americans who wanted "in" or wanted it abolished was a major diplomatic goal of the EEC at the UNCC. Throughout the life of the 1962 ICA and, again, in the 1968 renewal negotiations, the Latin Americans tried to use the mechanism of the ICO as a means of reshaping EEC coffee policy.

Within the EEC, the French had a strong diplomatic interest in fighting for the preference, since it benefited the former French colonies. The Germans were less interested in defending the preference than the French, but, in the interests of EEC unity, did support the French demands for the preference. The primary goal of Germany, Italy, the Netherlands, and Belgium was to satisfy local trade interests, which wanted a minimum of red tape and enough "loopholes" in the ICA to permit them to cheat.

The European Free Trade Association

The Nordic countries of the European Free Trade Association (EFTA), while recognizing the necessity of policing, tried to reduce administrative obligations to a minimum. The United Kingdom had a strong diplomatic interest in supporting its Robusta-exporting East African territories and an economic interest in assuring Robusta

supplies for its soluble coffee industry. It, therefore, joined with
the French and the West African Robusta exporters in arguing for a
selectivity pricing system in the ICA (i.e., pricing by submarkets).

The lack of a "preference" and a smooth exporting relationship
with the Latin Americans allowed the EFTA members to work as
mediators in the ICO between the Africans and the Latin Americans,
a position that the EEC, with its preference, was naturally unable to
fill.

The Other Importers

The remaining importing countries saw the ICA as an innovative
cooperative mechanism that was capable of ameliorating long-standing
LDC problems and as a reinforcement of the commodity agreement
idea as a solution to their own problems. Canada, for example,
joined as a means of getting support for the International Wheat Agreement. Argentina joined for the same reason, in addition to its desire
to increase stability in Latin America.

THE UNCC REGULATORY PROVISIONS*

Export Quotas

The central mission of the ICA was to check price declines and
instability in the world coffee market. The regulatory provisions of

---

*The legal principles guiding the drafters of the ICA were those
of the Final Act of the Havana Conference, known as the Havana
Charter. Havana Charter for an International Trade Organization
Incorporated in the Final Act of the United Nations Conference on
Trade and Employment, U.N. Doc. E/Conf. 2/78 (1948), also contained in Havana Charter for an International Trade Organization,
presented March 24, 1948, Department of State, Pub. 3206 (Commercial Policy Series 114). The Havana Charter set up an international
trade organization, to complement the activities of the International
Bank for Reconstruction and Development and the International Monetary Fund. Despite the fact that the international trade organization
never became a reality, many of the principles it enunciated did
later provide legal guidelines for international trade policy.

This was particularly true in the area of commodity policy.

the ICA, i.e., the system of administered export quotas, were designed to do this by limiting the offerings of coffee on the international
market.

The export quota mechanism dealt directly with the oversupply
problem by controlling the flow of coffee to the market and was
relatively simple to administer. In addition, its essential workability
had been proven in former short-term agreements. Thus, as the
negotiating records of the UNCC make clear, there was no debate
over the operating mechanism of the ICA at the UNCC. There were,
however, four separate issues that bedeviled the lawyers and diplo-
mats negotiating the ICA export quota provisions at the UNCC—methodology, the small country problem, political complications, and
statistics.

Methodology

Of prime importance to the producing countries was their share
of the total export quota. Hanging on the resolution of this question
was, of course, the size of the total annual quota, which could then
be expanded or contracted, according to market conditions.

The first problem was the sequence of calculating quotas.
Either a "reasonable" estimate of total world demand could be made,
with the total then to be divided up among exporting political action
units or the approach of "acceptable" export quotas could have been
used. This latter method would have involved adding up all the
"acceptable" basic export quotas and was "virtually certain to produce an unrealistic total quota figure."[4]

The second problem was the manner in which the individual

Despite the general free-trade orientation of the Havana Charter and
its condemnation of private monopolies and cartels, certain exceptions
were recognized for trade in primary commodities. The modalities
for commodity agreements were spelled out in Chapter VI of the
Havana Charter.

Although the Havana Charter was not ratified by enough governments, the rules of Chapter VI were agreed upon in the Economic
and Social Council of the U.N. as the terms of reference for the
conclusion of international commodity agreements between U.N.
members. For further details on the Havana Charter, see Clair
Wilcox, A Charter for World Trade (New York: The Macmillan
Company, 1949), pp. 114-26.

(basic export quota shares) quotas were to be derived.* Either the historical share approach or the flexible approach could have been used.

The historical share approach would have projected historical export quota patterns into the export quota mechanism of the ICA. This methodology was favored by Brazil and Colombia, which wanted to keep the status quo and to preserve their market shares for as long as possible.

The flexible approach was favored by the Africans, as they were confident that Robustas would continue to be demanded by consumers. Consequently, they favored a system based on flexible adjustment for the different submarkets coffee, i.e., a selectivity pricing system.

The methodological controversy masked the real battle. The participants at the UNCC wanted to export as much coffee at reasonable prices as possible. The historical approach became a euphemism for supporting the oligopolists—the flexible approach for support of the African position.

The Small Country Problem

The small countries contended that they should receive special consideration on export quota allocations. El Salvador argued that the economic dependence of small countries on coffee production "should also be a basic principle"[5] in the determination of export quotas. And India proposed that quota restrictions should not apply to producers whose output represented less than 5 percent of world production, arguing that this would allow the small producers "to stabilize their economies and to obtain the foreign exchange they

---

*The negotiation of export quotas, prices, and obstacles to trade and consumption was done in Economic Committee II, which was established by and reported to the Executive Committee of the UNCC. Economic Committee II had a limited membership (Brazil, Colombia, Mexico, Costa Rica, El Salvador, Tanganyika, Portugal, Ivory Coast, India, and the United States, United Kingdom, France, Italy, Sweden, Australia, and Germany) and was the only major conference committee to work without summary records of its meetings, which was done to ensure secrecy and frank discussion within the Committee. An unfortunate side effect of this extreme secrecy was that many participants at the UNCC often did not understand the rationale behind Economic Committee II's decisions.

needed to buy manufacturing articles from the industrial countries."[6]
Had such a quota exemption been adopted, only Brazil and Colombia
and, in some years, the Ivory Coast would have been subject to the
quota system. For obvious reasons, India's proposal was not happily
received by the dominant oligopolists.

Political Complications

No country wanted to sign an agreement that gave it a smaller
quota than it had under the short-term agreements, even if it had not
filled its quota under former agreements.

In addition, a "technical" solution could not be fairly applied to
countries that had experienced abnormal political difficulties (e.g.,
a civil war) during the historical period selected as the base period
for quota determination. The Congo Kinshasa, for example, recover-
ing from its civil war, asked for a "realistic" setting of export quotas
for "equitable" reasons.

The delegates knew that after the UNCC, they would have to
"sell" the ICA to their parliaments for ratification. Thus, they
tended to demand basic quotas approximating their "best-ever" export performance.

Statistics

The fourth problem in the quota negotiations was the lack of
agreement on an acceptable set of statistics on which to base an historical analysis. At the UNCC, fortunately, the U.S. Department of
Agriculture's estimates of world coffee production and exports,
based on attache reports, were available for use. The accuracy of
these export and production estimates, however, was bitterly con-
tested by many countries.

These problems of export quota allocation delayed consideration
of negotiated basic quota shares until the last three days of the UNCC
(the conference was scheduled for six weeks). It was obviously
absurd to believe that the delegates in the space of three days could
review the negotiated quotas with their governments in detail.

The delay, however, did allow time for writing a complicated
text of seventy-four articles and three annexes. George V. Robbins
of General Foods, an industry "advisor" to the U.S. delegation,
described the final scene:

Needless to say . . . very few countries were happy at the
suggested quotas and when they received them it was something

like a nuclear explosion . . . The arguments back and forth,
the debates, the compromises offered and rejected, consumed
many hours and many meetings of many types. At midnight on
the next to last day of the conference, the various producing
groups were meeting in different room with liason provided
by myself, the U.K., and U.S. delegates among others. If you
ever saw trading on any exchange this was it. Finally, at 5
A.M. agreement on quotas was reached. [7]

Annex

The complex formula devised to solve the export quota problem
had the following elements: (1) each country's quota share was based
on its average exportable production (total annual production minus
domestic consumption) in its choice of either the two coffee years
1961/62 and 1962/63, or the four coffee years 1959/60-1962/63, the
last year in each case being an estimate; (2) the base average was
then reduced by ascending percentages of retention. The figures were
6 percent up to 500,000 bags, 8 percent up to 1 million bags, 10 percent up to 2 million bags, and 12 percent up to 10 million bags; and
(3) actual quotas then were adjusted to reflect the special problems
of particular exporters. [8]

The result of the UNCC quota negotiations was, then, a complex
three-tiered system of administered export quotas. The first operational quota was the basic export quota. This represented each member's percentage share of the world market. This quota came to be
known as the Annex A quota, as the market shares hammered out at
the UNCC were listed in Annex A of the Agreement. (See Table 6.)
The second quota was the annual export quota, fixed by the ICC at the
beginning of each coffee year, based on the Council's estimate of
total world imports and probable nonmember exports for that year.
Finally, the quarterly export quota aimed at ensuring orderly marketing throughout the coffee year. [9]

Could any export quota system, however, no matter how finely
tuned a political compromise in the year of its inception, be fluid
enough to equilibrate the dynamic low-cost African Robusta producers
and other exporter members dissatisfied with their assigned basic
quota shares? Five possible equilibrating mechanisms, four written
into the Agreement and one tacit, could, it was hoped, release the
tensions of the Annex A settlement.

The first equilibrating mechanism written into the ICA was a
provision for the ICC to review the Annex A basic quotas during the
last six months of the coffee year ending on September 30, 1965,
"in order to adjust them to general market conditions."[10] This

TABLE 6

1962 International Coffee Agreement Quota Allotments—Annex A Quota*

Exporting Country	Basic Export Quotas In Bags of 132.276 Pounds	Percentage of Total
Colombia	6,011,280	13.053
Tanganyika	435,458	0.947
Kenya	516,835	1.123
Burundi and Rwanda	340,000	1.085
Costa Rica	950,000	2.063
Cuba	200,000	0.430
Dominican Republic	425,000	0.923
Ecuador	552,000	1.199
El Salvador	1,429,500	3.105
Guatemala	1,344,500	2.919
Haiti	420,000	0.912
Honduras	285,000	0.619
India	360,000	0.782
Mexico	1,509,000	3.277
Nicaragua	419,100	0.910
Panama	26,000	
Peru	580,000	1.259
Venezuela	475,000	1.031
Brazil	18,000,000	39.088
Ethiopia	850,000	2.551
Cameroun	762,795	1.657
Central African Republic	150,000	0.326
Congo-Brazzaville	11,000	
Dahomey	37,224	
Gabon	18,000	
Ivory Coast	2,324,278	5.047
Malagasy Republic	828,828	1.800
Togo	170,000	0.369
Uganda	1,887,737	4.100
Portugal	2,188,648	4.830
Congo-Leopoldville	700,000	2.476
Indonesia	1,176,000	2.549
Nigeria	18,000	
Sierra Leone	65,000	
Trinidad	44,000	
Yemen	77,000	
Grand Total	45,587,183	

*Special provisions for possible upward adjustments were made for Haiti, Dominican Republic, Congo-Leopoldville, Rwanda, and Burundi.

quota review, however, could not provide instant relief. For this
purpose a second equilibrating mechanism, the waiver, was introduced. The waiver allowed a member to export more if it was subject
to "exceptional or emergency circumstances."11 The third equilibrating mechanism, Article 41, pledged relief to consumers hard pressed
to obtain needed supplies. By a distributed two-thirds majority vote
(i.e., two-thirds of both the exporting and importing members), the
ICC was empowered to expand or reallocate basic quotas. While
apparently aimed at consumers, this Article could strengthen the
hand of the revisionists within the Agreement, namely the Africans,
by permitting them to argue that, as consumer demand grew for their
Robustas, the negotiated export quotas should be revised accordingly.

The most drastic equilibrating mechanism written into the
Agreement was a provision for voluntary withdrawal available for
dissatisfied members.12

The fifth equilibrating mechanism was a tacit one—the construc-
tion of the system to enforce the ICA quotas. To the degree that
quotas could be overshipped, desires for renegotiation of quotas might
be abated. On the other hand, a porous system, liable to undermine
the Agreement, could not be sanctioned.

THE ENFORCEMENT SYSTEM

Obligations of Importing Countries

The extent of the obligations of importing member countries
was a subject of great controversy at the UNCC and, obviously, of
paramount importance in the establishment of a viable control system.
The first set of issues at the UNCC covered importer participation
in a certificates of origin system to regulate the exports of members.
On this enforcement question, as on others at the UNCC, the importers
wanted to "do their duty" with as few burdensome obligations as
possible. Thus, several European maritime countries (Holland,
the United Kingdom, Belgium, and Germany) opposed the administrative burdens of checking certificates of origin and furnishing verification of certificates of origin to the ICO.13

Opposing the maritime questions on this question was a coalition
led by the United States and Brazil, which argued that the certificates
were essential for ICO enforcement of the export quotas established
at the UNCC. This issue was "lost" by the maritime countries, as
the ICO adopted a seemingly workable certificates of origin system.

Under the certificates system, every exporting member was obligated to send certificates of origin along with all coffee shipments[14] and copies of all such documents to the ICO in London.[15] The certificates were to be issued by a qualified agency chosen by the member,[16] and the member was obligated to keep the ICO apprised of the name of its designated agency.[17]

Of greater importance to the ICO enforcement system was the extent of _importer_ enforcement. Here, the Agreement provisions appeared to be relatively strict, stating that "each Member shall prohibit the entry of any shipment of coffee from any other Member which is not accompanied by a certificate of origin or a certificate of re-export."[18] The Agreement authorized—as a backstop for the importers' policing efforts—ICC intervention to verify the certificates of origin in order to ascertain any possible irregularities.[19] The Council was also given the power to declare certification by a particular agency unacceptable to it.[20]

A graduated system of sanctions was established for exporter members to ensure compliance with these treaty provisions. If an exporter member exceeded its quota for any quarter, the Council was authorized to deduct from one or more future quotas an amount equal to that excess.[21] If the offense was repeated, the Council was authorized to deduct double the excess from future quotas.[22] If direct overshipments occurred a third time during the duration of the accord, the Council was authorized to again deduct double the excess shipment and was also permitted to take action to require the withdrawal of the offending member from the ICO.[23]

The certificates of origin system was far from watertight. Despite the fact that certificates of origin were required to accompany shipments, the system could be defeated merely by not sending in certificates to the ICO secretariat in London, or by sending them in after long delays. Secondly, the simple model of the certificate of origin could be easily forged either in or outside of the original exporter's territory. Finally, two loopholes in the system emerged from the provisions themselves. Article 44 of the ICA prohibited importing members only from accepting shipments unaccompanied by a certificate of origin. But what if the accompanying certificate were clearly invalid? Certain importing and exporting members later argued—with the greatest of sophistry—that _any_ certificate, even if forged, was permissible under the ICA. Otherwise, it was argued, the word "valid" would have been inserted before the word "certificates" in Article 44. Perhaps, the most glaring omission, however, was the absence of provisions for penalties to be assessed against importing members for aiding violators of the ICA. Domestic legal sanctions within many importing countries later proved to be inadequate, raising the question—who was going to police the policeman?

The second set of issues related to importer obligations on
coffee imports from nonmembers. This problem obviously had to be
dealt with in some manner, or coffee-exporting countries would have
had little incentive to join the ICA. Nonmember exports at below
agreed minimum prices might then have undermined the market shares
of the ICA members.

Debate on the subject split the UNCC into two groups. In favor
of strict limitations on imports from nonmembers were most prospective producer members (for example, Brazil, Colombia, Guatemala,
and Mexico) and some consumer countries (for example, the United
States and Australia). They argued that: (1) regulation of imports
from nonmembers would add to the effectiveness of the ICA control
system and that, without such regulation, the ICA might go the way
of earlier short-term agreements; (2) it would be inequitable for nonmembers to be allowed to gain in market shares at the expense of
member countries; and (3) such regulation could coerce countries
into joining the ICA. [24]

Those opposed to limiting imports from nonmembers—Norway,
Sweden, the Netherlands, and Japan—argued that (1) any historical
span used for reference as a base period would be of limited utility
in a changing world market; (2) the principle of free trade should be
interfered with as little as possible; (3) members of the ICA should
wait and see what percentage of nonmember producing countries
would join the Agreement: (4) such regulation would limit the growth
of world demand and slow structural improvement of the world coffee
market; and (5) nonmember limitations would complicate existing
bilateral arrangements. [25]

The result of the debate on limitations of nonmember coffee exports was Article 45 of the 1962 ICA. This allowed the ICC to limit
total annual imports from nonmembers to a quantity not in excess of
its average annual imports from nonmember countries as a group
during the three year prior to the date the ICA entered into force
if it found that "exports from nonmember countries as a group"[26]
were distributing the exports of members. Limited punitive sanctions
were also granted to the ICC. *

Article 45 left open an obvious conduit for "tourist coffee," as
pundits later quaintly dubbled ex-quota coffee shipments. By not

---

*If an importing member failed to comply with Article 45 require-
ments, the ICC was empowered, by a distributed two-thirds majority
vote, to suspend both its voting rights in the ICC and the Executive
Board of the ICO. International Coffee Agreement, Art. 45 (8).

imposing a <u>present</u> prohibition against unlimited member imports
from nonmembers, the door to massive triangular transshipments of
coffee through nonmembers—clearly not within the spirit of the ICA—
was opened. Article 45 represented more than a victory for the maritime powers favoring minimal administrative obligations—it represented
the possible undoing of the ICA.*

New Markets

The third area of controversy dealt with the concept of "new
markets." The exporters claimed that, for promotional purposes,
they wanted to increase their coffee sales on an ex-quota basis in
markets with low consumption and the possibility of market growth.
They argued fervently that nonquota exports would not destabilize the
world coffee market. Unspoken was the exporters' desire to use nonquota markets also as entrepôts for triangular shipments to traditional
markets, i.e., as a mechanism for "cheating."

---

*Coping with nonmembers has traditionally been a difficult
problem for commodity agreements. Under the International Tin
Agreement, the International Tin Council in 1958 reached an agreement with the U.S.S.R. under which exports of tin from the Soviet
Union to certain markets were temporarily limited. In 1966, the
International Tin Council reached an agreement with the United States,
in which the United States undertook in principle to moderate its program of stockpile sales of tin should it prove to be inconsistent with
the objectives of the Agreement. On earlier difficulties in securing
U.S. cooperation with the International Tin Agreement, see J. W. F.
Rowe, <u>Primary Commodities in International Trade</u> (Cambridge: University Press, 1965), p. 173.

The 1958 International Sugar Agreement—unlike the 1962 ICA—
imposed limitations on nonmember imports as of the treaty's entry
into force. Members agreed not to permit the imports of sugar from
nonmembers as a group during any quota year to exceed the total
quantity imported from those countries as a group during any one of
the three calendar years 1951, 1952, and 1953. Waivers were available
to moderate possible detrimental effects of the limitations on nonmember exports. The absence of the United States and the EEC from the
1968 International Sugar Agreement is certain to hamper its operations.
In the 1968 Agreement, members are obligated not to increase their
imports from nonmembers and not to import at all from nonmembers
when the world sugar price drops below 3.25 U.S. cents per pound.

The importers were lukewarm to the nonquota market concept.
The United States led the opposition to the Annex B list of nonquota
markets, arguing that it made little sense to endanger 95 percent of
the world coffee market for 5 percent of it in Annex B sales.[27] It
cited the participation of Bulgaria and East Germany in triangular
shipments under the short-term agreements.

The exporters "won" on this issue, as the Annex B list was codified into the Agreement.* The key points of the Annex B provisions
were as follows: (1) exports to countries listed in Annex B were not
to be charged to export quotas; (2) exporting members obligated themselves not to export to the countries listed in Annex B in the aggregate
more than the ICC's estimated total internal consumption of the Annex
B countries;[28] and (3) the ICC was given authority to charge to the
quota of exporting members the amount of coffee re-exported to members by the Annex B country in question, [29] to delete offending countries
from the Annex B list, [30] to require that coffee bags destined for
Annex B markets be specially marked, and to require that exporting
countries receive banking and contractual guarantees to prevent the
re-exportation to countries not listed in Annex B.[31] Finally, the
Council could, "whenever it deems necessary," engage the services
of an internationally recognized private concern to investigate any
irregularities in the Annex B countries.[32]

Those producing countries that intended to cheat under the ICA
"won" important victories in the UNCC negotiations by the nonlimita-
tion on nonmember exports and the insertion of the Annex B list.
Both, later, were prime sources of "cheaters' coffee" through transshipments. On the other hand, the certificates of origin system was
important to a viable export control system, as it allowed importing
countries to police exporting members of the Agreement.

The enforcement system, in short, left sizable loopholes for exporters wishing to cheat and for importers willing to assist cheaters.
As with most international agreements, the critical variable would
be the deeds of the signatories under the Agreement rather than the
words themselves.

-----

*International Coffee Agreement, 1962, Art. 40. Annex B coun-
tries were Bahrein, Basutoland, Bechuanaland, Ceylon, China (Taiwan),
China (People's Republic), Federation of Rhodesia and Nyasaland,
Hungary, Iran, Iraq, Japan, Jordan, Kuwait, Muscat and Oman, Phil-
lipines, Poland, Qatar, Republic of Korea, North Korea, South Viet-
Nam, North Viet-Nam, Rumania, Saudi Arabia, Somalia, South-West
Africa, Sudan, Swaziland, Thailand, Republic of South Africa, and the
U.S.S.R.

PRICES

The exporters had an interest in seeing coffee prices return to their high levels of the early 1950's, while the importers' interest was limited to a stabilization of coffee prices at "reasonable" levels. Only the French among the importers, for political reasons related to their desire to retain French influence in Africa and the developing world generally, were interested in having coffee prices raised. Within the exporters, a split developed between Brazil and Colombia, in favor of an export quota system with only pro rata distributions based on the Annex A quotas, and the African Robusta-exporting countries, which favored a flexible system based on linking quota expansion and reduction to price performance by submarket ("selectivity").

The U.S. position was that a price system which would equitably establish price ranges for the different coffees was an undertaking that was impossible in view of the short time at hand. Therefore, the United States pressed for an ICA that would rely on market forces under the quota system established in Annex A. The split in opinion among the UNCC participants produced a variety of "selectivity" plans, none of which were adopted. [33]

The result of the debate on pricing under the ICA was Article 35, which stated only that annual and quarterly export quota changes would be "applied pro rata" by the ICC, according to a distributed two-thirds majority vote. [34] There is no mention of a selectivity system in the 1962 ICA. But Article 41 in the 1962 ICA, later relied upon by the Africans as support for their claim of the legality of a selectivity system, stated that the ICC should try to ensure that the consumers obtain the kinds of coffees that they need. [35] The ICC was allowed to "decide to use whatever methods it considers practicable." Thus, the ICA—despite Article 35—was a model of equivocality on the pricing issue. The back door, at least, was left open for selectivity in the 1962 ICA.

The delegates could not even bring themselves to make a concrete promise on a price floor for coffee, agreeing only "on the necessity of assuring that the general level of coffee prices does not decline below the level of such prices in 1962." [36]

STRUCTURAL PROVISIONS

The heart of the 1962 ICA was its regulatory provisions aimed at checking price declines and the instability of the world coffee market. The structural provisions were, however, of equal long-run importance, as an objective of the Agreement was to establish a rough equilibrium between production and consumption in the world coffee economy.

Obstacles to Consumption

The obstacles issue resulted in a confrontation between the Latin American producers and the African producers in alliance with the European Common Market. At issue was the "EEC preference" for its African associate members under the terms of the Yaounde Convention which, as of July 1, 1964, was to leave the Latin Americans confronting a 9.6 percent tariff on green coffee exports, while the African associate members were to have free entry. A separate issue was the internal tax structure within the EEC, which placed heavy taxes on green coffee.

The Latin American coffee producers presented a common front on the obstacles issue. They argued that (1) regionalism had no place in global regulation of the coffee market; (2) discrimination practiced against Latin American coffee exports was in effect a subsidy by the Latin Americans to the Africans; (3) an expansion of the EEC that would take in the United Kingdom or the Scandinavian countries would further disadvantage the Latin Americans; and (4) preferential entry aided the European consumer, whereas "aid" should be the other way around, i.e., from Europe to Latin America.[37]

The United States supported the Latin American position, but was unwilling to abort the ICA over the problem of obstacles to consumption in the developed countries. It tried to persuade the Latin Americans to discuss export quotas instead of the alleged obstacles.

The EEC argued that it did not have the competence to collectively negotiate at the UNCC, that the most effective way to a global solution of the coffee problem was through regional means, and that there was little statistical proof that the EEC preference was a real hindrance to internal consumption of Latin American coffees, due to a lack of agreement on the price elasticity of demand.[38]

The African associates of the EEC vociferously defended their right to the EEC preference. They argued that the preference ensured fair terms of trade for them and was part of a whole series of benefits and responsibilities that could not be modified in part without upsetting the whole structure.[39]

Following a five-day Brazilian walkout over the obstacles issue, Article 47—a decisive victory for the African/ECC coalition—was agreed upon. It recognized "the utmost importance" of the "progressive removal of any obstacles" that might hamper increases in consumption. In its operative provisions, however, it only pledged members "to take into account the results" of an ICC review of obstacles to consumption. In short, the Article did not pledge members to specific actions to remove obstacles, but only noted that they were bad things.

Stocks

Brazil and Colombia—holders of most of the world's stocks—wanted a form of stock regulation that would amount to burden-sharing by the other producing countries.

The negotiations on stocks assumed a slightly unreal character, as participants quarreled over whether the ICC should "establish" or "recommend" a policy concerning stocks. Ecuador, for example, felt that "establish" sounded supranational and, therefore, preferred "recommend."[40] The debate seemed to lose further touch from the realities of the world coffee market when the delegates discussed how the policy that the ICC would establish (or recommend) would be implemented. The United States recalled its World War II experiences of interallied cooperation, when periodic reports of supply usage served to "incur public odium," and argued that similar results would follow if the coffee stock situation was reported within the ICO. Sweden and Norway backed up the U.S. rationale.[41]

The result of this debate was Article 51, which called upon the ICC to "establish a policy relative to such stocks," but said that "each producing Member shall be entirely responsible for the measures it applies to carry out the policy thus established by the Council."[42] This article was complemented by Article 52, which obliged each producing member to "submit written reports to the Council" on what it was doing to carry out the ICC's policy relative to stocks.

Production Goals

In the debate on production goals, the specter was again raised of a supranational ICO interfering in matters of domestic jurisdiction. Nicaragua complained that small countries would not have the economic resources to diversify as rapidly as the large countries and that production goals would, therefore, be unfair to them.[43] The United States also did not lobby for structural reforms to be written into the ICA and settled for a lowest common denominator agreement. The production goals debate thus ran along similar lines to the debate on stocks and had equally negligible results.

Article 48 of the ICA called on producing members to undertake to adjust their production in accordance with the ICC's policy relative to stocks, but again left to each producing member the complete responsibility for its policies and procedures that "it applies to achieve these objectives."

The weak production control and stock provisions of the 1962 ICA deferred immediate action on the oversupply problem. By seeming to promise some action while legally providing none, the provisions on stocks and production goals may have done more harm than good.

The International Coffee Fund

An international coffee fund for diversification was also discussed at the UNCC. There were three possible alternatives: (1) a strong diversification fund (with compulsory contributions), (2) a weak diversification fund (to be funded by voluntary contributions), and (3) no fund.

The countries in favor of a fund—Mexico and Brazil—argued that it could achieve the following: (1) make a modest start towards a structural reform of the world coffee economy; (2) assist other international agencies interested in LDC economic development; (3) result in burden-sharing for the needed diversification in Brazil; and (4) tie in with the recently launched Alliance for Progress as an instrument of development.

The antifund forces—Indonesia, the Netherlands, the United Kingdom, and Australia—argued that (1) the U.N. had many agencies to handle commodity problems; (2) resources for development should not be dispersed so broadly; (3) levies for such a fund would raise the price of coffee to the consumers; and (4) the fund would only complicate an already complex accord.[44]

The key to the debate was the attitude of the United States, which argued that it was already assisting LDC's through other programs and that a fund, if set up, should have voluntary contributions. Canada was also anxious to avoid using the ICA as a vehicle for resource transfers.

The result was Article 57, which permitted the ICC, if it wished, to set up an International Coffee Fund, for the purpose of diversification or for "the achievement of the other objectives of the Agreement."[45] Contributions to the Fund were to be voluntary.[46]

The Fund, then, was more goal than reality. The debate on the Fund was another reflection of the general lack of interest at the UNCC in structural reform of the world coffee economy.

Promotion

The other side of the coin in structural improvement of the world coffee market is increasing the consumption of coffee. The debate on promotion of coffee at the UNCC was fairly limited, with the French argument—that promotion should be continued as under the short-term agreement—carrying the day.[47] A limited article permitting the ICC to set up a World Coffee Promotion Committee if it "so decides" was adopted.[48] No concrete proposal was made in the Agreement, however, for a promotion program.

ORGANIZATIONAL ASPECTS

Voting

The debate on voting at the UNCC was between the large countries, which wanted their predominant place in the world coffee economy recognized, and the medium-range and small countries, which were afraid of being left out of the decision-making processes of the ICO.

The United Kingdom and France proposed that the United States and Brazil be limited to 300 votes out of a 1,000 possible on each side. The United States and Brazil felt that at least 400 votes were needed if their respective parliaments were to approve the ICA.[49] The smaller countries lobbied for a form of weighted voting that would protect their interests (Indonesia, India, Dominican Republic, and Spain).[50]

The solution was an ingenious form of weighted voting in the ICC. Brazil and the United States were limited to 400 votes each within the producing and consuming groups in the ICC, respectively, 150 votes were to be allocated equally to the members of each group, and the remaining votes were to be distributed on a weighted voting basis, in which importing countries would have votes in relation to their imports in the preceding three-year period and exporters would have votes based on basic export quotas.[51] A distributed two-thirds majority (that is, two-thirds of both the exporters and the importers) of the ICC would be needed for the most important decisions, such as annual quotas and waivers.[52] The negative votes of two countries would be required to veto a proposal.[53]

The intention of the solution was to provide for a meaningful form of democracy in an international organization where the accouterments of power are market shares. During the life of the ICA, voting was avoided whenever possible, due to its possible divisive effects within the ICO.

Powers of the ICC and the Executive Board

The ICO had to divide its responsibilities between its "legislative" organ, the ICC, and its "executive" branch, the Executive Board. It was clear that the members of the Executive Board, to be elected by the ICC,* would need at least minimal powers to "run" the ICO between the ICC's biannual sessions. [54] Nevertheless, a broad coalition including the United States and the smaller powers—which feared underrepresentation on the Executive Board—favored granting practically all important decisions to the ICC.

The result was that the ICC was granted sole responsibility for the most important operational aspects of the Agreement. Furthermore, it was prohibited by the Agreement from delegating in a principal/agent relationship powers over such key matters as quotas, enforcement measures, waivers, and stocks to the Executive Board. [55] As the Agreement evolved, it became clear that this was a key weakness in the organizational structure. Frequently, postal votes had to be taken to poll ICO members, which would have to make decisions without the benefit of ICC debate. This time-consuming process rendered the ICO incapable of moving decisively to check sudden price fluctuations.

Two issues—the 1963/64 price rise and the festering problem of enforcement—exposed the power vacuum created by the ICA. The next two chapters analyze these issues and the ICO's response to them.

NOTES

1. The designation of political action units in this chapter owes much in terminology to Richard B. Bilder, "The International Coffee Agreement: A Case History in Negotiation," Law and Contemporary Problems, XXVIII (Spring, 1963), 328-91.

---

*The election procedure was complex. The voting was for seven exporting members and importing members to be elected each coffee year. See International Coffee Agreement, 1962, Art. 15.

2. J. W. F. Rowe, The World's Coffee (London: H.M. Stationery Office, 1963), p. 27.

3. Ibid.

4. Bilder, op. cit., p. 356.

5. "Provisional Summary Record," Executive Committee, UNCC, August 25, 1962.

6. Ibid., September 28, 1962.

7. George V. Robbins, "The United Nations Coffee Conference," George Gordon Paton and Co. Coffee Annual, 1962 (1963), p. 61.

8. See Bilder, op. cit., p. 357, and U.N., United Nations Coffee Conference 1962, Summary of Proceedings, E/Conf. 42/8 (1962), p. 49.

9. On the annual export quota, see International Coffee Agreement, Art. 30 (1963), 14 U.S.T. 1911, T.I.A.S. No. 5505, 469 U.N.T.S. 169 (effective provisionally July 1, 1963, and definitively December 27, 1963) (hereafter cited as International Coffee Agreement, 1962). On the quarterly export quota, see ibid., Art. 31 (2).

10. Ibid., Art. 28 (2).

11. Ibid., Art. 60 (1).

12. Ibid., Art. 68.

13. Robbins, op. cit., p. 60. Unless otherwise noted, the citations of countries taking a given position are meant to be exclusive. See, generally, Bilder, op. cit., on the politics of the enforcement system established at the UNCC.

14. International Coffee Agreement, 1962, Art. 44 (1).

15. Ibid.

16. Ibid.

17. Ibid., Art. 44 (3).

18. Ibid., Art. 44 (6).

19. Ibid., Art. 44 (1).

20. Ibid., Art. 44 (3).

21. Ibid., Art. 36 (3).

22. Ibid., Art. 36 (4).

23. Ibid., Art. 36 (5).

24. "Provisional Summary Record," Economic Committee I, UNCC, July 19, 1962.

25. Ibid., August 6, 1962.

26. International Coffee Agreement, 1962, Art. 45 (3).

27. Bilder, op. cit., pp. 360-61.

28. International Coffee Agreement, 1962, Art. 40 (1).

29. Ibid., Art. 40 (1)(f).

30. Ibid.

31. Ibid., Art. 40 (1)(d).

32. Ibid.

33. See Conference Paper c 3/26, UNCC (the French selectivity proposal), Conference Paper c 3/36, UNCC (the United Kingdom selectivity proposal), Conference Paper c 3/12 and Add. 1, UNCC (United Kingdom exporting territories' selectivity proposal), and Conference Paper c 3/21, UNCC (West and East African Robusta exporters' selectivity proposal).

34. International Coffee Agreement, 1962, Art. 35 (2).

35. Ibid., Art. 41.

36. Ibid., Art. 27 (2).

37. "Provisional Summary Record," Executive Committee, UNCC, July 18, 20, and July 25, 1962.

38. Ibid., July 20, 1962.

39. Ibid., July 24, 1962.

40. "Provisional Summary Record," Economic Committee I, UNCC, August 17, 1962.

41. Ibid., July 17, 1962.

42. International Coffee Agreement, 1962, Art. 51 (2) and (4).

43. "Provisional Summary Record," Economic Committee I, UNCC, July 16, 1962.

44. Ibid., July 19, 1962. Both the pro- and antifund arguments listed were in this session.

45. International Coffee Agreement, 1962, Art. 57 (1).

46. Ibid., Art. 57 (2).

47. "Provisional Summary Record," Administrative and Legal Committee, UNCC, July 17, 1962.

48. International Coffee Agreement, 1962, Art. 46 (4).

49. "Provisional Summary Record," Administrative and Legal Committee, UNCC, August 25, 1962.

50. Ibid., July 16, 1962.

51. International Coffee Agreement, 1962, Art. 12.

52. On waivers, see ibid., Art. 60; on quotas, see ibid., Arts. 28-35.

53. Ibid., Art. 14.

54. Ibid., Art. 11.

55. Ibid., Art. 17 (2).

One charge frequently leveled at export quota commodity agreements is that, while they may arguably be effective in limiting price declines by constricting supplies, they are ineffective in limiting price rises. It has been argued, in other words, that commodity agreements are a one-way street for the LDC's. This chapter examines a "prototype" price rise, the 1963/64 price rise due to natural disasters in Brazil. It concludes that export quota commodity agreements can be effective in limiting price rises on the world market. It is true that much of a commodity agreement's utility in a price rise situation is informational and psychological; it does not follow, however, that a commodity agreement is dysfunctional in a price rise situation.

THE CHALLENGE

On August 5, 1963, as the ICC was sorting out a host of waiver requests from exporting members dissatisfied with their basic quota shares, it was learned that serious damage had been done by frost to the coffee trees in the state of Parana in Brazil. The Brazilian Coffee Institute (hereafter cited as IBC) quickly confirmed the dimensions of the frost—over 50 percent of the coffee trees in Parana had been damaged. On September 9, 1963, another disaster struck—a series of fires broke out in Parana as a result of the prevailing drought conditions in parts of that state. It was estimated that the natural disasters would reduce Brazilian exportable production from 18 million bags in 1962/63 to 3 million bags in 1963/64. The market reacted predictably, as prices rose sharply for Brazils and Robustas. The price rise confronted the ICA with an unexpected early test. The Agreement—which had been negotiated primarily to put a floor under a dangerously declining market—had for its first challenge, ironically, to dampen, not raise, prices.

CONSUMER DEFEAT AT THE NOVEMBER, 1963, ICC MEETING

The price rise overshadowed all other business, including the many waiver requests from dissatisfied members, at the November, 1963, ICC meeting.

Positions at the ICC meeting were not polarized strictly along producer/consumer lines. Predictably, the importing members wanted an increase in the annual quota—which had earlier been set at 99 percent of the Annex A allotments. The exporting countries, however, were badly divided.

Brazil was in favor of expanding the annual quota. It recognized that without the U.S. implementing legislation for the ICA—still to be passed by the Congress—there could be no effective enforcement system. This was because legislation was needed to empower the Executive to control coffee imports at the U.S. border. With strong demand for Brazils in both the actual and futures market, Brazil believed that it could weather an annual quota increase.* This would be a minor price to pay for the survival of the ICA.

Colombia, on the other hand, opposed expansion of the annual quota to dampen prices, since its Milds had not risen by November, 1963, in contrast to the Robustas and Brazils.** The ICA was meant, Colombia frankly argued, to be a one-way street to help the developing countries.[1]

The Other Milds also opposed an expansion of the annual quota, as their coffees—like the Colombian MAMS (Manizales, or Colombian Milds coffee)—had declined in 1963.*** Many Other Mild producers were, however, anxious for waivers for their submarket.

---

*Although the average price (in U.S. cents) for Brazils rose only 0.4 percent in 1963 over 1962 (1962, 33.96; 1963, 34.11), spot prices for Santos 4s had risen 10 percent between January and December, 1963. (See the price narrative in Table 2.)

**Prices for Colombian MAMS declined 3 percent in 1963 from 1962 (in U.S. cents—1962, 40.77, 1963, 39.55). MAMS in September, 1963, were 2.3 percent below the January, 1963, level.

***Other Milds declined by 1.2 percent from 1962 (in U.S. cents—1962, 35.83; 1963, 35.40).

The Africans, with the exception of Portugal, were in favor of an annual quota increase. Their Robustas—directly competitive with the Brazilian coffees—were sharply rising, due to the Brazilian disasters. * It was, therefore, in their economic self-interest to have the annual quota expanded to permit more of their supplies to reach the market. The result was an unusual alliance between Brazil and the African revisionists (excluding Portugal, which preferred a waivers-only solution to the price rise).

On the importing side, the United States took the position that the ICO should expand the annual quota, since the ICA was not meant simply as a foreign aid device. Importers had a right to know, it argued, that the ICO would move to check sudden price rises. The U.S. position was dictated by domestic politics. The implementing legislation for the ICA was before Congress. Without the legislation, the State Department knew the ICA would be ineffective. Anxious legislators pointing to the Agreement as the "cause" of the price rise could kill the implementing legislation. The EEC and EFTA countries also spoke out in favor of an annual quota expansion. [2]

Finally, the Executive Director, Joao O. Santos, was opposed to a large annual quota increase that would be, he argued, difficult to reverse. He favored either a transfer of coffees from the second to the first quarter or a small annual quota increase.

Maneuvering within the ICC took place against the backdrop of these positions, and traders around the world waited anxiously to see if decisive action would be taken by the ICO to limit the price rise. On November 23, 1963, the ICC, after extended debate, rejected a proposal to expand the annual quota by 2.25 percent. Voting for the annual quota increase were all consuming countries and a clear majority of the producing countries. The only opponents of the resolution for annual quota expansion were the Mild producers and Portugal. With the producer vote 623 to 348, the resolution failed by 25 votes to gain the needed two-thirds distributed majority.

The four major results of the November, 1963, meeting of the ICC were as follows:

1. The meeting crystallized the tensions between the consumers and many producers in the ICA; it focused attention on the price rise

---

*In 1961, Robustas were selling at 10 cents per pound. Annual Robusta prices in 1963 averaged 30 percent above the levels of 1962. By December, 1963, Robustas were 40 percent above January, 1963, levels.

problem; notice was served that consumer interests had to be protected under the Agreement.

2. The negative vote delayed the adoption of the U.S. implementing legislation; its introduction before the Senate Finance Committee was postponed from December, 1963, to February 1964, due to administration fear of adverse Congressional reaction.

3. The market remained unsettled, and retail coffee prices continued to rise; green coffee prices did not begin to dip until April, 1964.

4. The meeting showed that the consumers did not understand that submarket price performance was the controlling factor in the producers' diplomacy; allowance should have been made, but was not, for the essentially short-run producer perspective.

The second mistake of the consumers was to underestimate the sensitivities of their adversaries in the negotiating process. The U.S. delegate, for example, stated in strident tones—under instructions from Washington—that, unless the annual quota was expanded, the Agreement would be meaningless. This overstatement irritated the producers. The amateur diplomacy of the "advisors" to the U.S. delegation from the coffee trade also irritated the producers. They rushed from delegation to delegation, bullying, threatening, and negotiating directly with the delegates (arguably in violation of the Logan Act).

The November ICC meeting had an appropriate finale. After the emotion-charged vote, George Robbins of General Foods rushed over to the Portuguese delegate, shook his fist in the astonished delegate's face, and stated that General Foods would not buy another bag of coffee from Portugal for the rest of the year.[3] After the wreckage of the November ICC meeting, the U.S. government and nongovernment representatives were more restrained.

COUNTERVAILING CONSUMER POWER: THE FEBRUARY, 1964, ICC MEETING

The rising actual and futures market for coffee prompted the importing members to call for another special session of the ICC in February, 1964, to again consider annual quota expansion. The special session followed a week of meetings of the Executive Board.

The passage of several months had brought the exporters closer together. Brazil was still anxious for the U.S. implementing legislation to pass. As Santos 4s were 10 cents a pound higher than August, 1963, levels, Brazil felt strong enough to withstand an annual quota increase. Colombia was the pivotal political action unit. Its representative, Hernan Jaramillo, was amenable to a "reasonable" annual quota increase. The Colombian switch can be ascribed to the increases in prices for its Milds since the November, 1963, ICC meeting and to the fact that the Senate Finance Committee was meeting at the end of February, 1964, to consider the U.S. implementing legislation.

The consumers—led by the United States—again argued that more coffee should be put on the market. This time, their argument carried the day. Over a one and one-half year period, the ICO called into play a host of equilibrating mechanisms to combat the price rise and deal simultaneously with the problem of market allocations among producers.

Annual Quota Expansion

The dual problems of the early waiver requests and the 1963/64 price rise were attacked by Resolution 35 of the ICC, adopted on February 12, 1964. (See Table 7.)

Section I of Resolution 35 increased the 1963/64 annual quota from 99 percent to 102.15 percent of the basic quotas. This action raised the quotas by 1.4 million bags. The addition was distributed pro rata in the remaining quarters of the coffee year 1963/64.

Resolution 35, however, was a "package deal," as the countries wanting waivers had to have assured extra distributions before they would vote for the annual quota increase.

Waivers

The second equilibrating measure approved by the ICC was a 948,000-bag grant of waivers—with the lion's share going to the Robusta-exporting countries. The effect of the waiver distribution was to placate the Other Milds and Robusta revisionists at the expense of Brazil and Colombia.

The vote on the final waiver distribution was overwhelmingly in favor, with the only opposing votes coming from Ecuador, El Salvador, Nicaragua, and Portugal. The unanimous vote by consumers showed that they regarded waivers as another equilibrating mechanism to dampen still rising prices. [4]

TABLE 7

Waivers—International Coffee Council Resolution 35

Country	Waiver Granted	Waiver Request	Retention Rate[a] (In Percent)
Guatemala	115, 000	200, 000[b]	12
Honduras[c]	43, 000	92, 850	9
OAMCAF[d]	310, 000	400, 000	
Peru	40, 000	120, 000[e]	6
Portugal	120, 000	185, 478	19
Trinidad and Tobago	30, 000	56, 000	34
Uganda	300, 000	e	33

[a]Ratio of excess exportable production to basic quota share of 1963/64 annual quota (prior to waiver).

[b]ICO, ICC (ICC-3-2, February 5, 1964).

[c]A nonmember at the time of the waiver distribution.

[d]Includes Cameroun, Central African Republic, Ivory Coast, Malagasy Republic, and Togo. The Organisation Africain et Malgache du Cafe (OAMCAF) retention rate was probably about 25 percent.

[e]No specific request.

Annual quota additions plus waivers amounted to almost 2.4 million bags, or 5.5 percent over the total fixed in August, 1963.

Shortfalls

The price situation resulting from the February ICC meeting was mixed. Retail prices continued to climb through March, 1964. By the end of April, 1964, however coffee futures were down by about 2 cents per pound, indicating that pressure on supplies was lessening. In this context, one more move, the distribution of shortfalls permitted by the ICA,[5] seemed capable of beating down the price rise.

At this point, both Brazil and Colombia wanted tighter supplies and were opposed to another annual quota increase. They were also worried about the distribution of shortfalls to the African Robusta exporters and its effect on their market shares. Finally, they were wary of the precedent of substantial shortfalls distributions.

The Africans, on the other hand, at first saw shortfalls as a way of getting larger market shares, easing the Ivory Coast overproduction problem, and meeting consumer demand for Robustas. They thus favored an early substantial shortfalls distribution.

The consuming countries favored a large shortfalls distribution, wanting to establish the principle that sharp price rises were unfair and should be equilibrated.

On May 1, 1964, the ICC provisionally accepted the estimate that 725, 000 bags of 1963/64 quotas would be unfilled due to shortfalls. These bags were to be distributed the first week in June, 1964, pro rata among members, with surpluses available for export by the Executive Board. *

1964/65 Annual Quota

The 1963/64 price rise could not yet fairly be considered to be over Retail coffee prices continued to march upwards after the June, 1964, distribution of shortfalls. The consumers, therefore, pushed for a large annual quota for the following marketing year as a "final solution" to the price rise. Brazil, backed up by Colombia, the Central Americans, and the Africans, fought for a small annual quota.

The countervailing power of the consumers was demonstrated by Resolution 52 of the ICC, passed in August, 1964. This resolution set the annual quota at 102. 67 percent of basic quotas, or 47. 5 million bags. It called for an increase of 500, 000 bags in the annual quota on January 8, 1965, unless the ICC decided otherwise in the light of the market situation, and stipulated that if any waivers were to be granted before then, quotas would be increased only by the difference between the amount of the waivers granted and 500, 000 bags. It obligated the ICC to "ascertain . . . the need for a supplementary distribution of 0. 5 million bags"[6] by April 30, 1965. **

---

*Resolution 40, May 1, 1964. By June 1, 1964, the market had weakened, and the original African proponents for the shortfalls distribution turned against the proposal. Both OAMCAF and Uganda opposed the June, 1964, release of the shortfalls, despite their early endorsement of the idea. Many Executive Board members indicated that the controlling factor was the still unpassed U. S. implementing legislation. Shortfalls actually distributed were those of Costa Rica (20, 425), Cuba (204, 300), Rwanda and Burundi (83, 923), Haiti (109, 836), Honduras (16, 706), and Venezuela (97, 947). Notification of Shortfalls, ICO Doc. No. EB-100/64 (June 7, 1964), passim.

**Only Congo-Leopoldville voted against Resolution 52.

Neither stipulation of Resolution 52 came into effect. Due to declining prices, particularly in the Robustas, the annual quota was slashed by 4 percent on March 5, 1965. The 1963/64 price rise had ended.

RESOLUTION 67: THE ORGANIZATIONAL RESPONSE
TO THE PROBLEM OF PRICE REGULATION

Despite early disappointments, the consumers finally succeeded in obtaining from the ICC an expansion of the annual quota and waiver and shortfall distributions. While the dimensions of the price rise in the absence of an agreement are impossible to know, it is probable that prices would have risen much higher without an ICA than they in fact did. The 1963/64 experience compares favorably to the 1954 price rise (also caused by natural disasters in Brazil) when, with no agreement, prices were almost double the maximum of the 1964 ceiling. The performance of the ICA was especially remarkable in view of the fact that Brazil retained its price defense policy, under-selling its basic quota by 2.2 million bags, or about 12 percent, in 1963/64, and by 4.3 million bags, or 25 percent, in 1964/65. This caused additional tension, leading to African demands for a piece of the unused quotas.

Could dextrous coffee diplomacy again forestall a sharp price rise? The 1963/64 experience showed that the straight annual quota mechanism—due to its time-consuming features—could actually destabilize prices. Improvements in the pricing mechanisms of the ICO were clearly necessary. Brazil made the first move towards a pricing system by calling for a price floor/ceiling arrangement, coupled with a buffer stock for coffee. The "normal stocks" would be financed by initial direct contributions of all the members of the ICO. The buffer stock would buy and sell in relation to market movements.[7] While not supporting the Brazilian proposal, the United States did support some form of price regulation. Furthermore, the quotas-only approach was an administrative nightmare for the United States, which hoped that a price ceiling might help sell the ICA to Congress.

A working group was set up within the ICO to consider the Brazilian plan for an indicator price system and a buffer stock. The proposals of the group limited the fund for the buffer stock by making it voluntary and approved a price floor/ceiling arrangement with levels of 40 and 44 cents. *

---

*The representatives of Brazil, Colombia, Guatemala, OAMCAF,

Resolution 67, passed by the ICC on March 16, 1965, contained only the price floor/ceiling idea and dropped the buffer stock concept. Its key provisions were as follows:

1. For the 1964/65 coffee year, a price floor (38 cents per pound) and ceiling (44 cents per pound) was established; a single price, based on the arithmetic average of Mild Arabicas, Unwashed Arabicas, and Robustas, would move within the range.

2. If the indicator price averaged below the floor of the range for fifteen consecutive market days, the annual quota would be contracted; if the price averaged above the ceiling for that period the annual quota would be expanded—these expansions or contractions would take place on a pro rata basis (i.e., according to the basic quota shares in Annex A).

3. Resolution 67 adjustments were made by the Executive Board—they were limited to 6 percent of the annual quotas fixed under article 30; for the 1964/65 year, the maximum permissible adjustment was set at 4.5 percent.

4. If the Executive Board did not reduce quotas within six calendar days of the fifteen-day period, then the Executive Director was empowered to adjust quotas up to one-third of the required amounts under the resolution.

5. The Executive Board was instructed to continue to search for a way to fit selectivity into the ICA, "if possible within the provisions of the Agreement as they exist at present but otherwise as they may subsequently be amended."[8]

Resolution 67 eased the process of price regulation by establishing a semi-automatic mechanism for the adjustment of the annual quota. It also strengthened the ICO by dispersing control over the quota mechanism among the Executive Board, the Executive Director, and the ICC. * The new pricing system, however, could not solve the basic problem of reallocation of quota shares from the "haves" to

---

Uganda, Australia, Belgium, Germany, the United States, and the United Kingdom were on the working group.

*The delegation of authority to the Executive Director and the Executive Board was an apparent violation of article 17 of the ICA, which prohibited the ICC from assigning its functions over the quota process.

the "have nots." The Robusta producers feared—and the operation of
Resolution 67 confirmed their premonition—that Brazil could manipulate the pro rata system to its ends by dropping its prices when the
annual quota seemed in danger of expanding.* Resolution 67 also
disregarded the different price movements of the various submarkets,
thus shorting consumers of needed supplies (often, African Robustas).

The African Robusta exporters—under pressure from continued
overproduction and consumer demand—felt justified in taking advantage
of certain loopholes in the 1962 ICA to circumvent their basic export
quotas. The issue was whether the seemingly irreconcilable conflict
between the revisionists and the oligopolists over market shares could
be worked out within the confines of the Agreement.

NOTES

1. Artur Gomez Jaramillo, "ICA Quotas Must Not Exceed
World Demand," in George Gordon Paton and Co. Coffee Annual, 1963
(1964), p. 55.

2. See, in general, George V. Robbins, "The Meetings in
London," in George Gordon Paton and Co. Coffee Annual, 1963,
(1964), p. 60.

3. Information based on an interview with a high U.S. official.

4. See "Summary Record," Second Plenary Meeting of the
Third Session of the ICC, ICO Doc. No. ICC-3-m-8 (February 20,
1964).

5. See International Coffee Agreement, 1962, Art. 33.

6. ICC Resolution 52, August, 1964.

7. Proposals Submitted by the Brazilian Delegation for
Improvement of the System of Stabilization in the International Coffee
Agreement, ICO Doc. No. ICC-4-1 (April 27, 1964), p. 8.

8. ICC Resolution 67, March, 1965, para. 11.

---

*Brazil dropped its prices—thereby losing foreign exchange
receipts—on May 4, 1965, in order to stop the ICA from expanding
annual quotas under Resolution 67.

6

This chapter explores the enforcement problem by focusing on the first three years of the ICA. Subsequent difficulties with the enforcement system are considered in tandem with the 1965/66 crisis on quota revision in the next chapter.

THE ENFORCEMENT PROBLEM

Under the 1962 ICA, exporting members were to send certificates of origin with all shipments and to send copies of the original documents to the ICO in London. Importing members were obligated to report coffee imports as required by the ICO, which would match the figures and assure compliance by a graduated scale of penalties. The first quarterly overshipment was to be countered by a deduction of an equal amount from future quotas, and second and third overshipments were to have double deductions. Expulsion was an alternative penalty for the third offense.

Three loopholes through the seemingly workable enforcement system established by the 1962 ICA soon developed.

The first was simple overshipment of export quotas. This was clearly illegal and required complicity between exporting and importing members. Another conduit was the "new market" mechanism established under Article 40 of the ICA, which allowed nonquota exports to countries "having a low per capita consumption and considerable potential for expansion." Coffee often never reached the new market or was redirected en route through new markets to importing members. A third loophole was the transshipment of coffee via nonmember countries, whose shipments did not require certificates of origin.

Movement of coffee along these avenues of escape was fueled by fundamental economic, political, and legal problems. The economic issue revolved around the conflict between the largest coffee producers (Brazil and Colombia, exporters of about a half the world's coffee), interested in higher prices and constant market shares, and smaller new entrants, mainly concerned about a larger market share. Brazil and Colombia shared a desire to maximize foreign exchange earnings, to stabilize foreign exchange receipts, and to minimize the loss of market shares. The revisionists, on the other hand, had a vested interest in circumventing their basic export quota shares. The African countries, in particular, wanted to continue their impressive advances on the world coffee market. African exports had grown from 21.9 percent of the world coffee market in 1957 to 27.9 percent in 1962. Meanwhile, Western Hemisphere exports had declined from 74.3 percent of the world's coffee exports in 1957 to 68.9 percent in 1962.

The oligopolist/revisionist conflict was worsened by continued excess production and inadequate storage facilities. This combination created almost irresistable pressures for smaller producers to export coffee in excess of assigned quotas.*

A more technical economic problem was the two-price system created by Article 40 ("new markets"). Due to the limitations on exports to quota markets, virtually the entire pressure of oversupply shifted to nonquota markets, with the result that prices were much lower ex-quota. This encouraged cheating, as brokers could make profits by arbitrating coffee from new to traditional markets. The following estimates of coffee prices in traditional and new markets[1] tend to confirm this hypothesis:

Average Import Unit Values in U.S. Dollars per Bag, 1963/65

Western Europe, United States, and Canada	
(main traditional markets)	48.80
Japan (new market)	42.30
Underdeveloped (traditional markets)	39.70
Underdeveloped (new markets)	32.90

The second aspect of the enforcement problem was political. The revisionists maintained that they could not be responsible for the final destination of Annex B and nonmember shipments, due to the malleable nature of documents. They also argued that they were

---

*Brazil and Colombia have traditionally had adequate storage facilities.

given low basic quota shares at the 1962 UNCC, which gave them a "moral right" to cheat.*

Many brokers and processors in importing countries also refused responsibility, arguing that looking behind documents would clog up business channels. In this context of shared but unfelt guilt, few members were willing to expel violators, a sanction that, ironically, could only weaken the enforcement mechanism.

Enforcement, finally, was a legal problem. As noted, obtaining compliance with assigned export quotas was primarily a task for the importing members of the ICA under the certificates of origin system. But the ICA failed to provide sanctions for those importing members who were aiding violators of the ICA. The efficacy of importer participation depended on the passage of effective local implementing legislation (or the degree to which the ICA was incorporated by national laws).

The problem of obtaining such legislation was most acute in the United States, importer of about a half of the world's coffee. As the delay in the passage of implementing legislation held up the initiation of an effective ICO enforcement system until May 24, 1965, the U.S. experience in 1963-65 is worth considering in some detail.

The United States signed the ICA in New York on September 28, 1962, and the treaty was ratified by the Senate on May 21, 1963, after intensive questioning in the Foreign Relations Committee and two days of debate on the Senate floor.** The ICA was handled as a treaty

---

*Contrast this with enforcement of a pact calling for economic sanctions against a hated enemy, a cause that could arouse moral fervor among the signatories. The ICA could not point to a higher morality, only to the possibility of its dissolution unless members stopped cheating. I am indebted to Charles Burton Marshall of the John Hopkins School of Advanced International Studies for this idea.

**On June 24, 1963, the United States informed the Secretary General of the U.N. that it would be necessary to secure domestic legislation to police imports entering the country. Many producer countries were surprised that ratification of the treaty alone would be inadequate to permit U.S. enforcement. As The Economist wagged:

Their regard for the sophistication of government in developed countries has taken a rude shock; but it will be restored if the President swiftly arms himself with powers to control imports

rather than as an executive agreement because of (1) its intrinsic importance, (2) the precedents established by the wheat and sugar agreements, and (3) the desire to have the two-bite process of a treaty followed by implementing legislation. [2] The last rationale was premised on the assumption that Senators would be less reluctant to vote for the ICA if implementing legislation remained to be approved. The legislative strategy of the Department of State—while probably legally correct*—proved to be a political disaster, as rising prices

---

from non-members . . . and to assure that certificates of origin accompany imports from members.

The Economist, (June 15, 1963), p. 1172.

*The threshold legal question was whether the ICA was a self-executing treaty. The Department of State argued that it was not a self-executing treaty:

> The Department of State agrees with the Committee on Foreign Relations that this treaty, if approved by the Senate, will not be self-executing. Since the United States cannot meet its obligations under the treaty without implementing legislation, the passage of such legislation is a prerequisite to active participation by the United States . . . It is the intention of the executive branch to submit a request for enabling legislation to the Congress immediately after favorable consideration of the treaty by the Senate. The executive branch will not attempt to make its participation in the agreement effective until implementing legislation is approved by the Congress.

109 Cong. Rec. 9126.

This appears to be a correct conclusion, under the logic of Foster v. Neilson, 1829 2 Pet. 253, 314, 7 L. Ed. 415:

> [A treaty is] to be regarded in courts of justice as equivalent to an act of the Legislature, whenever it operates of itself, without the aid of any legislative provision. But when the terms of the stipulation import a contract—when either of the parties engages to perform a particular act, the treaty addresses itself to the political, not the judicial department; and the Legislature must execute the contract, before it can become a rule for the court.

As the United States was undertaking to "perform a particular act," implementing legislation was apparently necessary to secure full participation in the ICA. See Abram Chayes, Thomas Ehrlich, and Andreas F. Lowenfeld, International Legal Process (Boston: Little, Brown and Company, 1968), pp. 588-89. Furthermore, the wording of the ICA itself does not appear to make the treaty self-executing.

due to frosts and droughts in Brazil caused enough consternation in
Congress to delay eventual adoption until May 24, 1965.* This presented the United States with the following dilemma: How could it
discharge the international obligations it had assumed under the terms
of the ICA and, at the same time, not go beyond its domestic authority?

The United States tried to put a brave face on matters by devising
an interim system of collecting certificates of origin and by reporting
imports to the ICO in London. This might, it was thought, embarrass
exporter members who were transshipping large amounts of coffee
into the U.S. market. Customs officials, however, lacked the
authority to reject shipments without certificates, in effect "opening"
the U.S. market to tourist coffee. The administration's agony ended
when the House of Representatives, on May 12, 1965, [3] and the Senate
on May 13, 1964, [4] passed the required implementing legislation.
Whether active U.S. participation in the ICA would prove to be a
sufficient counterpoise to the other elements of the enforcement problem
remained, however, to be seen.

DISEQUILIBRIUM: THE ICA IN OPERATION,
OCTOBER, 1963—August, 1966

Coffee Year 1963/64**

The ICA enforcement system was implemented at a snail's
pace. It took the ICO until October 1, 1964, to rule that importing

---

Jerome Jacobson, the man operationally in charge of the ICA/U.S.
relationship in the State Department, as U.S. Deputy Assistant
Secretary of State for Economic Affairs, opposed seeking implementing legislation for the ICA. He argued that, in this area, implementing legislation was superflous, that there would be great difficulty in
obtaining it, and that, in the meantime, the ICA would be without an
effective enforcement system. Nevertheless, he deferred to the
Office of the Legal Adviser when it argued for the need for implementing legislation. Interview with Jerome Jacobson, in Washington, D.C.,
June 16, 1969.

*The arguments marshalled against the implementing legislation
in the Senate were that the Agreement had helped to cause the price
rise, that it was a cartel abetting Brazil's price defense policy, and
that, once the United States joined the ICA, it would be difficult to
leave it or to resist the precedent when other commodities became
depressed.

**The "coffee year" under the ICA runs from October 1 through
September 30.

members could not admit coffee exports from members without a certificate of origin, [5] and the effect of this minimal move was vitiated by the absence of full U.S. participation at this point. [6]

Without importer policing, there were many overshipments in 1963/64. The OAMCAF, Nigeria, Ethiopia, Ghana, Peru, and India substantially overshipped their basic quota shares. Simple overshipments in 1963/64 in thousands of bags of 132.276 pounds[7] are as follows:

Country	Excess Exports Above Final Quota
Dominican Republic	6
India	23
Nicaragua	2
Peru	46
Ethiopia	150
Ghana	37
Nigeria	62
OAMCAF	551
Sierra Leone	1

Little tourist coffee was shipped via Annex B countries, as actual Annex B shipments were only slightly above the ICC estimate.* This had the effect of dampening desires to implement the U.S. proposal[8] to interpret Article 40 "strictly" to mean that aggregate exports to each Annex B country should not exceed a quantity set by the ICC.

Coffee Year 1964/65

In marketing year 1964/65, the ICO still lacked a viable export control system. Many countries failed to send in copies of certificates of origin** or improperly filled out their forms.

---

*Annex B exports were estimated at 1.7 million bags of green coffee in Resolution 9 of the ICC. Some 1.95 million bags were shipped in 1963/64 to Annex B markets.

**As of March, 1965, the following members were not even submitting copies of certificates of origin to the ICO: Congo-Kinshasa, Cuba, Dominican Republic, Cameroun, Dahomey, Ethiopia, Ivory Coast, Sierra Leone, Trinidad and Tobago, Argentina, Austria, Australia, Finland, Japan, New Zealand, Spain, Tunisia, and the U.S.S.R. Report of the Executive Director, ICO Doc. No. ICC-6-3 5 (March 10, 1965).

Relatively few deductions were made in 1964/65 for earlier overshipments. Deductions were made only for Tanzania (11, 733 bags), [9] the Dominican Republic (304, 580 bags), [10] and the OAMCAF (551, 141 bags), [11] all in the first half of 1965. The sting was taken out of OAMCAF's deduction by a waiver of 550, 000 bags in January, 1965.

Low exportable production in 1964/65 (35. 5 million bags) permitted this administration lethargy. Undershipments were more common in 1964/65 than were simple overshipments. Simple overshipments in 1964/65 in thousands of bags of 132. 276 pounds[12] are as follows:

Country	Excess Exports Above Final Quota
Ecuador	182
Peru	59
Ghana	5
Indonesia	46
Sierra Leone	1
Uganda	6

(Brazil undershipped its basic quota by 4. 3 million bags; total ICO undershipments in 1964/65 were at 5. 7 million bags.)

But Annex B shipments were at 2. 2 million bags, 400, 000 bags above the ICC estimate.* This was an indication that the Annex B mechanism was already being used for tourist coffee.

Coffee Year 1965/66

In contrast, 1965/66 was a "boom" year in the coffee cycle, with exportable production up to 66. 2 million bags. Brazilian exportable production alone was nine times larger than in the preceding year (its crop reflecting a recovery from the disastrous frosts of 1963/64). This oversupply, coupled with a failure to resolve the quota revision crisis rapidly, ** led to a rise in tourist coffee to about 2. 5 million

---

*The ICC's Annex B estimate was 1. 8 million bags (ICC, Resolution 53, August 8, 1964).

**See the next chapter on the politics of the quota revision process in the ICO. This was closely linked to the enforcement problem, as countries unhappy with their quota shares—and unsatisfied by quota revisions—were more prone to cheat.

bags, or 6 percent of the final annual quota. [13] About 1 million of
these bags were in simple overshipments of basic quota shares.
Simple overshipments in 1965/66 in thousands of bags of 132. 276
pounds[14] are as follows:

Country	Excess Exports Above Final Quota
Tanzania	216
Costa Rica	1
Dominican Republic	1
Ecuador	115
El Salvador	112
Guatemala	388
Nicaragua	34
Panama	11
Ghana	56
Indonesia	253
Nigeria	78
Sierra Leone	114

Annex B shipments in 1965/66, at 4.2 million bags, were 2.2
million bags above the staff estimate of imports by Annex B countries,
indicating large transshipments. [15] Exporting members with sharply
increased Annex B exports included the OANCAF, Uganda, Colombia,
Guatemala, and Mexico. *

Nonmember above quota shipments were also commonplace in
1965/66. The Ivory Coast shipped most frequently to consumers via
nonmembers in 1965/66. It used Liberia, Morocco, and other nonmembers as entrepôts for shipments to consuming members of the
Agreement.

Liberia, which averaged 57, 000 bags in exportable production**
from 1963/64 through 1966/67, exported 798, 000 bags of green coffee

---

*Those countries diverted at least the following quantities
(in thousands of bags of 132. 276 pounds each) to traditional markets:
OAMCAF, 8; Uganda, 2; Colombia, 4; Guatemala, 62; and Mexico,
97. Other diversions registered were from Costa Rica, 4; Dominican
Republic, 2; Ecuador, 8; and Tanzania, 1. Annex B transshipments
registered by the ICO were 186, 000 bags, an obvious understatement
of the true figure. Exports from Certain Producing Countries to
Annex B Countries Diverted to Traditional Markets, ICO Doc. No.
EB-514/67 1 (May 17, 1967).

**Exportable production is the difference between total pro-
duction and the quantity retained for domestic consumption.

to the United States in the first nine months of 1966. At Least 479,121 bags of Liberian coffee went in a block deal to General Foods[16] importer of one-sixth of the world's coffee and the Ivory Coast's best American customer—on false certificates of origin printed in Liberia.[17] As this figure is for Atlantic ports only, it substantially understates nonmember imports by the companies listed.* Other U.S. companies imported lesser amounts from Liberia in 1965/66, including The East Asiatic Company, Inc., with at least 61,335 bags; H. L. C. Bendiks, Inc., with at least 11,334 bags; A. C. Israel, with at least 4,200 bags; Rayner and Stonington, Inc., with at least 3,360 bags; and C. A. Markay, with at least 3,340 bags.

Ivory Coast transshipments via Morocco—a nonmember and non-producer of coffee—were also substantial. General Foods was again an accomplice of the Ivory Coast in thwarting the ICO enforcement system, importing 99,858 bags in 1966 from Morocco.[18]

Uganda, another large Robusta exporter, used Kenya, a non-member producer, as its conduit to the United States. In 1966, about 40 percent of all Ugandan coffee imported into the United States was estimated to have come under Kenyan certificates of origin.[19]

Nonmember transshipments were also made by the Milds producers. Colombia, for example, used Aruba as a base for exports to the United States. This wind-swept isle in the Netherlands Antilles, without a single coffee tree, exported at least 300,000 bags of coffee to the United States in 1965 and 1966. Coffee shipments via the Netherlands West Indies to U.S. Atlantic ports in 1961-66[20] are as follows:

Year	Exports
1961	—
1962	552
1963	1,713
1964	6,834
1965	207,290
1966	82,230

The smuggled coffee was transported by coffee producers in small

---

*New York is the principal customs district for the entry of coffee into the United States, with 43 percent of total coffee imports in 1969. New Orleans, San Francisco, and Houston are, in that order, the ports of next importance. Pan American Coffee Bureau, 1969 Annual Coffee Statistics (New York: 1970), p. 67.

boats to Aruba, only 45 miles west of Colombia, to avoid high Colombian export taxes.* The coffee went through Aruba in bond and untaxed to U.S. importers, such as General Foods, which imported at least 21,082 bags of coffee from the Netherlands West Indies in 1966.[21]

Measures to deal with the enforcement problem took place against the background of these extensive above quota shipments.

Colombia, supported by Brazil, made the first move, proposing that a worldwide verifying agency be set up in exporting countries to police shipments.[22] The Executive Board formalized Colombia's plan by asking the General Superintendence Company, Ltd., of Geneva, to act as the verifying agency.[23]

These moves were assailed by revisionist countries, which argued that an enforcement system run by a private agency would be costly, of dubious legality, and politically unacceptable.[24]

Meanwhile, as a partial result of the failure of the December, 1965, ICC meeting to revise basic quota shares, Resolution 92 absolved exporting members of all past and prospective penalties for overshipments prior to October, 1965. Further agreement on tightening the enforcement system was not possible.

The United States broke the impasse between oligopolists and revisionists by proposing what later became known as "the stamp plan." Under this plan, the ICO would give exporting members each quarter enough stamps to match its quota, and importing members would refuse to accept coffee shipments without stamps.[25] The Executive Board promptly adopted the U.S. proposal and submitted the stamp plan to the ICC meeting in September, 1966.[26] This set the stage for firm administrative action to handle simple overshipments.

Nonmember exports, however, were a continuing problem. Under urging by the ICO staff and Brazil, the ICC warned members to make preparations under Article 45 of the ICA to limit nonmember imports.[27] A working group of the Executive Board, the ICO staff, and the Executive Director subsequently swung to the view that Article 45 should be put into effect to check the nonmember conduit.**

---

*This is to be contrasted with the motivation of the Ivory Coast government, which permitted transshipments via nonmembers to escape tight export quotas.

**Other arguments advanced in favor of the application of Article 45 were that the ICO annual quota cuts disadvantaged producing

The result was a draft resolution submitted by the Executive Board to the September, 1966, ICC meeting recommending, as per Article 45, that nonmember imports to consuming members be limited to the three-year average prior to 1963. The debate and draft resolution on nonmember limitations had the desired effect, as Honduras, Jamaica, Kenya, and Liberia applied for accession to the ICA before the door was shut on them. 28

SUMMARY

Enforcement was the most difficult problem the ICA had to face. The ICO had to avoid the Scylla of underenforcement of export quotas— which would have imperiled—the desired price-stabilizing effects of the accord—and the Charbydis of zealous overenforcement, which by removing overshipments as an equilibrating mechanism might have also wrecked the Agreement.

The response of the Executive Board by September, 1966, to the enforcement crisis was to recommend to the ICC that the Agreement be tightened by putting all quota shipments under stamps and by limiting nonmember imports.

The Robusta exporters, however, maintained in the ICC that their coffee was in demand and, with the Other Milds exporters, that they had been given low export quotas in the 1962 game of fair division. If export quotas could be realigned to their satisfaction, then a "swap" might be arranged in which a viable enforcement system could be set up in return for quota reallocation. In the 1965/66 quota crisis, this trade-off was engineered in a complex package that solved both the problems of enforcement and quota revision.

NOTES

1. Source for data is Shamsher Singh, International Coffee Agreement, 1968 (Washington, D. C.: International Bank for Reconstruction and Development, 1968), p. 14.

---

members vis à vis nonmembers (there were two such cuts in 1964/65); availability of nonmember transshipments was disturbing plans for the implementation of production goals; and nonmembers, such as Bolivia, Paraguay, Rhodesia, South Africa, and Ceylon, were expanding coffee production.

2. Richard B. Bilder, "The International Coffee Agreement: A Case History in Negotiation," Law and Contemporary Problems, XXVIII (Spring, 1963), 328-91.

3. The House bill, H.R. 8864, 88th Cong., 2d Sess. (1964), was passed by a vote of 300 to 97.

4. The Senate vote was sixty-one to nineteen. The law is now codified in 19 U.S.C., Section 1356 (a)-(e) (1965).

5. Implementation of the System of Certificates of Origin and Re-export, ICO Doc. No. EB-151/64 (E) (September 11, 1964).

6. See pp. 137-38.

7. Source for data is Singh, op. cit., Tables 4 and 5, Appendix.

8. Comments on Staff Interpretation of Article 40 of the Agreement, contained in Document EB-78/64, ICC Doc. No. EB-107/64 (E) (June 16, 1964).

9. ICC, Resolution 66, March 18, 1965.

10. ICC, Resolution 69, March 19, 1965.

11. ICC, Resolution 74, June 26, 1965.

12. Singh, op. cit., Tables 4 and 5, Appendix.

13. Singh, op. cit., p. 15.

14. Ibid., Tables 4 and 5, Appendix.

15. "Estimate of Imports for Consumption by Countries Listed in Annex B in 1965/66," Staff Paper, ICO Doc. No. EB-297/65 Appendix (July 12, 1965).

16. "Annual Summary of Imports into U.S. Atlantic Ports, January 1 to December 31, 1966" (information courtesy of the Green Coffee Association of New York City). This is herinafter cited as "Annual Summary." (Mimeographed.)

17. The Economist (February 26), pp. 828-30.

18. "Annual Summary."

19. Lane Vanderslice, "The International Coffee Agreement

and Control of Coffee Overproduction, " (<u>unpublished</u> Ph. D. dissertation, University of Michigan, (in process).

20. Source for data is "Annual Summary of Imports into U.S. Atlantic Ports, January 1 to December 31, 1966" (information courtesy of the Green Coffee Association of New York City).

21. "Annual Summary."

22. <u>Comments Made by the Colombian Delegation on the Working Group Report on Certificates of Origin,</u> ICO Doc. No. Eb-298/65 (July 16, 1965), p. 2.

23. <u>Draft Resolution, Verification of Certificates of Origin,</u> ICO Doc. No. EB-290/65 (August 13, 1965).

24. <u>Legal Considerations on the Question of Verification of Origin,</u> ICO Doc. No. EB-326/65 (September 6, 1965).

25. <u>Draft Resolution Submitted by the Delegation of the United States, Strengthening of Certificates of Origin System,</u> ICO Doc. No. EB-420/66 (August 29, 1966).

26. <u>Draft Resolution Submitted by Executive Board, Strengthening of Certificates of Origin System,</u> ICO Doc. No. EB-420/66, Rev. 2 (September 2, 1966).

27. ICC, Resolution 84, August 18, 1965.

28. Honduras applied on September 9, 1965, for ICO membership; Jamaica on March 30, 1966; Kenya on March 30, 1966; and Liberia on September 2, 1966.

THE SELECTIVE QUOTA CASE

The seeds of conflict over quota revision were sown at the UNCC in 1962. Both Brazil and Colombia won large basic quota shares at the UNCC, while the Africans received smaller shares and failed in their efforts to have an explicit selective quota expansion proposal written into the Agreement.

Resolution 67 (effective March 19, 1965), which established a pro rata floor/ceiling price system, did not meet continuing African demands for selectivity; it did, however, instruct the Executive Board to search for ways to fit selectivity into the ICA, "if possible within the provisions of the Agreement as they exist at present but otherwise as they may subsequently be amended. "*

The working group appointed by the Executive Board pursuant to Resolution 67 deadlocked over the legality of selectivity. On July 22, 1965, the Executive Board admitted to the ICC that it had failed to resolve the issue and asked for a clarification of the legal problems raised by selectivity (i. e. , the concept of regulating quotas by submarket rather than on a pro rata basis).

In the ensuing ICC debate, Brazil argued that Article 35 of the 1962 ICA, which stated that "general changes in all quarterly export

---

*On Resolution 67 and the events that preceded it, see Chapter 5.

quotas . . . shall be applied pro rata to individual quarterly export quotas," was controlling. It also argued that selectivity would create technical problems of implementation, and that, if adopted, it would require an amendment, a procedure the Council had already decided would not be allowed in connection with the three-year review called for by Article 28 of the Agreement. Confident of its legal position and anxious to avoid a direct confrontation with the Africans, Brazil supported the proposal advanced by the consumers and the Africans calling for the establishment of a legal advisory panel (as allowed by Article 61 of the 1962 ICA)* to study the legality of selectivity.

The Africans rested their case on Article 41 of the Agreement:

In addition to ensuring that the total supplies of coffee are in accordance with estimated world imports, the Council shall seek to ensure that supplies of the types of coffee that consumers require are available to them. To achieve this objective, the Council may, by a distributed two-thirds majority vote, decide to use whatever methods it considers practicable. [Italics added.]

While selectivity had not been written into the ICA, the Africans argued, it had, at a minimum, been left in the Agreement as an option for the ICC to use to meet the needs of the world coffee market. This was shown, it was argued, by Article 42, which allowed the Council to: " . . . recommend a scale of price differentials for various grades and qualities of coffee which Members should strive to achieve through their pricing policies."

The Africans, realizing that Brazil would not willingly adopt selectivity, hoped to "win" through a legal panel what they had "lost" at the UNCC and had since been unable to obtain by negotiations.

---

*Article 61 reads as follows:

Any dispute concerning the interpretation or application of the Agreement which is not settled by negotiation, shall, at the request of any Member party to the dispute, be referred to the Council for decision.

(2) In any case where a dispute has been referred to the Council under paragraph (1) of this Article, a majority of Members, or Members holding not less than one-third of the total votes, may require the Council, after discussion, to seek the opinion of the advisory panel referred to in paragraph (3) of this Article on the issues in dispute before giving its decision.

Accordingly, the ICC accepted the proposal of the Africans and the consumers, and instructed the Executive Board to set up an advisory panel of international jurists to consider the legality of selectivity. The Board, on October 12, 1965, appointed the following members to the legal panel: Jose Nabuco (nominated by Brazil); M. Andre Philip (nominated by OAMCAF); Richard Bilder (nominated by the United States), and Paul de Visscher (nominated by Belgium). The panel later selected Abram Chayes (United States) as Chairman.

The advisory panel, according to its terms of reference given by the Executive Board, was to:

Give a legal opinion as to whether the adoption, by means of a further Resolution of the Council, of a selective system for the upward and downward adjustment in the annual quotas of the Members comprising any one of the three groups listed in Annex 1 to Resolution No. 67 would be compatible with the provisions of the Agreement as it now stands. [1]

A selective system would be, the Executive Board continued:

One which, as a result of relative or absolute changes in the price levels of the various types of coffee, permits the upward or downward adjustment of the annual quotas of countries listed as exporting any given one of the three types of coffee shown in Annex 1 of Resolution No. 67. [2]

The panel found "for" Brazil and "against" the Africans, or for a pro rata system of quota expansions and against a selectivity system (i.e., expansions by submarkets). It noted that the UNCC minutes showed that selectivity had been considered and rejected "by the Conference as a whole." In any case, a pro rata quota system was "the heart of the Agreement." Articles 27-35 of the Agreement confirmed that "in comprehensive and detailed terms that leave no room for doubts."[3] Other equilibrating mechanisms for difficulties with the quota system were pointed out by the panel: Article 28 (2)—which allowed a revision of basic quotas after three years, waivers, and quarterly quota extensions.* The panel concluded

_____

*The panel did not rule out, however, the possibility that selected quota increases might be made in "emergency" circumstances to meet "consumer needs" under the provisions of Article 41. Report of the Advisory Panel on the Legality of a System for the Selective Adjustment of Quotas, ICO Doc. No. ICC-7-60 (November 30, 1965), p. 8.

that "the balance among such interests struck at the last Conference and embodied in the Agreement should not be altered in the guise of legal interpretation. [4]

It remained to be seen whether the moral authority of the advisory panel's answer to the legal challenge to the pro rata system could be translated into sufficient political influence by Brazil and Colombia to hold off revisionist demands in the December, 1965, ICC meeting.

RESOLUTION 92

The ICC confronted two problems after the selective quota case: the review of basic quotas required by Article 28 (2) and the mandate of Resolution 67 to fit selectivity into the Agreement. To a degree, action on one problem could satisfy the other, since either could result in a reallocation of market shares. *

Rigid positions presaged divisive conflict over quota revision.

Brazil was disinterested in changing "any part of the Agreement, which might upset the still precarious relative balance already achieved, " especially Resolution 67, "basic reform" of which "now, might be self-defeating. "[5] Its defense of the status quo was underlined by the IBC, which dropped the export price of green coffee to keep the ICO price mechanism from triggering, reversed its policy of undershipping annual quotas by filling its first quarter quota, and cabled the Brazilian delegation at the ICO not to agree to a lowering of Brazil's annual quota. If Brazil took a cut, the cable admonished, the "farmers" would want to return to the free enterprise system, an explicit threat of dumping.

Colombia aligned itself with Brazil by proposing that the quota review be postponed for two years, due to the delayed U.S. implementation of the Agreement. [6]

The Robusta and Other Milds exporters wanted their basic export quotas enlarged. Legal technicalities should not impede the Article 28 (2) quota revision, the Africans argued. As the delegate of OAMCAF stated:

---

*Pressure for a solution to the producer game of fair division was increased by heavy exportable production in 1965/66; at 66.35 million bags, it was nearly double that of the preceding year.

If Article 28 was contained in the Agreement it was for
a reason, an inescapable reason. When the negotiations
in New York took place the French-speaking countries in
Africa lacked experience in the field of international negotiations, being either not yet independent, or newly independent. Those negotiations were their first steps in
international life but there was a limit to what they were
prepared to pay for this experience. Article 28 was in
the Agreement as recompense reserved for the inexperi-
enced . . .   The Ivory Coast, like Ethiopia, was asking
for a just sharing of sacrifices and a just distribution of
the market. The existing overproducing resulted from
coffee planted before the Agreement was signed. The
beans now in hand had nothing to do with the Agreement. [7]

The Africans continued to press for the inclusion of selectivity
in the ICA, despite the negative holding of the selective quota case.
Their indignation was fueled by the presence of large local surpluses.
As the delegate from Portugal pointed out:

Portugal, a major African producer, could not accept
the arguments that all variation of annual quotas must
be on a pro rata basis. This was prejudicial to the
African producers . . .   There was at the moment a
real shortage of Robusta coffees. No government could
accept an International Agreement which prevented a
partial solution of a situation like this. If there continued to be a shortage on the international market very
serious political problems would arise. It was therefore indispensable to establish selective quotas for all
types of coffee. With this solution the problem of basic
quotas itself would be very much reduced in importance. [8]

Among the consumers, the United States expressed no specific
public position on basic quota reallocations, while the French[9] and
the British[10] favored the institutionalization of a selectivity system.

Sparring within the ICO took place against the background of
these national positions. After the Executive Board ruled that Article
28 (2) did not require revision of basic quotas but only admitted that
such revision might be necessary, [11] the Council, on August 13, 1965,
set up a special working group to review quotas. [12]

The working group calculated alternative sets of figures based
on exportable production for six years (1959/60-1964/65) and two
years (1960-62), but was unable to reach agreement on a revision of
basic quotas, since no country was willing to accept a reduction of
its quota.

Waivers, however, could temporarily equilibrate the Agreement in the absence of an overall quota revision and avoid the political "stigma" of permanent market share loss. For these reasons, Resolution 92, which granted waivers, introduced a limited version of selectivity, and dropped penalties on enforcement violations, was adopted (without vote) at the December 12, 1965, meeting of the Council. Its relevant aspects are described below. (See Table 8.)

Waivers

Waivers were given to the Robustas (615,000), Mild Arabicas (667,000), and Unwashed Arabicas (75,000) totaling 1.3 million bags. Considering the size of the revisionists' basic quota requests, these grants were not unreasonable.

Selectivity

A limited selectivity system for the waivers was established, as they were granted on the condition that, if the price in the submarket for which the waiver was given averaged for fifteen consecutive market days below its price of December 10, 1965, the portion of the waiver applying to that quarter would be suspended immediately. If, however, the price responded by averaging at or above that level for fifteen consecutive market days, the waiver would be restored.

The grant of waivers under selectivity conditions was broadly compatible with the ruling of the advisory panel. Although the panel denied that the Agreement permitted selectivity as "a regular procedure with established standards," it did not foreclose the possibility that

in certain circumstances the Council could properly decide under Article 41, on an ad hoc basis and in order to meet emergency conditions of a short term character affecting consumer needs, [decide] to alter the quota of one or more producing countries without undertaking a general quota adjustment. [13]

Penalties

Finally, Resolution 92 suspended "all deductions already effected or liable to be effected in quarterly quotas resulting from excess exports made prior to 1 October, 1965." This particularly aided OAMCAF, which had overshipped its basic quota by 500,000 bags in 1963/64.

TABLE 8

International Coffee Council Resolution 92 Waivers[a]

Country	Basic Quota Request[b]	Waiver	Retention Rate Prior to Waiver[c] (In Percent)
Dominican Republic	125,000	40,000	35
Ecuador	200,000	50,000	38
El Salvador	494,250[d]	225,000	20
Ethiopia	[d]	75,000	5
Ghana	13,500	5,000	29
Guatemala	455,500[d]	135,000	31
Haiti	[d]	30,000	2
India	190,000	50,000	39
Nicaragua	211,000[d]	70,000	19
OAMCAF		300,000	41
Peru	325,000	17,000	21
Portugal	187,352[d]	150,000	26
Tanzania		50,000	36
Trinidad and Tobago	76,000[d]	25,000	0
Uganda		135,000	31

a In bags of 132.276 pounds each.
b For additions to basic quotas.
c For coffee year 1965/66.
d No specification required.

Sources: Information on basic quota requests from the ICO. Waiver data from ICC Resolution 92. Retention rate calculations based on exportable production data from the Pan American Coffee Bureau.

Resolution 92, at best, was a patchwork decision. As the Chairman of the Council for 1965/66, Roger Mukasa, stated:

> Attempts to revise basic quotas at the current meeting had now been abandoned because it had not been possible to narrow the differences between different groups. Efforts would continue to find a solution to the basic quota ques—tion but these should be forgotten for the time being. Per—haps producing members could meet before the next regu—lar session, but there was no point in convening until March or April (1966). Meanwhile care had to be taken to show the outside world that talks had not broken down.[14]

Resolution 92 did, however, meet many of the needs of the revisionists and the oligopolists. Revisionist demands for a larger market share were met through waivers granted "notwithstanding" the rules set forth in Article 60 on waivers, i.e., as a political solution. The insistence of the Robusta producers on the principle of selectivity was met by the limited application to the waiver grants. This set a precedent for the application of the principle by the ICC in the later years of the accord. *

The waivers, for Brazil and Colombia, were preferable to large quota evasions that would have undermined the ICA; it was wiser to "legitimate" what the revisionists were going to do anyway (or had done—hence, the absolution on penalties for overshipments prior to October 1, 1965). Nor was selectivity a great concession for the oligopolists, although they tried to make it sound like a key victory for the revisionists. With their well-developed price control systems, they could manipulate selectivity better than the revisionists— this had already been shown under Resolution 67. **

---

*From an organizational point of view, the incremental adoption of selectivity was probably a healthy development. As John M. Pfiffner notes: "What is probably needed is an index of organizational health. Incremental change should probably be the strategy for only healthy organizational systems. Massive change is probably the only appropriate strategy for unhealthy organizations." In Foreward of Garth N. Jones, Planned Organizational Change (New York: Frederick A. Praeger, 1969).

**This was later demonstrated under Resolution 92, when Brazil caused its group (Unwashed Arabicas) to lose its waiver, much to Ethiopia's anguish, and then to have it restored on May 20, 1966.

Resolution 92 had a firming effect on the coffee market until February, 1966, when all submarkets, weakened by large tourist coffee shipments and overproduction, began a steady decline. Additional moves by the ICO to shore up the market and check the rising ex-quota shipments were clearly needed.

THE PACKAGE

Joao O. Santos, the Executive Director of the ICO, tried to pick up the pieces of the December, 1965, Council meeting by canvassing members for suggestions on the quota review required by Article 28 (2) of the ICA. His active secretariat brokerage resulted in a plan for quota review—known as the "Santos document"—which served as a useful lightning rod in the ensuing discussions. [15]

The Santos solution was to keep the pro rata pricing system and to alter the basic quota shares by adding to the basic quota share all of either the Resolution 92 waivers or the total of the Annex B exports in the most recent marketing year and one-half of the smaller figure of the two. The proposal was a clever ploy designed to please the oligopolists, which did not approve of selectivity, and the revisionists, which benefited from Resolution 92. It would have also gotten rid of the troublesome Annex B conduit.

The Santos document displeased all major producer interests equally. The Africans immediately rejected it, calling for larger basic quotas and for full adoption of selectivity. The Inter-African Coffee Organization (IACO) further recommended that Article 45, limiting nonmember imports, be implemented only if a satisfactory arrangement on "revision of Annex A" could be made, and that Annex B be kept. The items, however, "might become part of a package deal." IACO threatened to leave the ICA unless its "minimum" requirements on selectivity and Annex A revision were met. [16]

Brazil countered the Africans with dextrous backstage diplomacy. Publicly, it matched African intransigence by denying any need for basic quota revision. [17] Privately, however, Brazil moved to flank the Africans by enlisting the support of the United States behind a compromise solution. Thus Brazil and the United States—in a separate and secret bilateral negotiation—agreed that a partial selectivity system should be established to more accurately reflect market forces. But Brazil could not agree to even limited selectivity without strict enforcement provisions to ensure that the Africans would be limited to the extra authorizations granted them. Accordingly, Brazil switched from opposition to support of the U.S. proposal limiting total quota exports to stamps issued by the ICO each quarter ("the stamp plan"). The "big two" also agreed on the necessity of limiting nonmember imports to check transshipments. Finally, Brazil and the United States agreed on the need for structural reform of the world coffee market. The concept of a Diversification Fund and the proposal that 20 percent of waiver proceeds should be used for purposes of diversification by recipients were endorsed by the two parties.[18]

The key convert to the U.S./Brazilian "package" was Colombia, which stated, on August 18, 1966, that it would be willing to shift to a limited selectivity system, if it could have a category separate from the Other Milds, as their weak marketing facilities might, it was feared, depress Colombia's prices.

Colombia's unexpected move prompted Fedecame, the representative of the Other Milds group, to reverse its earlier position and oppose selectivity. The Other Milds argued that the UNCC in 1962 had decided "to reject the principle of selectivity, " and that the legal advisory panel had found "that selectivity was incompatible with the Agreement. " Selectivity was "illegal, " Fedecame argued, and would be opposed "resolutely. "[19]

When it became apparent to the Other Milds that they were going to be outvoted on the selectivity issue, they shifted their attention to the revision of Annex A. On August 30, 1966, the delegate from El Salvador synthesized the situation facing the Council:

> This session was not making progress, and would not, because the positions on Annex A were well defined. IACO and the Fedecame countries were in favor of the revision of Annex A and other countries outside these groups had supported this view. On the other hand the delegations of Brazil and Colombia before coming to this session had said they were against revision of Annex A. The two countries with the majority of votes were against. The consumers had said they regretted the views of Brazil and Colombia not to revise Annex A but implied that they would accept them. They would be wasting time to listen again to the positions of the two different sides. It looked more and more difficult to find a solution, due to the rigid position taken up by both sides.[20]

El Salvador then proposed that "they should suspend the meeting so that IACO and Fedecame and all other groups in favor of revision could form a joint proposal. "[21] The proposal of El Salvador was formalized into a draft resolution calling for the creation of a

representative working group to consider basic quota requests before
the end of the plenary session. The resolution passed, becoming
Resolution 107. [22] Included in the working group established pursuant
to Resolution 107 were Brazil, Colombia, Fedecame, IACO, one
country not from any producing group, the United States, the Federal
Republic of Germany, the United Kingdom, and Sweden. Fedecame
thus coalesced the revisionists within the context of the ICO to confront
the oligopolists. The stage was now set for secret and intense
multilateral negotiations on a package to settle the outstanding issues
of quota revision, enforcement, and structural reform.

The private negotiations that followed in the working group
and in the corridors of the ICO framed the following "package" that
the Council eventually passed.

Annual Quota

The Council first placed parameters on the package by limiting
total quota exports in 1966/67 to 46.5 million bags. [23] It then set
the annual quota for 1966/67 at 43.7 million bags. [24] The issue was
how the remaining 2.8 million bags of coffee would be distributed
among the members.

Selectivity

A limited selectivity system was established, replacing the
pro rata mechanism of Resolution 67. [25] The Council distributed
1.0 million bags pro rata to exporting members and set up four
price ranges. (See Table 9.)

TABLE 9

1966/67 Selectivity Price Ranges
(In U.S. Cents per Pound)

Type	Floor Price	Ceiling Price
Colombian Milds	43.50	47.50
Other Milds	40.50	44.50
Unwashed Arabicas	37.50	41.50
Robustas	30.50	34.50

Source: ICC Resolution 115, September, 1966.

If the daily "indicator price" for a group averaged below its price floor for fifteen consecutive market days, the groups' distribution would be contracted by 2.5 percent of the member's total authorized exports for the 1966/67 coffee year. If the indicator price averaged above its price ceiling for the same period, the distribution of the group—called "special export authorizations," to distinguish them from waivers—would be expanded by 2.5 percent of the member's total exports for the 1966/67 marketing year. The operations of the selectivity system were not to cut into the basic quota shares. Within six days of the end of the fifteen-day marketing period, the Executive Board could decide, by a two-thirds distributed majority (i.e., two-thirds of both consumer and producer members), to make no adjustment or a different adjustment to the group's Special Export Authorizations.

Waivers

The next part of the package was a grant of waivers totaling 1.7 million bags. [26] The primary recipients of the waivers were the Other Milds and the Robustas exporters (Other Mild Arabicas, 719,000, and Robustas, 938,000). Resolution 114 waivers (in bags of 132.276 pounds) are as follows.

Type	Waiver
Other Mild Arabicas:	
Dominican Republic	40,000
Ecuador	58,000
El Salvador	225,000
Guatemala	135,000
Haiti	30,000
India	50,000
Nicaragua	70,000
Peru	61,000
Tanzania	50,000
Total	719,000
Unwashed Arabicas:	
Ethiopia	75,000
Total	75,000
Robustas:	
Ghana	6,000
OAMCAF	414,000
Portugal	279,000
Sierra Leone	17,000

Type	Waiver
Trinidad and Tobago	25,000
Uganda	197,000
Total	938,000
Grand Total	1,732,000

The waivers were also regulated by the selectivity mechanism established in Resolution 115 and were granted on the condition that 20
percent of the foreign exchange value of the coffee granted as waivers
would be placed in a fund under the joint control of the member and
the Executive Director of the ICO for financing "schemes of diversification and development." The latter condition was attacked by Ethiopia,
India, and Trinidad and Tobago as an illegal compulsory "backdoor"
Diversification Fund. Nevertheless, the resolution obtained the
required two-thirds distributed majority vote in the Council. [27]

The composite formula for quota revision was, therefore, as
follows: Annual Quota + Special Export Authorizations + Waivers =
Demand. [28]

Enforcement

Having given up market shares through selectivity and waivers,
the oligopolists wanted assurances that their remaining markets
would not be undermined by tourist coffee. Having obtained additional
market shares, the revisionists were willing to agree on a series of
far-reaching enforcement measures.

The first check on quota evasion was the establishment of
a stamp system to regulate members' exports. [29] Under this plan—
aimed at eliminating simple overshipments by members—all exporters,
as of April 1, 1967, were given stamps by quarters, matching the
total of their quotas and were required to affix them to certificates
of origin accompanying the coffee shipments. Importers were to
admit only the amount of coffee corresponding to the weight of coffee
covered by the certificate. *

---

*The stamp plan represented an accrual of power to the Exec-
utive Director of the ICO. Paragraph 8 of Resolution 118 authorized
the Executive Director to take "all necessary steps to cope with
administrative problems and unforeseen practical difficulties which
may arise during the first six months of operation of the system . . ."

If direct overshipments were reduced, the pressure on nonmember transshipments would be greatly increased. It was, therefore, necessary to limit them as well. This was accomplished by the invocation of Article 45; nonmembers were thus limited to the annual average of their total imports into consumer members for the period 1960/62. This was to be applied as soon as possible after October 1, 1966, but not later than January 1, 1967.[30]

The third move to improve the enforcement system was to get as many nonmembers as possible into the ICA, to ease the problem of enforcing the import restrictions of Article 45 against nonmembers. Accordingly, the ICC passed resolutions of accession for Bolivia,[31] Honduras,[32] and Kenya.[33] Thus, while the quota reallocation issue was contingent on the passage of strong enforcement measures, the efficacy of those enforcement measures depended on agreement with nonmembers over terms of accession.

Finally, in an attempt to cut off Annex B transshipments, the ICC declared that the provisions of Article 40 were mandatory and that coffee shipped by an exporting member would be charged automatically to the quota of the exporting member concerned.[34]

Structural Reform

The package was completed by moves towards structural reform of the world coffee economy. The first has been mentioned, the use of 20 percent of all waiver proceeds for projects of diversification. The Council also approved in principle the establishment of a Coffee Diversification and Development Fund "as a means of helping to bring equilibrium to the world coffee economy."[35] The question of contributions to the Fund was left unresolved.

ANALYSIS OF THE PACKAGE

The 1965/66 quota crisis had a more balanced result than the 1962 UNCC and reflected the shift of market power in the interim to the African Robusta exporters. The Africans gained extra export authorizations—a de facto quota revision in their favor—and the acceptance of the principle of selectivity. On the other hand, the Robustas did not benefit from selectivity until late in marketing year 1966/67[36] (due to their high price ceiling),* and they were to be

---

*In the political bargaining over prices Brazil insisted that the Robusta ceiling be set at 34.50 cents per pound, although at the time Robustas were selling at about 31 cents per pound.

limited henceforth by the stamp plan adopted to buttress the ICO
enforcement system.

Brazil also had reason to be pleased with the package. Its
concessions, e.g., on selectivity, were more apparent than real (it
did not suffer any quota cut during the life of the 1962 ICA, due to
its efficient internal market controls). By agreeing to waivers and
special export authorizations, Brazil probably conceded to the revisionists the minimum possible to keep the Agreement operational.

The Milds producers were the immediate losers. Split off
from the Colombian Milds and divided among themselves, the Other
Milds declined in price, and took five cuts in waivers and special
export authorizations in 1966/67. [37] With adequate supplies available,
Colombian Milds also took five cuts in additional export authorizations
in 1966/67. [38] Unlike the Other Milds, however, Colombians recouped
their fortunes under selectivity in 1967/68. *

In a macro sense, the package gave a new lease on life to the
ICO and to the world coffee market. With stricter enforcement
provisions, basic quotas became progressively harder to evade, although the late date of entry of the stamp system gave certain countries
time to put overshipments in the "pipeline." As a result—of the late
date of entry with the Other Milds as the worst offenders—almost 1
million bags of coffee were shipped over quotas in effect for 1966/67.
Simple overshipments in 1966/67[39] (in bags of 132.276 pounds) are
as follows:

Country	Excess Exports Above Final Quota
Bolivia	74,559
Costa Rica	3,727
El Salvador	778,714
Ghana	3,156
Guatemala	124
Indonesia	5,182
Liberia	9,070
Tanzania	31,058
Uganda	2,895
Total	908,485

Unfortunately, the effectiveness of Article 45 was also limited.
Many consumer members, including the United States, the Federal

---

*On November 30, 1967, and on July 15, 1968, the Colombian
Milds received an increase of 177,558 bags in special export authorizations, due to the triggering of their target price.

Republic of Germany, France, the United Kingdom, Switzerland, Sweden, and Finland, imported substantial amounts of coffee above the nonmember quotas assigned by Article 45 in 1966/67.

Excess of imports above nonmember limitations*
in effect in 1966/67[40]
(in bags of 132. 276 pounds) are as follows:

Country	Excess Imports Above Nonmember Limitations
Argentina	3, 486
Australia	975
Austria	1, 919
Belgium/Luxembourg	6, 998
Canada	4, 267
Denmark	11, 883
Germany	144, 511
Finland	13, 242
France	50, 710
Italy	11, 730
Netherlands	2, 706
Spain	7, 869
Sweden	13, 261
Switzerland	28, 667
United Kingdom	29, 723
United States	337, 832
Total	649, 757

Finally, although Annex B shipments dropped from the preceding year (from 4. 2 million bags in 1965/66 to 3. 7 million bags in 1966/67),[41] substantial amounts were transshipped into member markets. Among the exporter members guilty of diverting Annex B shipments into the markets of consumer members were Costa Rica, Indonesia, Mexico, OAMCAF, Portugal, Tanzania, and Uganda. Annex B shipments diverted in 1966/67[42] (in bags of 132.276 pounds) are as follows:

Country	Quantity Diverted in 1966/67
Costa Rica	21,127
Indonesia	32,108
Mexico	15,324
OAMCAF	52

---

*Calculations include Jamaica, Portuguese territories other than Angola, and Liberia and Honduras as nonmembers.

Country	Quantity Diverted in 1966/67
Portugal	683
Tanzania	3,495
Uganda	78,332
Total	132,332

Tourist coffee in 1966/67—as in 1965/66—was estimated at about 6 percent of annual quotas. [43] This performance, despite the decline in direct overshipments and Annex B transshipments, was unimpressive, considered in light of the decline in world exportable production from 66 million bags in 1965/66 to 44.2 million bags in 1966/67.

In 1967/68 the ICO enforcement system finally began to take hold. Early in the coffee year, the ICC authorized the Executive Director to withhold 10 percent of the coffee export stamps to be released to a member for its next quarter's shipments, if it failed to—

1. Submit certificates of origin within three weeks from the date of issue:

2. Advise the ICO by the fifteenth day of each month of the amount of coffee for which stamps were used during the preceding month:

3. Submit a report of exports to Annex B countries by countries of destination within 30 days of the close of each month. [44]

With the improved stamp system, direct overshipments fell to 18,327 bags, an all-time low for the ICA, in 1967/68. Simple overshipments in 1967/68[45] (in bags of 132.276 pounds) are as follows:

Country	Excess Exports
Brazil	67
Burundi	7
Ghana	17,897
Liberia	4
Panama	352
Total	18,327

Moreover, nonmember above quota exports to member importing countries were down more than three-quarters from the year before, a significant improvement. (See Table 10.) The effect of the reduced

TABLE 10

Excess of Imports Above Nonmember Limitations
in Effect, 1967/68

Country	Period Covered	Excess Imports Above Nonmember Limitations
Argentina	January	1,186
Canada	May	2,978
Germany	April	27,786
France	April	8,590
Italy	March	16,718
Norway	April	530
Sweden	May	34,189
Switzerland	May	5,261
United Kingdom	April	1,420
United States	May	103,869
Total		149,695

Note: Figures not available for periods beyond dates listed. Calculations include Bolivia, Cyprus, Guinea, Israel and Paraguay as nonmembers.

Source: Limitation on Imports of Coffee by Importing Members from Nonmember Countries for Coffee Year 1968-69, International Coffee Organization Doc. No. EB-679/68 (August 8, 1968).

overshipments and nonmember transshipments was to put additional pressure on the importing countries themselves to act as entrepôts for tourist coffee. As a result, an amount of coffee estimated by the ICO at 882,944 bags in 1967/68 traveled under forged certificates of re-export, or "splits." Forged certificates were issued in the name of the Bremen Chamber of Commerce, the Swiss certifying agency, the Belgian certifying agency, the Chamber of Commerce in Vienna, and the London Chamber of Commerce. Quantity of coffee covered by forged certificates in 1967/68[46] (in bags of 132.276 pounds) is as follows:

Alleged Source of Documents	Total
Switzerland	268,635
Federal Republic of Germany	200,955
Belgium	24,068

Alleged Source of Documents	Total
United Kingdom	11,669
Italy	78,042
Tunisia	213,325
Argentina	86,250
Total	882,944

This was the last loophole in the ICO enforcement system, and it was effectively closed in 1969, when the ICC adopted stringent regulations to curb re-exports.

The ICO, by the end of coffee year 1967/68, had clearly reduced tourist coffee to a tolerable level. This was due both to more effective enforcement measures and to the de facto reallocation of quotas needed to meet emergent African interests. By a dynamic upgrading of organizational goals[47] profitable to all members, the ICO appeared to have been brought into equilibrium, ensuring its renewal in 1968.

NOTES

1. Terms of Reference for the Advisory Panel to Adjudicate on a Legal Dispute Arising Out of the Study of a Selective System for the Adjustment of Quotas as Required by Paragraph 11 of Resolution No. 67, ICO Doc. No. EB-331/65 (September 30, 1965), p. 1.

2. Ibid., p. 1.

3. Report of the Advisory Panel on the Legality of a System for the Selective Adjustment of Quotas, ICO Doc. No. ICC-7-60 (November 30, 1965), (hereafter cited as Report of the Advisory Panel . . .), p. 6.

4. Ibid., p. 8.

5. Review of the International Coffee Agreement: Proposals Submitted by Brazil, ICO Doc. No. EB-260/65 (June 1, 1965), p. 4.

6. Review of the International Coffee Agreement: Proposals Submitted by Colombia, ICO Doc. No. EB-247/65 (May 3, 1965), p. 2.

7. "Summary Record," Third Plenary Meeting of the Seventh Session of the ICC, ICO Doc. No. ICC-7-m-20 (August 5, 1965).

8. Summary Record, " Sixth Plenary Meeting of the Seventh Session of the ICC, ICO Doc. No. ICC-7-m-53 (August 12, 1965).

9. Review of the International Coffee Agreement—Proposals Submitted by France, ICO Doc. No. EB-271/65 (June 8, 1965), passim.

10. Review of the International Coffee Agreement, ICO Doc. No. EB-308/65 (July 22, 1965), p. 2.

11. Decisions Adopted (15), ICO Doc. No. EB-282/65, Rev. 1 (June 15, 1965), p. 7.

12. ICC Resolution 81, August 13, 1965.

13. Report of the Advisory Panel . . . , see citation at note 1, pp. 9, 10.

14. "Summary Record," Fifteenth Plenary Meeting of the Seventh Session of the ICC, ICO Doc. No. ICC-7-m-88 (December 11, 1965).

15. See Draft Comprehensive Plan for the Consideration of Pending Questions, ICO Doc. No. EB-403/66 (August 17, 1966).

16. Report of the Conclusions of the Board of Directors of the Inter-African Coffee Organization, ICO Doc. No. EB-404/66 (August 17, 1966), p. 5.

17. Brazil/Preliminary Memorandum, ICO Doc. No. EB-402/66 (August 17, 1966), p. 3.

18. Information about these negotiations was obtained in a series of interviews with one of the participants.

19. Statement by Member Countries of Fedecame with Regard to Selectivity, ICO Doc. No. ICC-8-9 (August 25, 1966). All quotations are from p. 1.

20. "Summary Record," Third Plenary Meeting of the Eighth Session of the ICC, ICO Doc. No. ICC-8-m-37 (September 14, 1966).

21. Ibid.

22. ICC Resolution 107, August 31, 1966.

23. ICC Resolution 108, August 31, 1966.

24. ICC Resolution 116, September 6, 1966.

25. ICC Resolution 115, September 6, 1966.

26. ICC Resolution 114, September 6, 1966.

27. For the debate on the waiver provisions, see "Summary Record, " Seventh Plenary Meeting of the Eighth Session of the ICC, ICO Doc. No. ICC-8-m-42 (October 9, 1966).

The vote on Resolution 114 (Source: ibid.) was as follows:

Vote	Exporters	Importers	
Yes	534	Yes	942
No	124	No	-
Abstain	342	Abstain	58

Breakdown by country vote is not available.

28. See Abram Chayes, Thomas Ehrlich, and Andreas F. Lowenfeld, International Legal Process (Boston: Little, Brown and Company, 1968), p. 617.

29. Resolution 118, September 6, 1966.

30. ICC Resolution 117, September 6, 1966, para. 2.

31. ICC Resolution 111, September 5, 1966.

32. ICC Resolution 112, September 5, 1966.

33. ICC Resolution 113, September 5, 1966. On the relationship of the problem of nonmember accessions to the problem of direct overshipments, see Chayes, Ehrlich, and Lowenfeld, op. cit., pp. 621-23. On the package in general, see Andreas F. Lowenfeld, "International Coffee Controls—Some Lessons from the Coffee Agreement, " The American Journal of International Law, LXI (July, 1967), 785-89.

34. ICC Resolution 122, September 6, 1966.

35. ICC Resolution 120, September 6, 1966.

36. The first selectivity quota expansion for the Robustas, on May 3, 1967, amounted to 117, 021 bags. Other quota expansions resulting from selectivity were on June 27, 1967 (161, 617 bags); November 30, 1967 (295, 154 bags); and 300, 002 bag expansions on February 12, March 11, and June 11, 1968.

37. Other Milds quota cuts were as follows: December 26, 1966 (233, 628 bags); January 23, 1967 (164, 319); February 20, 1967 (135, 054); March 20, 1967 (100, 126); and April 27, 1967 (217, 908).

38. Colombian Milds quota cuts were as follows: February 13, 1967 (120,622 bags); March 12, 1967 (16,703 bags); April 27, 1967 (152,014 bags); June 27, 1967 (20,141 bags); July 18, 1967 (3,537 bags).

39. Source for data is the International Bank for Reconstruction and Development.

40. Source for data is Limitation on Imports of Coffee by Importing Members from Non-member Countries for Coffee Year 1968-69, ICO Doc. No. EB-679/68 (August 8, 1968).

41. Shamser Singh, International Coffee Agreement, 1968 (Washington, D.C.: International Bank for Reconstruction and Development, August, 1968), Table 5.

42. Source for data is "Report on Quota Controls," Staff Paper, ICO Doc. No. EB-545/67 (September 21, 1967).

43. The Economist (September 2, 1967), p. 806.

44. ICC Resolution 141, September 10, 1967.

45. The data are preliminary. The source is the International Bank for Reconstruction and Development.

46. Source for data is Control System: Investigations (Report by the Executive Director), ICO Doc. No. EB-861/70 (February 12, 1970).

47. See Ernst B. Haas, Beyond the Nation-State (Stanford: Calif.: Stanford University Press, 1964), for a description of the process of organizational growth.

8

**THE 1968 INTERNATIONAL
COFFEE AGREEMENT:
REGULATORY, ENFORCEMENT,
STRUCTURAL, AND
ORGANIZATIONAL PROVISIONS**

The ICA was renegotiated in the last half of 1967 and the early months of 1968. This chapter analyzes most of the results of the renewal negotiations—the regulatory, enforcement, structural and organizational provisions of the 1968 ICA. The next chapter explores the soluble coffee controversy between the United States and Brazil, one result of which was Article 44 of the 1968 ICA on processed coffee. Since the dispute was strictly bilateral and had a denouement worthy of comprehensive analysis, it is considered separately.

THE POLITICAL ACTION UNITS REVISITED

The Major Trading Countries

The major trading countries were still interested in having their weight in the world market translated into influence in the 1968 ICA. They knew, however, that they would have to accomodate a number of countries that had been dissatisfied with quota shares and with their role in shaping ICO policy since 1962.

The Smaller Trading Countries

The smaller trading countries wanted a larger voice in the ICC and in the increasingly important Executive Board. The small exporters also wanted their advances in world trade to be reflected in a renegotiated Annex A List.

The Exporters

The exporters were in favor of renewing the ICA in 1968. To appreciate the dimensions of the assist given by the ICA to the exporters, it must be recalled that, preceding the Agreement, prices had declined steadily from the 1954 high of 79 cents per pound (Santos 4, New York spot price) to 34 cents per pound in 1962. In terms of foreign exchange lost to coffee-exporting countries, this meant a drop from $2,480 million in 1954 to $1,822 million in 1962. In contrast, since the ICA had been in effect, foreign exchange proceeds had risen remarkably,* in the following manner:

Year	Foreign Exchange Proceeds (In Millions of Dollars
1962	$ 1,822
1963	1,951
1964	2,315
1965	2,157
1966	2,331
1967**	2,217

Apart from the boost given to their foreign exchange proceeds by the ICA, the exporters also appreciated the fact that the statistical balance in the world coffee economy had steadily improved in their favor since 1962. (See Tables 11-13.) Exportable production had decreased from 73 million bags in 1962 to 69 million bags in 1968—compared to an increase from 38 million bags in 1952 to 73 bags in 1962. Meanwhile, world consumption had grown from 61 million bags in 1962 to an estimated 70 million bags in 1968.

The exporters—buoyed by the rhetoric of two U.N. Trade and Development conferences since the 1962 UNCC—did not question the need to keep the ICA as a "prototype" for other commodities that they were interested in having supported. They were, as usual, divided on the reallocation of market shares.

---

*African foreign exchange earnings increased most sharply, from $406 million in 1962 to $628 million in 1967. The other large gainer in foreign exchange was Brazil, with receipts from coffee exports rising from $643 million in 1962 to $732 million in 1967.

**Provisional.

TABLE 11

Coffee: Exports by Country of Origin, Average 1960-64, Annual 1966-70
(In Thousands of Bags of 132.276 Pounds Each)

Country of Origin	Average 1960-64	1966[a]	1967[a]	1968[a]	1969[a]	1970[b]
North America:						
Costa Rica	872	914	1,102	1,142	1,127	1,147
Dominican Republic	468	423	370	392	447	435
El Salvador	1,637	1,617	1,997	1,970	1,867	1,840
Guatemala	1,394	1,817	1,355	1,572	1,501	1,547
Haiti	405	349	311	292	297	260
Honduras	278	383	366	440	410	519
Mexico	1,436	1,537	1,241	1,588	1,565	1,348
Nicaragua	369	387	430	474	442	494
Trinidad and Tobago	43	40	43	72	46	34
Other[c]	119	46	131	261	56	40
Total North America	7,021	7,513	7,346	8,203	7,758	7,664
South America:						
Brazil[d]	16,925	17,031	17,331	19,035	19,613	17,164
Colombia	6,139	5,565	6,094	6,588	6,478	6,509
Ecuador	476	728	945	826	627	879
Peru	601	590	693	873	714	748
Venezuela	373	303	309	161	315	320
Other[e]	99	142	121	97	46	49
Total South America	24,613	24,359	25,493	27,580	27,793	25,669
Africa:						
Angola	2,125	2,607	3,275	3,144	3,047	2,943
Burundi[f]	[g] 243	246	314	313	247	288
Cameroun[h]	648	989	943	1,225	1,016	1,100
Central African Republic	131	189	152	137	152	156
Congo-Kinshasa	[i] 694	577	594	900	749	857
Ethiopia	1,019	1,224	1,227	1,338	1,473	1,548
Guinea	182	207	206	205	150	150
Ivory Coast	2,762	3,024	2,484	3,574	2,972	3,012
Kenya	571	908	846	627	850	829
Malagasy Republic	728	761	832	897	826	866
Rwanda[f]	[g] 76	147	187	201	193	189
Equatorial Guinea	118	150	120	120	110	110
Tanzania[j]	455	852	756	819	825	694
Togo	162	220	94	170	184	218
Uganda	2,146	2,788	2,658	2,533	3,010	2,919
Other[k]	302	524	331	508	344	300
Total Africa	12,362	15,413	15,019	16,711	16,148	16,179
Asia and Oceania:						
India	402	403	600	471	567	454
Indonesia	1,012	1,592	1,100	1,369	1,738	1,623
Malaysia[l]	717	562	820	620	700	400
Yemen	73	43	27	30	19	18
Other[m]	153	264	360	369	391	500
Total Asia and Oceania	2,357	2,864	2,907	2,859	3,415	2,995
Grand Total	46,353	50,149	50,765	55,353	55,114	52,507

[a]Revised.
[b]Preliminary.
[c]Includes Cuba, Guadeloupe, Hawaii, Jamaica, Panama, and Puerto Rico.
[d]Includes soluble coffee in green bean equivalent.
[e]Includes Bolivia, Guyana, Paraguay and Surinam.
[f]Prior to 1963, included in Congo-Kinshasa.
[g]Two-year average, 1963 and 1964.
[h]East Cameroun only.
[i]Includes Burundi and Rwanda prior to 1963.
[j]Prior to 1964-65 year, was shown as Tanganyika, now includes Zanzibar as well.
[k]Includes Cape Verde, Comoro Islands, Dahomey, Gabon, Ghana, Liberia, Nigeria, Congo-Kinshasa, Sao Tome and Principe, and Sierra Leone.
[l]Data for Malaysia represent estimated reexports not otherwise shown.
[m]Includes New Caledonia, New Hebrides, Papua and New Guinea, and Portuguese Timor.

Source: Foreign Agricultural Service, U.S. Department of Agriculture. Prepared or estimated on the basis of official statistics of foreign governments, other foreign source materials, reports of Agricultural Attaches and Foreign Service Officers, results of office research and related information.

TABLE 12

Coffee: Exports by Continents as Percentage of Total
World Exports, Average 1960-64, Annual 1966-70

Continent	Average 1960-64	1966	1967	1968	1969	1970
North America	15.1	15.0	14.5	14.8	14.1	14.6
South America	53.1	48.6	50.2	49.8	50.4	48.9
Africa	26.7	30.7	29.6	30.2	29.3	30.8
Asia and Oceania	5.1	5.7	5.7	5.2	6.2	5.7
Total	100.0	100.0	100.0	100.0	100.0	100.0

Source: Foreign Agricultural Service, U.S. Department of Agriculture.

TABLE 13

Coffee: Exports by Nine Principal Producing Countries as
Percentage of World Exports, Average 1960-64, Annual 1966-70

Country of Origin	Average 1960-64	1966	1967	1968	1969	1970
Angola	4.6	5.2	6.5	5.7	5.5	5.6
Brazil	36.5	34.0	34.1	34.4	35.6	32.7
Colombia	13.2	11.1	12.0	11.9	11.8	12.4
El Salvador	3.5	3.2	3.9	3.6	3.4	3.5
Ethiopia	2.2	2.4	2.4	2.4	2.7	2.9
Guatemala	3.0	3.6	2.7	2.8	2.7	2.9
Ivory Coast	6.0	6.0	4.9	6.5	5.4	5.7
Mexico	3.1	3.1	2.4	2.9	2.8	2.6
Uganda	4.6	5.6	5.2	4.6	5.5	5.6
Total	76.7	74.2	74.1	74.8	75.4	73.9

Source: Foreign Agricultural Service, U.S. Department of Agriculture.

The Latin Americans

The Latin Americans wanted larger basic quota shares and the dilution or elimination of selectivity. They argued that selectivity had been politically divisive, pitting all producers against each other on a yearly basis, and had resulted in the LDC's bargaining for lower prices in order to assure quota expansions.

Brazil

Brazil, despite its declining market share, had prospered under the ICA and wanted it renewed. * The decline in Brazil's market share, paradoxiocally, strengthened its bargaining position, as the confidence of the other coffee exporters in the continuation of Brazil's price support (i.e., nondumping) policy had eroded proportionately. Aware of growing pressures from the planters of Brazil for a more aggressive marketing policy, the other exporters were compelled to join a stabilizing agreement with Brazil as their leader for as good a bargain as they could drive.

Brazil championed a diversification fund, production goals, and strict export controls in order to force diversification in the other producing countries. It was interested in "improving" on selectivity and getting rid of the EEC preference for its African associates, [1] but did not insist as adamantly on the latter as it had in the 1962 UNCC.

Finally, Brazil hoped to preserve market access into the United States for its burgeoning soluble coffee industry. It wanted to confine the soluble issue to bilateral negotiations between the two countries.

Colombia

Colombia continued to have a strong interest in a quota agreement that would lock in potential market entrants and complement its price

---

*In 1962, Brazil exported 16.3 million bags—35.4 percent of the world market; in 1967, Brazil exported 17.3 million bags, with 34 percent of the world market. The average price of Brazils (Santos 4s) increased from 34.0 in 1962 to 37.8 (U.S. cents per pound) in 1967.

defense policy.* It urged that (1) selectivity be abolished, (2) tighter export controls be instituted, and (3) effective provisions for production goals and a diversification fund be negotiated.

Other Milds

The Other Milds—angered by their declining market share** argued that the "unfair" UNCC quotas should be reallocated in their favor. They also condemned selectivity, despite the increase in their prices from 1962. Their arguments against selectivity were given force by the substantial cuts inflicted on them by the system in 1966/67 and the narrow price differentials (1.5 cents) set between the Other Milds and the Colombian Milds in 1967, which allowed the Colombians to expand sales at their expense.

The Africans

The Africans had prospered under the 1962 ICA. The decline in world output since 1962 had been due mainly to climatic conditions and diversification in Brazil: African production and exports had continued to increase.*** The Africans, wary of a direct confrontation with Brazil in a free market, were thus anxious to renew the ICA. They pressed for (1) a revised Annex A list, (2) a continuation of selectivity (seen as helpful for their dynamic Robustas), (3) an extension of the Annex B list (seen as a vital conduit for anticipated tourist coffee, and (4) a more liberal application of quarterly quotas.[2] Due to their desire to expand Robusta production, the Africans wanted to dilute the diversification fund by making contributions voluntary.

---

*In 1962, Colombia exported 6.6 million bags—14.2 percent of the world coffee market; in 1967, Colombia exported 6.1 million bags, or 12 percent of the global total. Average prices for its Milds, however, were up during the ICA (In U.S. cents per pound—1962, 40.8; 1967, 41.9).

**Other Milds were down from 15.4 percent of the World market in 1962 to 14.8 percent in 1967.

***In 1962, Africa exported 12.9 million bags, with 28 percent of the world market. In 1967, Africa exported 15.3 million bags, or 30 percent of the world market.

The Importers

To promote long-range structural improvement in the world coffee economy, the importers advocated writing a diversification fund and production goals into the 1968 ICA.[3] They also wanted to reallocate market shares in such a way as to reflect the shifts in consumer demand that had taken place since 1962. Consequently, they endorsed revision of Annex A. To ensure that future demand changes would be reflected in exporters' quotas, the importers backed the concept of selectivity.[4] The only other particularized consumer interest was the desire of the United States to check rapidly rising Brazilian exports of soluble (instant) coffee, which had, the United States argued, flourished from "unfair" competition under the Agreement.

THE 1968 ICA

Regulatory Provisions

Basic Quotas

The 1968 ICA, despite a few alterations, is basically unchanged from the 1962 Agreement. The mechanism for ensuring a "reasonable" price to exporters is the three-tiered export quota system described earlier (see page 83), which is adjusted to meet market conditions.

Basic quotas, however, are revised substantially in the 1968 ICA.* (See Table 14.) The new Annex A reduces shares of the quota

---

*The methodological problems are not elaborated in this chapter. (See pages 74-83 on the 1962 UNCC negotiations for an explanation of the difficulties of drawing up the Annex A List.) The problems in 1968 were similar, with frequent threats to leave the ICO unless specific conditions were met. Final base year figures were best alternatives between the exportable production of 1959/60-1962/63 or 1961/62-1962/63, i.e., four-and two-year periods. This figure was then reduced for retentions: for countries producing less than 25,000 bags, no reduction; 25,000 to 500,000 bags, 6 percent; 500,000 to 1 million bags, 8 percent; 1 to 2 million bags, 10 percent; 2 to 10 million bags, 12 percent, and more than 10 million bags, 20 percent. Other factors, such as new coffee trees coming into bearing, surplus stocks, and the extent of dependence on coffee exports, were

TABLE 14

Comparison of Basic Coffee Quotas Under the 1968 International Coffee Agreement;
Basic Quotas Under the 1962 Agreement and 1967/68 Initial Effective Quotas

Country	1968 Agreement Basic Quotas		1962 Agreement Basic Quotas			1967/68 Initial Effective Quotas			Percentage Change Under the 1968 Agreement from:	
	In Thousands of Bags	Percent	In Thousands of Bags	Percent	Adjusted to 55.041 Million Bags	In Thousands of Bags	Per cent	Adjusted to 55.041 Million Bags	1962 Basic Quotas (1) - (5)	1967/68 Effective Quotas (1) - (8)
	(1)	(2)	(3)	(4)	(5)	(6)	(7)	(8)	(9)	(10)
Brazil	20,926	38.019	18,000	39.088	21,514	17,672	37.603	20,697	-2.73	1.11
Burundi	233	0.423	288	0.625	344	282	0.600	330	-32.27	-29.39
Colombia	7,000	12.718	6,011	13.053	7,185	5,902	12.559	6,912	-2.57	1.27
Congo-Kinshasa	1,000	1.817	1,140	2.476	1,363	1,129	2.402	1,322	-26.63	-24.36
Costa Rica	1,100	1.999	950	2.063	1,135	933	1.985	1,093	-3.03	0.64
Dominican Republic	520	0.945	425	0.923	508	458	0.975	537	2.36	-3.17
Ecuador	750	1.363	552	1.199	660	554	1.179	649	13.64	15.56
El Salvador	1,900	3.452	1,430	3.105	1,709	1,613	3.432	1,889	11.18	0.58
Ethiopia	1,494	2.714	1,175	2.551	1,404	1,230	2.617	1,440	6.41	3.75
Guatemala	1,800	3.270	1,344	2.919	1,607	1,395	2.968	1,634	12.01	10.16
Haiti	490	0.890	420	0.912	502	443	0.943	519	-2.39	-5.59
Honduras	425	0.772	285	0.619	341	412	0.877	483	24.63	-12.01
India	423	0.769	360	0.782	430	363	0.772	425	-1.63	-0.47
Indonesia	1,357	2.465	1,174	2.549	1,403	1,024	2.179	1,199	-3.28	13.18
Kenya	860	1.562	517	1.123	618	760	1.617	890	39.16	-3.37

	(1)	(2)	(3)	(4)	(5)	(6)	(7)	(8)	(9)	(10)
Mexico	1,760	3.198	1,509	3.277	1,804	1,444	3.073	1,691	-2.44	4.08
Nicaragua	550	0.999	419	0.910	501	471	1.002	552	9.78	-0.36
OAMCAF:	(5,383)	(9.779)	(4,236)	(9.199)	(5,063)	4,614[a]	9.818	5,404	(6.32)	0.39
Cameroun	1,000	1.817	763	1.657	912	b	b	b	9.65	b
Central African Republic	200	0.363	150	0.326	179	b	b	b	11.73	b
Ivory Coast	3,073	5.583	2,324	5.047	2,778	b	b	b	10.62	b
Malagasy Republic	910	1.653	829	1.800	991	b	b	b	-8.17	b
Togo	200	0.363	170	0.369	203	b	b	b	-1.48	b
Peru	740	1.344	580	1.259	693	617	1.313	723	6.78	2.35
Portugal	2,776	5.044	2,224	4.830	2,658	2,492	5.303	2,919	4.44	-4.90
Rwanda	150	0.273	212	0.460	253	209	0.445	245	-40.71	-38.78
Tanzania	700	1.272	436	0.947	521	441	0.938	516	34.36	35.66
Uganda	2,379	4.322	1,888	4.100	2,257	2,072	4.409	2,427	5.41	-1.98
Venezuela	325	0.591	475	1.031	568	466	0.991	545	-42.78	-40.37
Total	55,041	100.000	46,050	100.000	55,041	46,996	100.000	55,042		

[a]Excludes estimated quotas for Congo-Brazzaville, Dahomey, and Gabon.
[b]Included in OAMCAF total.

Source: Shamsher Singh, International Coffee Agreement, 1968 (Washington, D.C.: International Bank for Reconstruction and Development, 1968), Appendix, Table 6.

market for thirteen countries, ranging from a cut of 42.8 percent for Venezuela to 1.5 percent for Togo. Brazil and Colombia yielded 2.7 percent and 2.6 percent, respectively, with the remainder split among smaller countries.

Fifteen countries received quota increases, ranging from 39.2 percent for Kenya to 2.4 percent for the Dominican Republic. Principal beneficiaries of the quota reallocations were the revisionists in Africa and Latin America:

Country	Quota Increase in Percent
Africa:	
Kenya	39
Tanzania	34
Central African Republic	12
Ivory Coast	11
Cameroun	10
Ethiopia	6
Portugal	4
Latin America:	
Honduras	25
Ecuador	14
Guatemala	12
El Salvador	11
Nicaragua	10

All modifications in the 1968 Annex A compared to the 1967/68 marketing year, however, are minor, with the exception of the special status of Burundi, Rwanda, Congo-Kinshasa, and Venezula (discussed below), and Tanzania (+36 percent increased), Ecuador (+16 percent) Guatemala (+10 percent), Honduras (-12 percent), and Indonesia (+13 percent). The shares for Brazil and Colombia were slightly higher than their shares during the last year of the 1962 Agreement. The new Annex A thus formalized the additional export authorizations given on a provisional basis during the life of the 1962 ICA.

Export authorizations of small exporters were changed substantially in the 1968 Annex A. Thirteen small exporters (i.e., exporters

---

then taken into account. See Shamsher Singh, International Coffee Agreement, 1968 (Washington, D.C.: International Bank for Reconstruction and Development, 1968), p. 22.

of less than 100,000 bags) have export allotments for the 1968/69 coffee year in footnote 1 of Annex A.* These allotments will be increased annually by 10 percent until a maximun of 100,000 bags is reached, at which point a basic quota will be set. [5] This is a departure from the 1962 Agreement, which permitted exporters of less than 25,000 bags to be free from final basic quotas. [6] Footnote 1 of Annex A should be seen as a useful equilibrating mechanism to allow small exporters to legally expand market shares under the new Agreement.

Another equilibrating measure for certain small exporters is found in footnote 2 of Annex A. It grants Burundi, Congo-Kinshasa, Cuba, Rwanda, and Venezuela the possibility of larger basic quota shares if they can demonstrate that their exportable production is larger than their 1968/69 allotments.

Finally, the provision for the three-year review of the basic quota shares, which, as has been seen (see Chapter 7) did not work in the 1962 Agreement, was dropped.

Waivers

The waiver provision in the 1968 ICA is stricter than its predecessor. It forbids waivers for exporters basing their requests on overproduction or noncompliance with the production control aspects of the Agreement. [7] By closely defining "force majeure," the Agreement will lessen the number of waiver requests coming before the ICC.

Prices

The 1962 ICA conspicuously omitted any article specifically permitting the Council to establish a selectivity price system. That omission was over time resolved by Resolution 67, which established a price floor/ceiling system, and Resolution 115, which permitted both special export authorizations and waivers to be distributed on a submarket basis.

The 1968 ICA reflects this development of the treaty in an article that permits the Council to establish a selectivity system for

---

*Those exporters are Bolivia (1968/69 export authorization of 50,000 bags); Congo-Brazzaville, 25,000; Cuba, 50,000; Dahomey, 33,000; Gabon, 25,000; Ghana, 51,000; Jamaica, 25,000; Liberia, 60,000; Nigeria, 52,000; Panama, 25,000; Paraguay, 70,000; Sierra Leone, 82,000; and Trinidad and Tobago, 69,000.

the "principal types of coffee."[8] To placate the Other Milds, downward adjustments of annual quotas by more than 5 percent are prohibited.[9] There is, by implication, no limit on upward adjustments. If prices continue to drop after the downward limit of a submarket under selectivity has been reached, the Council is to decrease all quotas pro rata. The rather ambiguous general undertaking by members that they "agree on the necessity of assuring that the general level of coffee prices does not decline below the general level of such prices in 1962"[10] is retained.

Enforcement

The enforcement provisions of the new ICA are patterned on the certificates of origin system developed under the former Agreement. There are, however, a few minor changes. Coffee imported into the member countries must now be accompanied by a "valid" certificate or origin,[11] as opposed to one patterned on a model certificate. The validity of the certificate is to be determined "in accordance with rules established by the Council."[12] This was interpreted as a formalization of the stamp plan.[13]

Tougher penalties are provided than in the first ICA. The penalty for the first overshipment of a quarterly quota is a deduction of 110 percent of the excess, as opposed to a deduction of an equal sum under the 1962 ICA.* For a second offense, the ICC is authorized to deduct an amount equal to twice the excess.[14] For a third offense, the ICC is to make another double deduction and suspend the voting rights of the member until it decides whether or not to require the member's withdrawal.[15]

The 1968 ICA limits the annual imports of nonmembers to a quantity not in excess of the average annual imports of coffee from those countries into consumer members during the calender years 1960, 1961 and 1962.[16] These quotas are subject to suspension or variation by a two-thirds distributed majority of the ICC.[17]

Nonquota exports of coffee to certain countries with low consumption and considerable potential for expansion (listed in Annex B)

---

*International Coffee Agreement, 1968, Art. 38 (3). This penalty provision was introduced in the renewal negotiations as an amendment by Colombia. It is interesting to note that the dominant oligopolists, Brazil and Colombia, were generally in favor of strict enforcement measures throughout the history of the ICA.

are permitted in the 1968 ICA. [18] Mindful of past violations of Annex
B through transshipments, the farmers of the new ICA added a specific
prohibition against member importations of ex-quota coffees. [19] The
Annex B list, however, will probably continue to be a conduit for
evasion of basic export quotas.

Structural Provisions

Diversification Fund

   The key changes in the 1968 ICA are in new provisions aimed
at correcting the structural problem of oversupply and overdependence
on coffee as an earner of foreign exchange proceeds.

   The 1962 ICA made gestures toward the goal of diversification,
but presented nothing besides the quota system itself as a concrete
remedy for overproduction. Diversification was left to exporters to
complete on their own timetable. Fortunately, Brazil—with the most
to lose from a collapse of the world coffee market—unilaterally
diversified during the life of the 1962 ICA. One-third of all coffee
trees standing in 1961/62 in Brazil were eradicated. This amounted
to a net reduction in Brazil's production of 20 percent, equaling
between 5 to 10 percent of world production. [20] ICO initiatives were,
however, needed to finance diversification in the remaining producing
countries. Accordingly, the concept of a fund for diversification was
introduced by the United States in 1965 as a part of the Resolution
92 compromise and endorsed in principle in 1966 by the ICC. [21]

   The diversification fund that was drafted in a new article in
the 1968 ICA is a unique innovation in commodity agreements.* The
Fund is to be originally financed by contributions of the exporting
members of 60 cents a bag for all bags actually exported over 100,000
bags each year to quota market. [22] A particularly interesting aspect
of the Fund is that 20 percent of the total contributions must be in
convertible currency for use in the territory of any exporting member. [23] Most of the remainder of the proceeds of the Fund are to be
used for projects in the contributing countries, and a small percentage
of the total contribution is to be payable in convertible currency for
administrative expenses for the Fund. [24] The United States argued
that a larger share of the proceeds should be in convertible currency
to solve the "coffee problem" more effectively on a marcro basis,

----

   *International Coffee Agreement, 1968, Art. 54. It replaces
the voluntary fund concept outlined in Article 57 of the 1962 ICA.

but this was not acceptable to the smaller exporters, which feared domination of the Fund by Brazil and Colombia.

Production Goals

The new provisions on production goals attempt to meet the problem of autonomous national coffee policies by forcing exporting members to define national production goals. Exporters retain the power to "apply whatever policies and procedures" they deem necessary to carry out the production goals, but they are subject to a loss in additional quota exports if the Council determines that the steps taken are insufficient.[25]

Organizational Aspects

The 1968 ICA enlarges the Executive Board from seven importing and seven exporting members to eight importing and eight exporting members.[26] This move was a result of the demands of the small exporting countries, which had complained of big-power domination of the ICO. Secondly, the installation of selectivity is facilitated by a provision permitting the ICC to delegate to the Executive Board the administration of submarket quota expansions.[27]

By mid-January, 1968, the major substantive changes in the ICA had been settled. The only matter remaining to be solved was an article on processed coffee that would satisfy Brazil and the United States. The fate of the renewal negotiations thus hung on the successful resolution of the soluble coffee controversy.

NOTES

1. Extension, Renegotiation and/or Amendment, ICO Doc. No. ICC-9-5 (June 9, 1967). p. 5.

2. See Extension, Renegotiation, and/or Amendment of the Agreement: Statement Made by the Representative of Portugal, ICO Doc. No. ICC-9-24 (June 7, 1967), p. 6., and Extension, Renegotiation and/or Amendment, ICO Doc. No. ICC-9-5 (June 9, 1967), p. 10.

3. Statement by Consumers Group, ICO Doc. No. ICC-9-25 (June 6, 1967), p. 2.

4. Ibid., p. 2.

5. International Coffee Agreement, 19 U.S.T, T.I.A.S. 6584 (1968), Art. 21(2). Hereinafter cited as International Coffee Agreement, 1968.

6. International Coffee Agreement, 1962, Art. 39 (1).

7. International Coffee Agreement, 1968, Art. 57 (2).

8. Ibid., Art. 37 (2).

9. Ibid.

10. Ibid., Art. 27 (2).

11. Ibid., Art. 43 (1).

12. Ibid.

13. Abram Chayes, Thomas Ehrlich, and Andreas F. Lowenfeld, International Legal Process (Boston: Little, Brown and Company, 1968), p. 626. See Resolution 118, September 6, 1966, at pp. 176-77.

14. International Coffee Agreement, 1968, Art. 38 (4).

15. Ibid., Art. 38 (5).

16. Ibid., Art. 45 (1).

17. Ibid., Art. 45 (2).

18. Ibid., Art. 40. The Philippines, Jordon, and North and South Viet-Nam are deleted from the 1962 Annex B list.

19. Ibid., Art. 40 (d). Compare to the 1962 ICA: "The Council shall call any possible irregularity to the attention of the Members." International Coffee Agreement, 1962 Art. 40 (1) (d).

20. On the extent of the Brazilian diversification, see International Monetary Fund and International Bank for Reconstruction and Development Staff Study, "The Problem of Stabilization of Prices of Primary Products, Part I" (Washington, D.C.: IMF, IBRD, 1968), pp. 138-48. The base years used for the estimates are 1960/63 averages. The reason for the discrepancy in Brazilian figures is that the older trees were the first ones eliminated in the diversification program.

21. Resolution 120, September 7, 1966.

22. Ibid. , Art . 54 (3). This paragraph states that the Fund, by a two-thirds distributed majority vote, may increase the levy to a level not exceeding $1.00 per bag.

23. Ibid. , Art. 54 (4).

24. Ibid.

25. Ibid. , Art. 48 (6).

26. Ibid. , Art. 15 (1).

27. Ibid. , Art. 17 (2).

THE PROBLEM

The soluble coffee crisis started to brew (to use a bad pun) in 1960, when the Brazilian federal government made its first venture into the instant coffee export industry by establishing a series of incentives for soluble (instant) coffee production. These were equally available for nationals and foreign companies. * When eleven companies, all Brazilian, showed interest, the advantages were expanded by the IBC.[1] By the end of 1961, four companies had projects for soluble coffee plants approved by the Brazilian federal government. [2]

Due to a preoccupation with the 1962 ICA, ** and a desire not to irritate the American green coffee importers, many of whom also sell soluble coffee, only two factories, Cacique and Nestle, were

---

*Oddly enough, Brazil preferred to burn its excess green coffee (or store it) before 1960 rather than use it for soluble coffee exports. In 1960, the IBC issued Resolution 161, which offered incentives for new soluble industries in Brazil, the principal one being an IBC guarantee to buy the first 80 percent of the output of the plant in its first year and decreasing amounts thereafter.

**The 1962 ICA covered all forms of green coffee exports, including processed soluble coffee. A conversion factor of three was used to multiply the soluble coffee's net weight, which was then added to the sum of the member's green coffee exports. International Coffee Agreement, 1962, Art. 2 (g). Brazilian exportation of soluble powder was, therefore, legal under the terms of the ICA.

finished by 1964.[3]   Four additional plants were built by the end of 1967.[4]

Unencumbered by either internal Brazilian taxes or export taxes (so-called contributions) and aided by the accessibility of cheap local green coffee ("grinders") not put into international trade, Brazilian soluble exports to the United States soared from 1 percent of the U.S. solubles market in 1965 to 14 percent of the U.S. market in 1967.* (See Table 15.) The Brazilian soluble powder was purchased by almost every major coffee roaster in the United States.[5]

The NCA in the United States publicly condemned Brazil on June 13, 1966. Privately, however, the American coffee industry was divided on the Brazilian market moves.

General Foods, the largest producer of regular (29 percent of all industry sales in the United States)[6] and soluble (53.5 percent of all industry sales in the United States)** coffee in the United States, faced a particularly acute dilemma. Its overriding objective was to protect its share of the U.S. soluble coffee market. The question for General Foods—the prototype of a "mature" corporation[7]—was

---

*The average price of Brazilian soluble powder (selling at about 85 cents per pound ex-dock in New York) was about 50 cents below the U.S. export price of soluble per pound, indicating a substantial competitive advantage for Brazil in soluble production.

**J.C. Maxwell, Jr., "Overview: Trends in Coffee Marketing," World Coffee and Tea (May, 1970), p. 43. General Foods is the largest manufacturer of nationally branded packaged food in the United States, with annual net sales (for all products) exceeding $2,045 million. It is a publicly held corporation, with about 70,000 shareholders sharing the wealth. And it is diversified into nearly autonomous divisions, with products ranging from cosmetics to Kool-Aid.

But its "diversification" should not be overemphasized. The company's past and present growth has come largely from coffee, which has traditionally amounted to more than one-third of its sales and one half of its profits. Its heavy dependence on coffee has led General Foods to take a more active role in industry politics than companies such as Procter and Gamble or Standard Brands, for whom coffee represents a smaller share of net sales. On the issue of autonomy for its divisions within General Foods, see A. D. H. Kaplan, J. B. Dirlan, and R. F. Lanzilotti, Pricing in Big Business (Washington, D.C.: The Brookings Institution, 1958), p. 231.

TABLE 15

U.S. Imports of Soluble Coffee, 1965-67
(In Thousands of Pounds and Thousands of Dollars)

Imports	1965		1966		1967	
	Pounds	Dollars	Pounds	Dollars	Pounds	Dollars
Mexico	8	7	1,023	1,010	701	690
Guatemala	370	407	1,405	1,213	861	783
El Salvador	301	315	769	750	1,028	1,015
Nicaragua	1,858	2,360	864	1,135	228	278
Brazil	276	300	5,996	6,471	22,451	23,503
All Other	26	26	510	647	2,097	n.a.
France	-	-	321	507	1,725	3,390

Sources: Basic data from U.S. Department of Commerce. Alexander W. Shapleigh, "Soluble Coffee and the International Coffee Agreement, 1968," paper for Johns Hopkins School of Advanced International Studies (May, 1968).

whether it could best do this by vertically integrating, i.e., by buying
a solubles plant in Brazil to take advantage of the Brazilian incentives,
or by pressing the State Department for actions to limit the export of
Brazilian soluble powder to the United States.

Somewhat confused by the swift march of events, General Foods
commissioned a study by the Arthur Andersen & Co., auditors and
management consultants, on whether it should move some of its coffee
operations to Brazil. The Andersen study recommended that General
Foods not go to Brazil.

The Andersen recommendations coincided with the view of the
International Division of General Foods—held before the solubles
crisis—that its major problem was to rationalize and consolidate its
present overseas operations, not to extend them.[8] Moves into the
LDC's were particularly frowned upon by the International Division.
Most of these countries, it was thought, were unstable politically,
unfriendly politically, and excessively nationalistic with respect to
investment questions.[9]

The problems involved in moving to Brazil, in particular,
included, in addition to the investment climate issue mentioned above,
the fear of the rampant inflation in Brazil (which had made long-range
planning for General Foods' controlled subsidiary in Brazil, Kibon,
a "nightmare"),[10] the finding and training of adequate local personnel,
and the absence of a ready local market for instant coffee, due to the
Brazilian preference for strong "regular" brews.[11]

Finally, General Foods' top management[12] feared that any sizable diversion of economic resources from the United States to Brazil
resulting in plant closures would be met by nationwide strikes by
resentful employees.

Matters were less complex for the smaller (11.5 percent of the
regular coffee market in the United States and 1.75 percent of the
instant coffee market) closely held Hills Bros. Coffee Co., Inc.,
which was primarily interested in maximizing profits. As the importation of Brazilian soluble powder allowed Hills Bros. to compete
with the larger operations of the publicly held General Foods, it
favored the maximization of Brazilian soluble exports to the United
States. Hills Bros. was also less worried than General Foods about
potential labor difficulties; when the Brazilian soluble powder became
available, it closed down its soluble-producing plants on the West
Coast in order to market a largely Brazilian product. * Hills Bros.

---

*Arthur J. Cordell, "The Brazilian Soluble Coffee Problem:
A Review," The Quarterly Review of Economics and Business, IX

put direct pressure on the State Department to allow the continued
importation of Brazilian soluble, making the persuasive argument
that the lower-priced Brazilian soluble was a boon to the hard-pressed
American consumer.

The green coffee brokers lined up with General Foods on the
solubles issue.[13] They feared—probably correctly—that the importation of soluble powder would substantially reduce their green coffee
imports (on which they make turnover commissions).

A swirl of rumors soon arose out of these crosscurrents of
industry politics in the United States. One rumor was that General
Foods was going to move some operations to Brazil. This prompted
General Foods' principal African Robusta suppliers (including the
Ivory Coast) to warn the State Department that—the ICA notwithstand-
ing—they were prepared to offer massive discounts to the large U.S.
processors, then using Robustas for instant coffee to maintain their
U.S. market position.

The State Department thus faced an agonizing strategy problem.
It could let events take their course, in which case a coffee price war
(triggered by the threatened African discounts) might occur or the
wrath of the coffee trade in the United States might prevent an election-
year Congress from ratifying the 1968 ICA. Alternatively, it could
move to limit additional Brazilian soluble exports, with the wrath of
the Latin Americans certain to descend on the United States for
stopping the "industrialization" of Brazil.

(Spring, 1969), 32. The behavior of the Hills Bros. Coffee Co., Inc.,
deserves to be carefully scrutinized. For it is the archetype of the
"entrepreneurial" corporation, the closely held corporation whose
shares (or at least voting shares) are held by a single shareholder or
closely knit group of stockholders.

The structure of the closely held corporation differs markedly
from that of the publicly held corporation. There are usually no
public investors, its shareholders are active in the management of
the business, and emphasis is placed on simplified and informal
internal procedures. In short, members incorporate in order to
obtain the benefits of the corporate structure, such as limited liability,
while, at the same time, they are permitted to preserve many of the
internal characteristics of the individual proprietorship or partnership.
The information in this paragraph is from Harry G. Henn, Handbook
of the Law of Corporations and Other Business Enterprises (Minneap-
olis, Minn.: West Publishing Company, 1970), p. 507.

The State Department chose the latter option, in order to preserve the ICA and to placate the trade in the United States. The next key issue was whether the United States would attempt such a limitation unilaterally, bilaterally, or within the ICO. Unilateral action by the United States was limited by the legality of Brazil's actions under the ICA and by the Tariff Act of 1930, which prohibited the imposition of countervailing duties on "subsidized" imports that were not dutiable (the argument of many in the U.S. trade was that the lack of comparability in export taxes on green and soluble coffee in Brazil was a "subsidy").* Bilateral resolution of the controversy was precluded by Brazil's refusal to place "voluntary" restrictions on its soluble exports at the request of the United States. The only remaining alternative for the State Department was, therefore, to seek a cooperative solution within the multilateral context of the renewal negotiations of the ICA.

The reaction of Brazil to the desire of the United States for an amendment to the ICA to check "unfair" competition remained to be seen. Within Brazil, the political equation was also complex and uncertain. The financial interests that had invested in the soluble plants wanted to expand soluble exports, even at considerable risk to the ICA.[14] The planters, on the other hand, were split. Several cooperatives of coffee growers—which had either taken advantage of, or were planning to use, the Brazilian federal government incentives to invest in the soluble plants—urged the IBC to protect the soluble soluble industry, even at the risk of a price war.[15] The most powerful group representing the planters of the State of São Paulo (Federation of Agriculture of São Paulo), however, impressed upon the federal government the necessity for a continued ICA. They argued that the value of Brazilian soluble exports was only about 3 percent of the total value of Brazilian coffee exports and that, even under the best settlement possible, that percentage could not be expected to rise to much more than 10 percent, given the world pattern of soluble demand.[16]

Exposed to these conflicting pressures, the Brazilian federal government wavered. As noted, it first spurned a U.S. initiative for a "voluntary" restriction of soluble exports to the U.S. It then

---

*See the Tariff Act of 1930, Section 303, 19 U.S.C., Sec. 1303. It is questionable, in any case, whether the lack of comparability in export taxes and/or the availability of "grinders" could be considered a subsidy under Section 303. The United States had lifted its nominal 3 cents per pound tariff on soluble coffee on July 1, 1964, as a gesture of goodwill to the LDC's.

replaced the President of the IBC, Horacio Sabino Coimbra, who was sympathetic to, and financially involved with, the Brazilian soluble coffee industry, with an "outsider" with no links to the coffee industry, Caio de Alcantara Machado, on January 4, 1968.

The issue as Brazil went to the ICO in mid-January, 1968, was whether it could manage a settlement with the United States that could simultaneously placate its large and small planters, local financial interests, and domestic public opinion.

THE ARTICLE 44 COMPROMISE

The United States made the first move in the renewal negotiations on the solubles issue, proposing that importers should have the unilateral right to impose an import fee if an exporting member did not have "corresponding" export taxes for green and processed coffee. It also called for the prohibition of the denial of access to any grade of coffee used internally by an exporting member and for the use of an arbitration panel to adjudge discrimination under the Agreement. [17]

The net effect of the U.S. amendments would have been to force Brazil to put its broken beans ("grinders") on the market for foreign roasters and to impose a "corresponding" export tax on its soluble coffee (or to have the United States respond with a countervailing import fee).

Accompanying the U.S. proposal was a blunt warning that there could be no new ICA without some compromise by Brazil.

Brazil responded by arguing forum non conveniens, calling for the dispute to be handled bilaterally, outside of the ICO (conveniently overlooking its refusal to "voluntarily" limit soluble exports and the quirks of the U.S. tariff legislation, which prohibited the imposition of a countervailing duty against soluble imports).

The principle of comparability of export taxes, Brazil argued, was antithetical to the spirit of UNCTAD and the Alliance for Progress, counter to the law of comparative advantage, a 180-degree reversal of the U.S. endorsement of LDC industrialization of their agrarian sectors, [18] and did not take into account the fact that soluble and green coffee were two different classes of products (the former industrial and the latter an agricultural commodity. Unspoken, but important for Brazil, was its desire to use soluble exports as a "filler" for its large basic quota share and as a counter to growing Robusta exports (which were frequently converted into soluble powder).

With private negotiations between Brazil and the United States at an impasse, the Council appointed a mission on January 29, 1968, to visit the Brazilian and American governments to try to work out a solution.[19] The mission went to Washington, D.C., where it met with Secretary of State Dean Rusk, and, then, to Rio de Janeiro, where a final settlement was hammered out with the Brazilian federal government. The compromise, which became Article 44 of the 1968 ICA, was adopted by the Council on February 19, 1968.

Under Article 44, members are not to apply governmental measures affecting exports of coffee that amount to "discriminatory treatment in favour of processed coffee as compared to green coffee."[20] When a member believes that Article 44 is not being lived up to, it may file a complaint with the Executive Director.[21] If no solution is found in thirty days, the Executive Director must within forty days establish an arbitration panel to determine whether there is discriminatory treatment.[22] If the panel finds the complaint justified, then the member against which the charges have been made must within thirty days take action to correct the situation. The complaining member has the right to apply counter measures unilaterally immediately thereafter if no such action is taken.

With the solubles issue temporarily resolved, the last major roadblock to the renewal of the ICA was removed.[23] The final outcome of the solubles crisis was, however, still unknown.

THE SOLUBLE COFFEE CASE

Reaction to the uneasy compromise arrived at in Article 44 was varied in Brazil. Some newspapers argued that Brazil was the loser and criticized the government for ever having allowed the matter to enter the ICO negotiations. Other newspapers lauded the solution, but correctly noted that the final battle over the soluble export tax remained to be fought.

By November 27, 1968, the extent of Brazil's compliance with Article 44 was its cautious declaration that the commitment to tax soluble coffee exports was implicit in the 1968 ICA. Meanwhile, the Brazilian federal government announced that it had authorized the installation of five new soluble plants and the expansion of three existing ones.

Brazil's delay in doing anything to raise the price of its soluble exports prompted the United States, on December 2, 1968, to lodge a formal protest under Article 44 with the ICO Executive Director. The United States based its complaint on the lack of comparability of export taxes in Brazil between green and soluble coffee and on the lack of access to the cheap Brazilian grinders. [24]

The Executive Director established the arbitration panel required by Article 44, with one Brazilian member (Paulo Egidio Martins), one American member (David R. Herwitz), and a Swedish Chairman (B'engt Odevall). After three weeks of study and argument, the panel delivered its findings separately. [25]

The Brazilian delegate found no discrimination. He argued that Brazil could not be expected to put its grinders on the world market, as this would result in the paradoxical situation of Brazil storing its good coffee to support its price defense policy and selling its worst product on the world market. Furthermore, the United States refused to "discuss the profitability of its own soluble coffee industry for purposes of comparison," Martins noted, and had been unable to show that the Brazilian soluble exports had caused injury to the U.S. coffee trade. [26]

The American delegate, on the other hand, found that there had been a showing of discriminatory treatment:

The one inescapable fact in the situation is that as a result of the overall "system" stemming from the existence of the International Coffee Agreement and the governmental measures in Brazil previously referred to, the Brazilian producers of soluble coffee have an advantage in the acquisition of their raw material that is not available to producers of soluble coffee in the United States. [27]

The panel should not, Herwitz continued, attempt to establish a remedy for the United States (although he said a reasonable outer limit for U.S. counteraction would be a fee of 46 cents per pound on Brazilian soluble imports), but should rather rely "on the good will of the United States and the opinion of the international trading community." [28]

The swing figure on the panel was the widely respected Swedish Chairman, B'engt Odevall. He joined the U.S. member of the panel in finding in favor of the American position.

Brazil should, Odevall said, "take care of the situation," and if it did not do so, the "appropriate actions by the United States Government would be a natural course to follow." [29]

Odevall was particularly swayed by Herwitz's questioning of the Brazilian delegate. What if, Herwitz asked, Brazil had the techniques to manufacture roasted coffee and decided to expand roasted coffee exports under the ICA? Martins responded that Brazil would, of course, take over as large a share of the roasted market as it could. The principle involved—manufacturing a product of green coffee—was the same, the Brazilian delegate conceded. In a twinkling, Odevall saw that, unless the panel found in favor of the United States, a precedent would be established that might allow exporting members of the ICA to take advantage of its existence to "conquer" (a favorite Brazilian verb) the roasted coffee market as well.[30] Herwitz's clever analogy, based on an admittedly unlikely contingency, thus saved the day for the U.S. position.

Brazil "complied" with the arbitration panel's decision by imposing, as of May 1, 1969, an export tax of 13 cents per pound on soluble coffee exports to the United States. The United States stated that it anticipated that Brazil would raise its export tax on soluble coffee to about 30 cents per pound by May 1, 1970, while Brazil denied that "the tax level mentioned" by the United States would be guaranteed to be "acceptable" in 1970. The two governments agreed to meet "on or about January 15, 1970, to consult on developments in the soluble coffee market and seek agreement on further measures to be taken with respect to soluble coffee exports from Brazil."[31]

A SOLUBLE CONTROVERSY

The target date of May 1, 1970, passed with no serious negotiations between the United States and Brazilian governments on the solubles issue. Brazil argued the "hard line" that it would, under no circumstances, alter its 13 cent per pound export tax on soluble coffee sold to the United States. The principal Brazilian argument was that its solubles were selling on the U.S. market at about 30 cents per pound above the previous year's prices, due to the exhaustion of its cheap "grinders."

The United States, like Brazil, was not disposed to retreat on the solubles issue. Pressures from certain elements of the coffee trade, a sincere belief that the Brazilians were acting unfairly under the agreement, and the realities of a possibly protectionist Congress led the State Department to continue to press Brazil to raise the tax on its soluble coffee exports to the desired 30 cents level. Secretary of State Rogers explained the State Department's dilemma:

The joint review proved inconclusive. Brazil regarded its tax as sufficient while we maintained that additional steps were required. In the circumstances we were faced with three options: imposition of an import tax unilaterally by

the United States, * withdrawing from the International
Coffee Agreement, or further negotiations based on some
new approach. The first course would have had a delete-
rious effect on our relations with an important country of
Latin America. It would have also been opposed by elements of our own industry. The second course would have
meant the loss of an agreement which has benefitted many
developing countries and consumer and industry interests
in the United States. Under your directive we pursued the
third course—further negotiations—with results that are
satisfactory to all major countries concerned. [32]

Ironically, during the final, successful negotiations with Brazil,
the State Department pursued a harder line than many segments of
the industry it was "protecting." This unusual position resulted from
the vagaries of industry politics in the United States. The green coffee
brokers in the United States, both large and small, continued to
protest Brazilian "discrimination" under Article 44 of the ICA. But
their former ally on the solubles issue, the roaster-oriented NCA,
on May 4, 1970, voted to convert to the Brazilian position, expressing
"its opposition to increases in the Brazilian export tax on soluble
coffee into the United States and/or the institution of a duty in the
United States on imports of soluble coffee from Brazil. "[33]

Several factors explained the NCA reversal. First of all,
Nestle, which had once joined in asking for a higher Brazilian soluble
tax, changed its position. It recently had purchased a Brazilian
soluble coffee plant, to be used for export to the United States. Coca-
Cola (Tenco) had recently decided to expand its plant capacity for
exports to the United States.[34] And General Foods was, during the
NCA meeting, involved in a complex set of negotiations aimed at
buying a soluble plant in Brazil. Thus, while General Foods voted
against the NCA resolution, it did not lobby among the smaller processors as energetically as it might have otherwise. The net result
of the NCA reversal was that the State Department, which had battled
long and hard for Article 44 as a concession to the NCA, found itself
at odds with the group for which it had so strenuously fought!

-----

*This option was now open to the United States, due to authority
in the U.S. implementing legislation—the International Coffee Agreement Act of 1968, 19 U.S.C., Section 1356 (1968)—to impose a duty
on unfairly marketed processed coffee.

Following the NCA meeting, the negotiations of General Foods
for a plant in Brazil collapsed, due to its reluctance to accept the
Brazilian condition that the proposed soluble coffee plant would have
to be a "joint venture," with local participation. Down but not out
General Foods—now the primary antagonist to the Brazilian position
in the coffee trade—moved swiftly on two fronts to resume active
opposition to the Brazilian position. It tried to put direct pressure
on House Ways and Means Committee Chairman Wilbur Mills by
sending James W. Andrews, the President of its Maxwell House
Division, and a representative of the union involved in its soluble
coffee operations, the Amalgamated Meat Cutters and Butcher Work-
men to plead the company's case. The thrust of their presentation
to Mills was that the Ways and Means Committee should hold up on
the agreement's implementing legislation (expiring September 30,
1970) until the solubles crisis was resolved. Mills listened intently
to the company's emissaries and questioned them sharply. Following
this meeting with Mills, the union testified on the solubles issue before
the full House Ways and Means Committee. The Committee, impressed
by the union's plea and confident of being sustained by a protectionist-
minded House of Representatives, on the night of July 15, 1970,
rejected the implementing legislation needed to continue active U. S.
participation in the ICA. Finally, on December 31, 1970, the Senate,
by voice vote, renewed the implementing legislation until June 30,
1971, with the stipulation that there would be no further implementing
legislation unless the solubles controversy was settled by April 1,
1971.

Faced with the Congressional time deadline, Brazil and the
United States resumed negotiations on the solubles issue in earnest.
The negotiations ended with a "victory" for the United States, as
Brazil agreed to give the American importers an equal price advantage
by providing export-tax free the green coffee equivalent of Brazil's
soluble coffee exports to the United States during 1970. Thus, 560,000
bags of green coffee (132.276 pounds in a bag) are to be exported to
U.S. processors without the imposition of an export tax (presently,
about $17.75). In return, Brazil is permitted to drop the 13 cents
per pound export tax that it had imposed since April, 1969, on soluble
powder shipped to U.S. importers. [35]

The solubles agreement was also a "victory" for the large
publicly held corporations, such as General Foods, within the United
States. The 560,000-bag special allocation is to be made available
to U.S. soluble manufacturers on the basis of their average share of
soluble coffee production in the United States over the past two years.
The terms of the settlement thus give General Foods, with 53.5
percent of the U.S. soluble market, about 280,000 export-tax free
bags of green coffee from Brazil (a substantial bonus for its patient

exercise of pressure in the corridors of power). Nestle, whose share
of the market is estimated at about 25 percent, will receive about
140, 000 bags export-tax free. The closely held Hills Bros. Coffee
Co. , Inc. , which shut down its own soluble coffee plants in the United
States two years ago and imported the Brazilian product, will thus be
frozen out of the special allocation.[36] General Foods' and Nestle
executives, realizing the windfall given them by the settlement,
promptly hailed the accord, while the Pacific Coast Coffee Association,
under Reuben Hills' influence, attacked the agreement as "discriminatory. "[37]

    It appears—at least temporarily—that the solubles crisis has
been settled.[38] What preliminary observations can be made on the
behavior of the coffee industry in this political and economic controversy? If generalizations from one case can have much validity, it
would seem fair to hypothesize from this experience that there is a
basic identity of interests between the large publicly held corporations
(such as General Foods) and large states in international economic
organizations. Both are interested in obtaining "profits" from the
organization—although they define the term differently—in an orderly
manner in a stable world environment. Interviews at General Foods
and elsewhere in the coffee industry seem to indicate—the Andersen
study notwithstanding—that General Foods fought out the solubles controversy as a matter of principle, deeply convinced that the principle
of the sanctity of treaties—pacta sunt servanda—was at stake. Given
the ICA with Article 44, Brazil's behavior, as the executives at
General Foods saw it, was immoral; according to General Foods cost
estimates after the Andersen study, it was firmly believed by many
executives of General Foods that it was losing money by not moving
its operations to Brazil. But principle—and a desire for orderly
growth in a stable world environment where treaties would be respected—prompted General Foods to fight it out on the solubles issue.

    Secondly, how can the fact that the State Department and General
Foods "agreed" on the solubles issue be explained? It would seem
that the State Department—General Foods' entente could hardly warrant
a Marxist interpretation of the State Department's position. In fact,
the interests of General Foods coincided with those of the State
Department, which revolved around systems-maintenance for the
ICA. On other occasions—for example, the adoption of a selectivity
pricing mechanism (pricing by submarkets in the ICA)—the State
Department took a position opposed to that of the industry.

    Thirdly, what are the implications of the solubles controversy
for future efforts by the LDC's to attract American industry? One
can only conclude that the same issues of investment climate, fear
of inflation, and so forth will continue to haunt efforts to invest in the

LDC's.[39] But it is clear that the U.S. Government would not in other instances, as it did in the solubles controversy, discourage American industry from moving into the LDC's. The overriding concern of the State Department in the solubles crisis was to prevent a price war in green coffee that would have undermined the ICA. A General Foods move to Brazil might have precipitated that feared price war. In other words, the international economic organization in which this crisis over vertical integration was played out profoundly influenced the attitude of the U.S. Government. The solubles issue is, therefore, "atypical" in terms of implications for future vertical integration.

Finally, the most important questions raised by the solubles controversy are its implications for the future of developed country—LDC relations. Will the solubles agreement be a precedent for future developed country-LDC trade clashes? To phrase the question differently, will comparability of export taxes between raw materials and their processed products become a principle with a life of its own, even in the absence of a commodity agreement creating the opportunity for unfair competition? These are some of the questions being raised in many developing countries demanding—and obtaining—external tariff preferences to aid their industrialization, much of which must begin by the processing of raw materials near the source of production. If comparability does become a blanket precedent, then the net result of the soluble coffee controversy will have been a negative one, and the efforts of the negotiators on both sides will have been in vain.

If, however, the principle of comparability is seen only as a means of preventing unfair competition under commodity agreements, then the preservation of the 1968 ICA may be seen as not having been too big a price to pay.

NOTES

1. IBC Resolution 195, March 22, 1961. This resolution allowed an exemption of duties on capital equipment for the soluble coffee plants. It guaranteed all credits needed to get the project underway.

2. Those companies were Companhia Caçique de Café Solúvel, Companhia Campineira de Café Solúvel, Companhia Industrial e Comercial de Produtos Alimentares ("Nestle"), and Companhia Industrial de Café de Brasil.

3. Information kindly supplied by Cia Iguacu de Cafe Soluvel, "The Soluble Coffee Industry in Brazil." (Mimeographed.)

    4. Dominium (1964), Vigor (1966), Frusol (1966), Industrial de Café Soluvel (1967). All of the companies are located in the state of São Paulo, Brazil.

    5. Arthur J. Cordell, "The Brazilian Soluble Coffee Problem: A Review, " The Quarterly Review of Economics and Business, IX (Spring, 1969), 32.

    6. J. C. Maxwell, Jr., "Overview: Trends in Coffee Marketing, " World Coffee and Tea (May, 1970), p. 43.

    7. John K. Galbraith, The New Industrial State (New York: Signet, 1968) p. 325. General Foods also qualifies as a "multidivisional product organization." See Raymond Vernon, "Organization as a Scale Factor in the Growth of Firms, " in Jesse W. Markham and Gustav V. Papanek, eds., Industrial Organization and Economic Development (Boston: Houghton Mifflin Company, 1970), p. 63. Also, see Alfred Chandler, Strategy and Structure: Chapters in the History of the Industrial Enterprise (Cambridge: M.I.T. Press, 1962) for the classic description of the evolution toward the multidivisional firm in the American economy. From another point of view, General Foods also qualifies as a multinational enterprise, i.e., "a cluster of corporations of diverse nationality joined together by ties of common ownership and responsive to a common management strategy." Raymond Vernon, "Economic Sovereignty at Bay, " Foreign Affairs, XLVII (1968), 110 and 114.

    8. General Foods Corp., Harvard Business School Case Study No. ICH 10G104, AM-P, 188R2 (1964), p. 23 (on file in Harvard Business School Library).

    9. Ibid.

    10. General Foods Corp., International Division, Harvard Business School Case Study No. ICH 10G107, AM-P, 198R2 (1964), p. 14.

    11. Ibid., pp. 6-12, passim.

    12. The executives in charge of General Foods's policy during the solubles crisis were C. W. (Tex) Cook, Chairman of the Board; A. E. Larkin, President; M. R. Bohm, Executive Vice-President; James W. Andrews, President of the Maxwell House Division and Vice-President of General Foods; and Frederick J. Otterbein, Vice-President of General Foods's green coffee operations. General Foods Corp., Maxwell House Division of General Foods, Harvard Business School Case Study No. 4-371-479, AI 308 (1971), p. 2.

13. The Green Coffee Association of New York City, composed mainly of green coffee brokers, protested the Brazilian market moves on June 16, 1966.

14. The major organization defending the interests of the soluble coffee industry in Brazil was O Sindicato da Industria do Café Solúvel do Estado de São Paulo.

15. Those cooperatives included the Cooperative of Coffee Growers of the Garça Region and the Cooperative of Coffee Growers of Cornelio Procópio.

16. Alexander W. Shapleigh, "Soluble Coffee and the International Coffee Agreement, 1968" (unpublished paper, Johns Hopkins School of Advanced International Studies, 1968), pp. 15 and 16.

17. Amendment to the International Coffee Agreement (Submitted by the Delegation of the United States), ICO Doc. No. ICC-10-12, Rev. 2 (October 18, 1967).

18. President Lyndon B. Johnson, in April, 1967, at Punta del Este, pledged to "provide incentives for the industrialization of agricultural production" and to promote "exports of processed agricultural goods." See 56 Department State Bulletin (1967), pp. 712 and 718. The President's statement seemed somewhat out of place, with the United States now moving to check a Latin American country that had taken the President's advice too literally.

19. The mission included representatives from the Netherlands, Uganda, the United Kingdom, Guatemala, Uganda, Ivory Coast, and the Executive Director of the ICO, Joao O. Santos.

20. International Coffee Agreement, 1968, Art. 44 (1).

21. Ibid., Art. 44 (2) (a).

22. Ibid., Art. 44 (2) (b). The panel is to consist of three people, one person designated by the complaining member, one person designated by the member against whom the complaint has been made, and a chairman mutually agreed upon by the members in dispute or by the two designated members of the panel. Ibid.

23. Joao O. Santos, Executive Director of the ICO, resigned at the end of the renewal negotiations. He was replaced by Alexandre Fontana Beltrao, formerly head of the World Coffee Promotion Committee of the ICO.

24. Complaint by the United States of America against Brazil under Article 44 of the Agreement, ICO Doc. No. ICC-13-8 (December 18, 1968), passim.

25. Findings of Arbitration Panel Established under the Provisions of Article 44, ICO Doc. No. ED-397/69 (March 3, 1969).

26. Ibid., p. 29.

27. Ibid., p. 12.

28. Ibid., p. 9.

29. Ibid., p. 4.

30. Herwitz's argument is developed in ibid., pp. 14 and 15.

31. The Brazilian-U.S. agreement was expressed in an exchange of diplomatic notes between the two governments made on April 23, 1969. Newsletter (New York: NCA, April 30, 1969).

32. Letter from Secretary of State William P. Rogers to President Richard M. Nixon, March 30, 1971.

33. Newsletter (New York: NCA, May 4, 1970.

34. See "U.S. Battles Brazil to a Coffee Break," Business Week (August 8, 1970), p. 15.

35. See "Brazil Solubles Issue: Did Settlement Clear the Way for USA Participation in the ICA?", World Coffee and Tea (May, 1971), p. 36.

36. Ibid.

37. Ibid.

38. The implementation of the solubles accord has, however, been delayed by the failure of the U.S. Congress to promptly renew the implementing legislation for the ICA after June 30, 1971. Following Congressional approval of the ICA implementing legislation, the solubles accord will go into operation, as the agreement, by its terms, is contingent upon U.S. participation in the ICA. See World Coffee and Tea, October, 1971, p. 74. The unexpected Congressional delay in dealing with the implementing legislation—which would extend U.S. participation in the ICA through September 30, 1973—was due to:

(1) a controversy between the U.S. and Brazil over the extent of Brazil's claims over its territorial waters and alleged firing in Brazilian waters on U.S. fishing vessels; (2) the relatively high prices for coffee during the latter half of 1971; and (3) Congressional preoccupation with President Nixon's "New Economic Program" announced on August 15, 1971.

39. On the general corporate problem of "investment climate" in the LDC's, see Robert B. Stobaugh, "How to Analyze Foreign Investment Climate," Harvard Business Review (September/October, 1969).

10

THE CURRENT MARKET SITUATION

The greatest problem faced by the world coffee market in the early 1960's was overproduction relative to consumer demand. Supplies in the early 1970's, on the other hand, are in approximate equilibrium with world demand. This fundamental shift in the world supply and demand equation is due to a series of short crops in the last four years of the 1960's (see Table 16), resultant stock drawdowns at the rate of 10 to 12 million bags per year (see Table 17), the run-down condition of much of the world coffee economy, * and frosts and droughts in Brazil in July, 1969 (see pages 156-57). It is clear, then, that a host of critical new problems will confront the ICA in the 1970's. In 1962, it was generally feared that the world coffee market might break without a price support mechanism. In the early 1970's, the problem will be how to stabilize prices at their current levels, not to raise them. These observations raise two inquiries of contemporary relevance: Has the ICA been successful enough to warrant its renewal in 1973? And what new features might a renegotiated agreement contain?

---

*Due to the generally lower coffee prices of the latter 1960's, many producers had little incentive to maintain their farms in optimum condition. Planters reduced their maintenance expenses in such areas as fertilizing, pruning, shade control, and regulation of diseases and pests.

TABLE 16

Recent Supply Availabilities
(In Thousands of Bags of 132.267 Pounds Each)

Production and Exports	1964/65	1965/66	1966/67	1967/68	1968/69
Exportable Production	35, 878	66, 244	44, 448	51, 776	43, 051
Total Exports	42, 148	50, 550	50, 944	54, 397	52, 702
	-6, 270	+15, 694	-6, 496	-2, 621	-9, 651

Source: The George Gordon Paton and Co. Coffee Annual, 1969 (1970), p. 41.

TABLE 17

Recent Stock Drawdowns

Year	Carryover Stocks (In Millions of Bags)	Percentage of Consumption Requirements
1963/64	72.2	135
1968/69	44.5	85
1969/70	38*	73

*Estimate.

Note: Complicating and adding to the seriousness of the stock situation is the lack of knowledge as to the quality of the remaining carryover stocks. Sources interviewed in the coffee trade indicated that between 10 and 40 percent of carryover stocks are unfit for human consumption.

Source: John I. Kross and J. Phillip Rourk, "Story of the 1960's: Coffee in World Trade," Foreign Agriculture (January 12, 1970), p. 8.

THE AGREEMENT IN OPERATION

Price Levels

The LDC's support commodity agreements primarily because they hope such arrangements will effectuate resource transfers from the developed countries to them. Many in the developed countries also view commodity agreements as a discrete surrogate for aid in an era of declining foreign aid. An important area of assessment, then, for the ICA, is that of resource transfers from the "North" to the "South" under the accord. None deny that the ICA has improved the foreign exchange earnings of the developing countries.[1] The nice—and ultimately unanswerable—question is how great the difference was between actual total coffee earnings and the earnings that would have been realized in the absence of the ICA. (See Table 18.) The General Accounting Office (GAO), in the only published estimates of the "coffee assistance" due to the ICA, has made the following findings:

1. Total [U.S. and other coffee-importing countries] coffee assistance averaged $601 million a year during 1964-67;

2. United States coffee aid averaged $314 million during 1964-67;

3. Inclusion of coffee assistance would increase reported foreign aid disbursements of the United States and other major aid donors by 8 percent a year; and

4. In 1967 Latin America accounted for 66 percent and Africa for 28 percent of United States coffee assistance.[2]

While the GAO deserves plaudits for its effort to estimate coffee assistance, * the results of its study point up the real difficulties in arriving at any realistic assistance figure:

---

*The supply of world coffee exports was estimated on the basis of the trend of exports in 1950-63; the demand for coffee exports was made a function of income in the importing countries and the export price of coffee. World prices for 1964-67 were estimated by using the trend values of exports in the world demand equation. See ibid., pp. 40-42.

TABLE 18

Estimates of Total and U. S. Coffee Assistance
(In Millions of Dollars)
(a)
Total

Year	Actual Revenue	Estimated Revenue	Estimated Coffee Assistance (Difference Between Actual and Estimated Revenues)
1964	$2, 301	$1, 733	$568
1965	2, 162	1, 691	471
1966	2, 320	1, 640	680
1967	2, 170	1, 484	686

(b)
United States

Year	Actual Revenue	Estimated Revenue	Estimated Coffee Assistance (Difference Between Actual and Estimated Revenues)
1964	1, 197	826	371
1965	1, 058	789	269
1966	1, 067	749	318
1967	963	665	298

Source: U. S. Congress, Foreign Aid Provided Through the
Operations of the United States Sugar Act and the International Coffee
Agreement, Report of the Congress by the Comptroller-General of
the United States (October 23, 1969), p. 43.

First, no model can make completely accurate assumptions
about the behavior of the exporting members in the absence of an
Agreement. Accepting the GAO results means hypothesizing that
Brazil, Colombia, and the other large exporters would have gone on
managing their stocks as they had during the years preceding the
Agreement.

Second, the trend of coffee exports and prices was based on
annual data on the quantity of exports for the period 1950-63. But the

years 1954-57 were omitted as abnormal, due to the 1954 frost in
Brazil; this is, however, an omission of an important part of the coffee
cycle.

Third, the study in no way took into account the 1963 frost in
Brazil, which prompted the 1963/64 price rise. This, probably more
than the Agreement, caused higher prices in the early stages of the
Agreement, as an effective control system did not evolve until at least
midway through the Agreement.

Despite these shortcomings in the study, even U. S. Aid for
International Development (U. S. AID) and the Department of State,
understandably reluctant for political reasons to concede the possibility
of resource transfers under the ICA, were forced to concede that the
basic point of the GAO study—that the ICA has probably increased the
foreign exchange earnings of the coffee-exporting LDC's—was correct.[3]

The strength of the coffee export prices under the ICA is shown
in Table 19. It reveals that, in terms of price levels, the greatest
gainer was the Robustas, with all submarkets, however, showing
substantial gains over their price levels under the 1957-62 period of
the short-term agreements.

The ICA has, then, successfully served as a "second best"
vehicle for resource transfers to the LDC's by raising coffee prices.
Whether this was an objective worth pursuing is a normative question.
The conclusion, however, that the commodity agreement mechanism
has, in this instance, served as a means of foreign aid seems too
clear to dispute.

Price Stability

As a prelude to analysis here, it must be remembered that from
the 1930's to the early 1960's the "boom/bust" cycle of coffee prices
predominated. The result was to cause uncertainty in the LDC's,
preventing them from planning ahead on the basis of any assured
revenue from coffee exports.

The ICA, in a welcome contrast to the previous trend, brought
relative price stability to the world coffee market from 1962 through
mid-July, 1969. One index of price stability—the price range of
coffee—shows that in the pre-Agreement years following World War
II, U. S. green-coffee import prices had a range of 41. 7 cents between
the lowest and highest average levels, as compared with a range of
only 11 cents from 1963 through March, 1970.

The ICA can only limit—not eliminate—price fluctuations. Two
market price fluctuations have taken place since the ICA went into

TABLE 19

Coffee Prices: Selected Periods, 1957-1972,
by ICO Indicator Groups

Coffee Years	Colombian Mild Arabicas	Other Mild Arabicas	Unwashed Arabicas	Robustas
5 Year Average, 57-58 to 61-62	46. 23	42. 50	39. 48	27. 05
5 Year Average 63-64 to 67-68	45. 68	42. 67	41. 43	33. 77
January, 1972*	51. 75	45. 25	44. 25	42. 19

*Citation is for January 4, 1972.

Source: Pan-American Coffee Bureau, Annual Coffee Statistics, 1968 (New York: 1969), A-95-A-99, and The Financial Times, January 4, 1972.

force. The first, the 1963/64 price rise, prompted by a frost in Brazil, was dealt with by the ICA through a series of equilibrating devices aimed at lowering the price of coffee on the world market: an increase in the 1963 annual quota, waivers, distribution of short-falls, and by a large 1964/65 annual quota. It is likely that the price rise would have been greater in the absence of an agreement as a symbol of cooperation among exporters and importers.

The second sharp price rise was sparked by a frost followed by droughts in Brazil in July, 1969. The physical effect of these natural disasters was to reduce Brazil's crop from an estimated 19 million bags in 1969/70 to an estimated 10 million bags in 1970/71. Predict-ably, all submarkets rose sharply. The ICA response was in three parts. The first move was in August, 1969, at the ICC meeting. A two-part package was agreed upon. The first element in the package was a basic quota reserve of 2 million bags to be released or deducted in accordance with certain price provisions.[4] In addition to the quota reserve of 2 million bags, automatic increases in market supplies under the selectivity pricing system were provided for. Under the 1969/70 selectivity system, up to 8.25 percent of a member's annual quota as of October 1, 1969 (or a total of 3.7 million bags) could be released, if prices for that submarket were at or above the ceiling of the price range for twenty consecutive market days. Thus, the ICC foresaw the possibility of a runup in prices and attempted to cope with the impending difficulties by setting out what was, in effect, a total of 5.7 million bags as a reserve to the annual quota. The second part of the ICA response was a producer victory for higher prices, as the producers, led by Brazil and Colombia, blocked consumer efforts in a March, 1970, meeting of the ICC to expand allocations for the world market.[5] The third part of the ICA response was a decisive consumer assertion of countervailing power at the August, 1970, meeting of the ICC, analogous to the consumer victory in the February, 1964, ICC meeting in the midst of the 1963/64 price rise. At the August, 1970, ICC meeting a complex annual quota formula, sufficient to meet world demand, was agreed upon, with a base figure for the quota at 54 million bags and possible upward adjustments of 4 million bags[6] and possible downwards adjustments of 3 million bags.[7]

That the ICA actions have served to limit the recent price rise is illustrated by a chronology of the market prices. Due to the natural disasters in Brazil, the price of Brazil's Santos 4s was 53.9 cents (U.S.) per pound in April, 1970, as compared to 38.0 cents one year earlier. In April, 1971, Brazils were selling at 44.5 cents per pound, a substantial decline.

In summary, it seems that the ICA has been a useful mechanism for price stabilization on the world coffee market. At the least, it can not be said that the Agreement has destabilized the coffee market, as many feared it would do.

Enforcement

The problem of enforcing the ICA has amounted to an attempt to contain the rivalry between the revisionists—the African Robusta producers and the Other Mild producers from Central America—and the large oligopolists (Brazil and Colombia), which are primarily interested in maintaining the status quo. (See Chapter 6.) When concessions from the oligopolists were not forthcoming—as during the first half of the 1962 ICA—the revisionists felt morally justified in overshipping their basic quota shares.[8] Resolution of this problem was complicated by exogenous factors, such as poor storage facilities, weak administrative capabilities in many LDC's, and a two-price market created by the quota system.

It follows from what has just been said that a rigid "legalistic" approach to enforcing the ICA would have been inappropriate. It is at this point that the traditional vocabulary of international law fails us. It is not enough to contend that commodity controls call for a "dynamic of accomodation."9 The elements of that dynamic must be defined and analyzed: they are boundary maintenance and equilibration.

All treaties have a tolerance level for noncompliance. Beyond a certain level of noncompliance, the treaty ceases to function as a behavior determinant. That point was never reached by the ICA, as overexports apparently never exceeded 6 percent of annual quotas. It thus may be said that its boundaries were effectively maintained during its duration.

Strict boundary maintenance in the ICA, however, would have been unfair and oppressive in view of the problems faced by the revisionists mentioned above. When basic export quotas could not be adjusted by assigned quota reviews, waivers, or pricing by submarkets, the enforcement system appropriately permitted some slack. Thus, by removing overshipments as an equilibrating mechanism prior to making quota adjustments in favor of the revisionists in 1965 and 1966, the large producers and the consumers might have destroyed the ICA.

It is clear that consumers were needed as policemen for the ICA. Otherwise, exporting countries could not have been relied upon to refrain from gaining market advantages by overshipping their assigned quotas. But consumer country participation raised additional problems for the ICA, such as obtaining effective implementing legislation and controlling profit-oriented businessmen in importing countries willing to help exporters evade their quota obligations. Thus, large corporations, such as General Foods, praised the ICA publicly, 10 yet were not averse to undermining it privately in order to maximize short-term profits.

Finally, the ICA managed to establish dual systems of control to check member and nonmember exports of coffee. This was necessary to check transshipments that would have undermined the quota system.

With cooperation from importing and exporting members, the ICA has been successfully enforced. It is true that some bureaucratic machinery has been required for the task, but it would seem that this is a lesser evil for the LDC's than the exposure of one of their key commodities to the vicissitudes of a totally unregulated world market.

Structural Reforms

The fourth major area of ICO activity was its creative organizational attempts to cope with the structural problem of surplus production. By way of brief review, four ICO moves should be noted.

Waivers

Waivers were granted to certain producing countries, as of September, 1966, on the condition that 20 percent of the foreign exchange value of the coffee granted as waivers would be placed in a fund under the joint control of the member and the Executive Director of the ICO.[11] The fund was to be used to finance plans for diversification out of coffee. The funds released for approved projects in Burundi, Ecuador, Guatemala, Ivory Coast, Uganda, and Trinidad and Tobago, amount to $3.6 million, or 56 percent of the total of the funds deposited in the joint funds.[12]

Diversification Fund

A Diversification Fund was written into the 1968 ICA. The Fund is financed by contributions of the exporting members of the ICO of 60 cents a bag for all bags actually exported over 100,000 bags each year to quota markets. Portion A monies under the Fund are to be used in the exporting members' territory only (78 percent of contributions), while Portion C monies (20 percent) are to be used for financing programs of any contributing exporter participant. Unfortunately, the Diversification Fund has made only one loan thus far, to Kenya ($460,000—a twenty-year, interest-free loan) to finance a livestock development project.[13] This was a Portion A loan. Due to disagreement among the producer countries over where Portion C loans should be made and how they should be funded, no Portion C loans have yet been made. It seems clear that greater use should have been made of the Diversification Fund. By the end of the 1968 ICA, there will be approximately $134 million in the Fund.

Production Goals

Production goals were written into the 1968 ICA. While exporters retained the power to apply whatever policies they deemed necessary to carry out their production goals, they were subject to a loss of additional quota exports if the Council found their steps to be insufficient.[14]

Promotion of Coffee Consumption

Promotion of coffee consumption was made an integral part of the ICA. On August 6, 1964, the Council created the World Coffee Promotion Committee (WCPC) as a standing committee within the framework of the Executive Board. Since 1965/66, nine exporting members have guided the WCPC. An average of $5.7 million per annum for coffee promotion has been allocated by the WCPC since 1964.

Apart from the programs mentioned above, the ICA enforcement system was a key agent of structural reform. Coffee exporters had little incentive to continue to produce supplies that could not move under ICO quotas.

POLICIES FOR THE FUTURE

The most urgent issue is whether the ICA should be maintained or scrapped, as the treaty expires on September 30, 1973. It would be unfortunate if the ICA were to be allowed to expire on that date. The Agreement's past performance in the areas of price maintenance and stabilization, enforcement, and structural reform merits its continuation, at least through 1978. Without a commodity agreement for the world coffee market, there would probably be a drift back to the boom/bust cycles that characterized the world coffee economy before the 1962 ICA. Assuming arguendo that the ICA should be kept, how can it be improved to make it relevant to the current near equilibrium of world supply and demand?

Quotas

Three schools of thought are to be found on what to do with the ICA quota-price system in view of the approximate equilibrium in world supply and demand. Some argue that now is the opportune moment to scrap the quota system and to place the ICA on a "stand-by" basis. Their arguments are that quotas are in themselves no solution to any problem, that the abolition of the quota system would release time and money needed to solve other problems, and that, in any case, the quotas are and always have been an unwanted interference with the normal free trade in coffee.[15] Others argue that, in the absence of basic and annual quotas, the whole control structure of the ICO would become irreparably paralyzed and that, without basic quotas enforced by consumers as checks, all producing countries would abandon efforts at production controls and plant coffee without restraint to fill a deficit, real or imagined, in world production.[16] The third group, represented by the President of the Brazilian Coffee Institute, Mario Penteado, appears to favor a return to a straight producer cartel, i.e., quotas without consumer country participation. [17]

Under the circumstances, it seems that the best course would be for the ICO to keep the quota system, based upon "realistic" annual quotas that would offer assurance of sufficient supplies to the consumer members and adequate prices for producers. The ICO should also keep its "extra quota" arrangement, by which, if any country fails to export its full quota, the "short fall" may be made available to other countries for export.

The quota mechanism could be improved by a provision that would require exporting members to market a certain percentage of their stocks, if prices rise above specified levels. This could serve as a guarantee of producer "best efforts" to ameliorate sharp price rises.

Finally, the option for the ICO to use a selectivity system to ensure that consumers are supplied with the types of coffee that they require should be written into the new treaty.

Enforcement

A key reform in the area of enforcement would be for the United States to obtain implementing legislation for the full duration of the new treaty. Obtaining such legislation—essential for the maintenance of the ICO enforcement system—has turned into an almost yearly hassle in the U.S. Congress, a process with many more costs than benefits. The most important cost is that, during the hiatus periods when the implementing legislation is allowed to lapse, the U.S. market is "opened up" to tourist coffee. The alleged "benefit" of informing Congress of U.S. participation in the ICA could be performed equally well by implementing legislation for the duration of the treaty, plus annual reports to the Congress.

Second, the Annex B list should be eliminated in the new ICA. All coffees should be put under quotas. This would eliminate the last sizable loophole for tourist coffee.

Third, all penalties should be mandatory when overshipments are discovered by the ICO staff in London. No ICC action should be necessary.

Diversification Fund

A policy review of the purpose of the Diversification Fund is required, in view of the changes in the market situation from the circumstances that called the Fund into being. The problem the Fund now faces is how to increase production in specific countries in the short run without seriously overburdening world coffee supply in the long run. Without a controlled recovery in world supplies, world oversupply may occur again before the end of the 1970's.

The question of Portion C monies—funds that can be used in the territory of any producing member—should be clarified. It would seem that maximum use should be made of the Portion C funds that are presently available. [18]

SUMMARY

Despite complex economic and political problems, the ICA has succeeded since 1962 in the areas of price maintenance and stabilization, enforcement, and structural reforms. It should, therefore, be renewed, at least until 1978.

Only a few changes in the ICA are recommended—the addition of a mandatory marketing provision to limit price rises, the omission of the Annex B list, and improvements in the administration of the Diversification Fund. "Outside" the ICA, the United States should make a maximum effort to obtain from its Congress implementing legislation for the duration of the treaty. It would seem unwise to either put the ICA on a "stand-by" basis (by suspending the quota mechanism temporarily) or to change the basic quota mechanism.

Clemenceau once said that war was much too important a matter to be left to generals. Similarly, we should be prepared to admit that the world coffee economy is much too important a matter to be left to the vicissitudes of a totally unregulated market. Despite our natural preference for completely free markets, we should be prepared to continue international collaboration in the world coffee market.

NOTES

1. For a clear analysis of how the ICA has boosted world coffee prices, see John I. Kross and J. Phillip Rourk, "Story of the 1960's: Coffee in the World Trade," Foreign Agriculture (January 12, 1970), p. 8. And see U. S. Congress, Foreign Aid Provided Through the Operations of the United States Sugar Act and the International

Coffee Agreement, Report to the Congress by the Comptroller-General of the United States (October 23, 1969), (hereafter cited as GAO Study), p. 5.

2. Ibid., pp. 1 and 2.

3. Ibid., p. 70.

4. See Resolution No. 216, September 3, 1969. These additions to market supplies were to be prorated to all producing members in accordance with their initial export quotas.

5. See "Summary Record," Plenary Meeting of the Sixteenth Session of the ICC, ICO Doc. No. ICC-16-1 (March 10, 1970).

6. See Resolution No. 225, September 8, 1970. If the composite price index remained at or above 52 U.S. cents per pound for fifteen consecutive marketing days after October 1, 1970, then there would be an upward adjustment of 2 million bags. If the price remained at or above 52 U.S. cents per pound for an additional twenty-one consecutive market days after October 1, 1970, another 2 million bag tranche was to be put on the world market.

7. Two levels of downward adjustments were permitted—removal of the upward adjustments if prices averaged below 50 U.S. cents per pound for the required marketing periods (i.e., removal of the 4 million bags added in the tranches described in footnote 6, above), and downward adjustments in two tranches of 1.5 million bags each if prices averaged first below 48 cents and then, 46 cents for the required marketing periods (i.e., down to a possible quota of only 51 million bags). There was, in other words, a "swing" factor of 7 million bags in the annual quota mechanism, which gave the ICO substantial flexibility to deal with price movements.

8. See Jerome Jacobson, "Difficulties in Framing Effective Commodity Agreements," International Development Review, X (June, 1968), 11.

9. See Andreas F. Lowenfeld, "International Coffee Controls—Some Lessons from the Coffee Agreement," The American Journal of International Law, LXI (July, 1967), 785, and Abram Chayes, Thomas Ehrlich, and Andreas F. Lowenfeld, The International Legal Process (Boston: Little, Brown and Company, 1968), p. 586. And see Charles G. Fenwick, International Law (New York: Appleton-Century-Crofts, 1965), p. 50: "International law, like national law, must be a dynamic system if it is to fulfill its high purpose."

10. George V. Robbins, of the Maxwell House Division of General Foods, on February 1, 1963, urged the Senate Foreign Relations Committee to report favorably on the 1962 ICA: "I respectfully urge your support of this effort to help stabilize this very important commodity in the international trade of the free world." Telegram from George V. Robbins to Sen. J. W. Fulbright, February 1, 1963, in Hearing before the Senate Committee on Foreign Relations on Executive H, 87th Cong., 2d Sess., 88th Cong., 1st Sess. (1963), p. 99.

11. See Resolution No. 114, September 6, 1966, and Resolution No. 157, December 4, 1967.

12. See Progress Report on the Utilisation of Waiver Funds Deposited Under the Provisions of Resolutions Numbers 114 (as Amended by Resolution Number 131) and 157, ICO Doc. No. EB-985/71 (E) (May 26, 1971), passim.

13. This was a 20-year, interest-free loan. The Board of Directors of the Diversification Fund, have however, recently approved five additional loans valued at $19.6 million. They are as follows: Brazil ($1.98 million, for coffeesector surveys and statistical technique improvement), Colombia ($7.2 million, for cocoa production development), Guatemala ($3.34 million, to diversify its coffee sector), Ivory Coast ($5.87 million, for a rice cultivation project), and Tanzania ($1.17 million, for small holder tea development). World Tea and Coffee (December, 1971), p. 70.

14. International Coffee Agreement, 1968, Art. 48 (8).

15. George Gordon Paton and Co. Coffee Annual, 1969, see arguments made on pp. 100 and 101, by John G. Lydall (1970).

16. Ibid., p. 79, arguments made by Arturo Gomez Jaramillo.

17. Mr. Penteado has suggested the creation of a new international coffee organization with the participation of the nine biggest producers to take the place of the present ICO. See World Coffee and Tea, (December, 1971), p. 44.

18. This would include the first tranche of a $15-million loan pledged to the Diversification Fund in convertible currency (dollars) by the United States.

A

**INITIAL
AND FINAL QUOTAS
UNDER THE
INTERNATIONAL
COFFEE AGREEMENT, 1962**

Initial and Final Quotas Under the International Coffee Agreement, 1962
(In Thousand 60-Kilo Bags)

Exporting Country	1962/63 Initial	Final	1963/64 Initial	Final	1964/65 Initial	Final	1965/66 Initial	Final	1966/67 Initial	Final	1967/68 Initial	Final[1]
Colombian Milds:												
Colombia	5,951	5,951	5,951	6,243	6,172	5,620	5,669	5,669	5,782	5,421	5,902	6,344
Kenya	512[1]*	512[1]*	512[1]*	528*	530*	483*	487*	487*	744*	698	760	817
Tanzania	431	431	431	452	447	407	411	436	469	401	441	508
Subtotal	6,894	6,894	6,894	7,223	7,149	6,510	6,567	6,592	6,995	6,520	7,103	7,669
Other Milds:												
Burundi	411[2]	411[2]	411[2]	424[2]	257	269	271	271	276	259	282	322
Costa Rica	941	941	941	971	975	888	896	896	914	855	933	932
Cuba	198	198	198	204	205	187	189	189	192	180	196	196
Dominican Republic	505	505	505	530	436	525	298	419	449	393	458	458
Ecuador	546	546	546	573	567	516	521	546	589	577	554	554
El Salvador	1,415	1,415	1,415	1,685	1,468	1,561	1,348	1,461	1,600	1,318	1,633	1,613
Guatemala	1,331	1,331	1,331	1,511	1,380	1,257	1,268	1,336	1,428	1,234	1,395	1,455
Haiti	499*	499*	499*	515*	431*	393	396	411	434	386	443	443
Honduras	282*	282*	282*	334*	293*	266*	269*	269*	404*	379	412	413
India	356	356	356	374	370	314	339	364	396	396	363	373
Jamaica										25	12	12
Mexico	1,494	1,494	1,494	1,567	1,549	1,411	1,423	1,423	1,451	1,355	1,444	1,444
Nicaragua	415	415	415	435	430	455	331	429	473	396	471	471
Panama	26	26	26	27	27	25	25	25	26	25	24	24
Peru	574	574	574	642	595	496	547	555	619	536	617	617
Rwanda	3	3	3	3	257	199	200	200	204	192	209	209
Venezuela	470*	470*	470*	485	488	444	448	448	457	429	466	466
Subtotal	9,463	9,463	9,463	10,277	9,728	9,206	8,769	9,242	9,912	8,935	9,912	10,002
Unwashed Arabicas:												
Bolivia	20*	20*	20*	20*	21*	25*	25*	25*	26*	25*	49*	49
Brazil	17,820	17,820	17,820	18,693	18,480	16,828	16,976	16,976	17,312	16,937	17,672	17,672
Ethiopia	1,010*	1,010*	1,010*	1,037*	1,206*	1,098	1,108	1,164	1,205	1,181	1,230	1,230
Paraguay											69	69
Subtotal	18,850	18,850	18,850	19,750	19,707	17,951	18,109	18,165	18,543	18,143	19,020	19,020
Robustas:												
Congo-Kinshasa	940	940	940	987	975	1,066	1,075	1,075	1,096	1,152	1,120	1,242
Ghana				44	44	40	41	46	47	48	43	47
Guinea											194	209
Indonesia	1,164	1,164	1,164	1,221	1,207	1,100	1,109	1,109	1,131	1,155	1,024	1,248
Liberia										60	60	66
Nigeria	18	18	18	25	25	25	25	42	42	43	38	42
OAMCAF	4,259	4,259	4,259	4,778	4,417		4,057	4,357	4,552	4,706	4,686	5,155
Portugal	2,167	2,167	2,167	2,393	2,247	2,045	2,064	2,214	2,384	2,542	2,492	2,741
Sierra Leone	64*	64*	64*	66*	68*	61	62	61	80	66	82	90
Trinidad and Tobago	44	44	44	65	45	61	42	67	67	71	60	76
Uganda	1,869	1,869	1,869	2,260	1,938	1,765	1,780	1,915	2,013	2,112	2,072	2,279
Subtotal	10,525	10,525	10,525	11,839	10,966	10,183	10,255	10,886	11,412	11,955	11,889	18,195
Total	45,732	45,732	45,732	49,089	47,550	43,850	43,700	44,885	46,862	45,553	47,924	49,886

*Signatory nonmember; such a member is one who signed the treaty but was unable to secure parliamentary approval for the treaty. Complete only through July 15, 1968.

[1]Excludes shipments to the United Kingdom.
[2]Includes Rwanda.
[3]Included in Burundi.

Source: International Coffee Organization.

INTERNATIONAL COFFEE AGREEMENT, 1962

Preamble

The Governments Parties to this Agreement,

Recognizing the exceptional importance of coffee to the economies of many countries which are largely dependent upon this commodity for their export earnings and thus for the continuation of their development programmes in the social and economic fields;

Considering that close international co-operation on coffee marketing will stimulate the economic diversification and development of coffee-producing countries and thus contribute to a strengthening of the political and economic bonds between producers and consumers;

Finding reason to expect a tendency toward persistent disequilibrium between production and consumption, accumulation of burdensome stocks, and pronounced fluctuations in prices, which can be harmful both to producers and to consumers; and

Believing that, in the absence of international measures, this situation cannot be corrected by normal market forces,

Have agreed as follows:

CHAPTER I - OBJECTIVES

Article 1

Objectives

The objectives of the Agreement are:

(1) to achieve a reasonable balance between supply and demand on a basis which will assure adequate supplies of coffee to consumers and markets for coffee to producers at equitable prices, and which will bring about long-term equilibrium between production and consumption;

(2) to alleviate the serious hardship caused by burdensome surpluses and excessive fluctuations in the prices of coffee to the detriment of the interests of both producers and consumers;

(3) to contribute to the development of productive resources and to the promotion and maintenance of employment and income in the Member countries, thereby helping to bring about fair wages, higher living standards, and better working conditions;

(4) to assist in increasing the purchasing power of coffee-exporting countries by keeping prices at equitable levels and by increasing consumption;

(5) to encourage the consumption of coffee by every possible means; and

(6) in general, in recognition of the relationship of the trade in coffee to the economic stability of markets for industrial products, to further international co-operation in connexion with world coffee problems.

CHAPTER II - DEFINITIONS

Article 2

Definitions

For the purposes of the Agreement:

(1) "Coffee" means the beans and berries of the coffee tree, whether parchment, green or roasted, and includes ground, decaffeinated, liquid and soluble coffee. These terms shall have the following meaning:

(a) "green coffee" means all coffee in the naked bean form before roasting;

(b) "coffee berries" means the complete fruit of the coffee tree; to find the equivalent of coffee berries to green coffee, multiply the net weight of the dried coffee by berries 0.50;

(c) "parchment coffee" means the green coffee bean contained in the parchment skin; to find the equivalent of parchment coffee to green coffee, multiply the net weight of the parchment coffee by 0.80;

(d) "roasted coffee" means green coffee roasted to any degree and includes ground coffee; to find the equivalent of roasted coffee to green coffee, multiply the net weight of roasted coffee by 1.19;

(e) "decaffeinated coffee" means green, roasted or soluble coffee from which caffein has been extracted; to find the equivalent of decaffeinated coffee to green coffee, multiply the net weight of the decaffeinated coffee in green, roasted or soluble form by 1.00, 1.19 or 3.00, respectively;

(f) "liquid coffee" means the water-soluble solids derived from roasted coffee and put into liquid form; to find the equivalent

of liquid to green coffee, multiply the net weight of the
dried coffee solids contained in the liquid coffee by 3.00;

(g) "soluble coffee" means the dried water-soluble solids derived from roasted coffee; to find the equivalent of soluble
coffee to green coffee, multiply the net weight of the soluble
coffee by 3.00.

(2) "Bag" means 60 kilogrammes or 132.276 pounds of green
coffee; "ton" means a metric ton of 1,000 kilogrammes or 2,204.6
pounds; and "pound" means 453.597 grammes.

(3) "Coffee year" means the period of one year, from 1 October
through 30 September; and "first coffee year" means the coffee year
beginning 1 October 1962.

(4) "Export of coffee" means, except as otherwise provided in
Article 38, any shipment of coffee which leaves the territory of the
country where the coffee was grown.

(5) "Organization", "Council" and "Board" mean, respectively,
the International Coffee Organization, the International Coffee Council,
and the Executive Board established under Article 7 of the Agreement.

(6) "Member" means a Contracting Party; a dependent territory
or territories in respect of which separate Membership has been declared under Article 4; or two or more Contracting Parties or dependent territories, or both, which participate in the Organization
as a Member group under Article 5 or 6.

(7) "Exporting Member" or "exporting country" means a Member or country, respectively, which is a net exporter of coffee; that
is, whose exports exceed its imports.

(8) "Importing Member" or "importing country" means a
Member or country, respectively, which is a net importer of coffee;
that is, whose imports exceed its exports.

(9) "Producing Member" or "producing country" means a
Member or country, respectively, which grows coffee in commercially
significant quantities.

(10) "Distributed simple majority vote" means a majority of
the votes cast by exporting Members present and voting, and a majority
of the votes cast by importing Members present and voting, counted
separately.

(11) "Distributed two-thirds majority vote" means a two-thirds
majority of the votes cast by exporting Members present and voting
and a two-thirds majority of the votes cast by importing Members
present and voting, counted separately.

(12) "Entry into force" means, except where the context
otherwise requires, the date on which the Agreement first enters
into force, whether provisionally or definitively.

CHAPTER III - MEMBERSHIP

Article 3

Membership in the Organization

Each Contracting Party, together with those of its dependent territories to which the Agreement is extended under paragraph (1) of Article 67, shall constitute a single Member of the Organization, except as otherwise provided under Article 4, 5 or 6.

Article 4

Separate Membership in Respect of
Dependent Territories

Any Contracting Party which is a net importer of coffee may, at any time, by appropriate notification in accordance with paragraph (2) of Article 67, declare that it is participating in the Organization separately with respect to any of its dependent territories which are net exporters of coffee and which it designates. In such case, the metropolitan territory and its non-designated dependent territories will have a single Membership, and its designated dependent territories, either individually or collectively as the notification indicates, will have separate Membership.

Article 5

Group Membership upon Joining the Organization

(1) Two or more Contracting Parties which are net exporters of coffee may, by appropriate notification to the Secretary-General of the United Nations at the time of deposit of their respective instruments of ratification or accession, and to the Council at its first session, declare that they are joining the Organization as a Member group. A dependent territory to which the Agreement has been extended under paragraph (1) of Article 67 may constitute part of such a Member group if the Government of the State responsible for its international relations has given appropriate notification thereof under paragraph (2) of Article 67. Such Contracting Parties and dependent territories must satisfy the following conditions:

(a) they shall declare their willingness to accept responsibility for group obligations in an individual as well as a group capacity;

(b) they shall subsequently provide sufficient evidence to the Council that the group has the organization necessary to implement a common coffee policy, and that they have the means of complying, together with the other parties to the group, with their obligations under the Agreement; and

(c) they shall subsequently provide evidence to the Council either:

(i) that they have been recognized as a group in a previous international coffee agreement; or

(ii) that they have:

(a) a common or co-ordinated commercial and economic policy in relation to coffee, and

(b) a co-ordinated monetary and financial policy, as well as the organs necessary for implementing such a policy, so that the Council is satisfied that the Member group can comply with the spirit of group membership and the group obligations involved.

(2) The Member group shall constitute a single Member of the Organization, except that each party to the group shall be treated as if it were a single Member as regards all matters arising under the following provisions:

(a) Chapters XI and XII;
(b) Articles 10, 11 and 19 of Chapter IV; and
(c) Article 70 of Chapter XIX.

(3) The Contracting Parties and dependent territories joining as a Member group shall specify the Government or organization which will represent them in the Council as regards all matters arising under the Agreement other than those specified in paragraph (2) of this Article.

(4) The Member group's voting rights shall be as follows:

(a) the Member group shall have the same number of basic votes as a single Member country joining the Organization in an individual capacity. These basic votes shall be attributed to and exercised by the Government or organization representing the group;

(b) in the event of a vote on any matters arising under provisions specified in paragraph (2) of this Article, the parties to the

Member group may exercise separately the votes attributed to them by the provisions of paragraph (3) of Article 12 as if each were an individual Member of the Organization, except for the basic votes, which shall remain attributable only to the Government or organization representing the group.

(5) Any Contracting Party or dependent territory which is a party to a Member group may, by notification to the Council, withdraw from that group and become a separate Member. Such withdrawal shall take effect upon receipt of the notification by the Council. In case of such withdrawal from a group, or in case a party to a group ceases, by withdrawal from the Organization or otherwise, to be such a party, the remaining parties to the group may apply to the Council to maintain the group, and the group shall continue to exist unless the Council disapproves the application. If the Member group is dissolved, each former party to the group will become a separate Member. A Member which has ceased to be a party to a group may not, as long as the Agreement remains in force, again become a party to a group.

Article 6

Subsequent Group Membership

Two or more exporting Members may, at any time after the Agreement has entered into force with respect to them, apply to the Council to form a Member group. The Council shall approve the application if it finds that the Members have made a declaration, and have provided evidence, satisfying the requirements of paragraph (1) of Article 5. Upon such approval, the Member group shall be subject to the provisions of paragraphs (2), (3), (4) and (5) of that Article.

CHAPTER IV - ORGANIZATION
AND ADMINISTRATION

Establishment, Seat and Structure of
the International Coffee Organization

(1) The International Coffee Organization is hereby established to administer the provisions of the Agreement and to supervise its operation.

(2) The seat of the Organization shall be in London.

(3) The Organization shall function through the International Coffee Council, its Executive Board, its Executive Director, and its staff.

Article 8

Composition of the International Coffee Council

(1) The highest authority of the Organization shall be the International Coffee Council, which shall consist of all the Members of the Organization.

(2) Each Member shall be represented on the Council by a representative and one or more alternates. A Member may also designate one or more advisers to accompany its representative or alternates.

Article 9

Powers and Functions of the Council

(1) All powers specifically conferred by the Agreement shall be vested in the Council, which shall have the powers and perform the functions necessary to carry out the provisions of the Agreement.

(2) The Council shall, by a distributed two-thirds majority vote, establish such rules and regulations, including its own rules of procedure and the financial and staff regulations of the Organization, as are necessary to carry out the provisions of the Agreement and are consistent therewith. The Council may, in its rules of procedure, provide a procedure whereby it may, without meeting, decide specific questions.

(3) The Council shall also keep such records as are required to perform its functions under the Agreement and such other records as it considers desirable, and shall publish an annual report.

Article 10

Election of the Chairman and Vice-Chairmen of the Council

(1) The Council shall elect, for each coffee year, a Chairman and a first, a second and a third Vice-Chairman.

(2) As a general rule, the Chairman and the first Vice-Chairman shall both be elected either from among the representatives of exporting Members, or from among the representatives of importing Members, and the second and the third Vice-Chairmen shall be elected from representatives of the other category of Members; these offices shall alternate each coffee year between the two categories of Members.

(3) Neither the Chairman nor any Vice-Chairman acting as Chairman shall have the right to vote. His alternate will in such case exercise the Member's voting rights.

Article 11

Sessions of the Council

As a general rule, the Council shall hold regular sessions twice a year. It may hold special sessions if it so decides. Special sessions shall also be held when either the Executive Board, or any five Members, or a Member or Members having at least 200 votes so request. Notice of sessions shall be given at least thirty days in advance, except in cases of emergency. Sessions shall be held at the seat of the Organization, unless the Council decides otherwise.

Article 12

Votes

(1) The exporting Members shall together hold 1,000 votes and the importing Members shall together hold 1,000 votes, distributed within each category of Members—that is, exporting and importing Members, respectively—as provided in the following paragraphs of this Article.

(2) Each Member shall have five basic votes, provided that the total number of basic votes within each category of Members does not exceed 150. Should there be more than thirty exporting Members or more than thirty importing Members, the number of basic votes for each Member within that category of Members shall be adjusted so as to keep the number of basic votes for each category of Members within the maximum of 150.

(3) The remaining votes of exporting Members shall be divided among those Members in proportion to their respective basic export quotas, except that in the event of a vote on any matter arising under the provisions specified in paragraph (2) of Article 5, the remaining votes of a Member group shall be divided among the parties to that group in proportion to their respective participation in the basic export quota of the Member group.

(4) The remaining votes of importing Members shall be divided among those Members in proportion to the average volume of their respective coffee imports in the preceding three-year period.

(5) The distribution of votes shall be determined by the Council at the beginning of each coffee year, and shall remain in effect during that year, except as provided in paragraph (6) of this Article.

(6) The Council shall provide for the redistribution of votes in accordance with this Article whenever there is a change in the Membership of the Organization, or if the voting rights of a Member are suspended or regained under the provisions of Article 25, 45 or 61.

(7) No Member shall hold more than 400 votes.

(8) There shall be no fractional votes.

Article 13

Voting Procedure of the Council

(1) Each representative shall be entitled to cast the number of votes held by the Member represented by him, and cannot divide its votes. He may, however, cast differently from such votes any votes which he exercises pursuant to paragraph (2) of this Article.

(2) Any exporting Member may authorize any other exporting Member, and any importing Member may authorize any other importing Member, to represent its interests and to exercise its right to vote at any meeting or meetings of the Council. The limitation provided for in paragraph (7) of Article 12 shall not apply in this case.

Article 14

Decisions of the Council

(1) All decisions of the Council shall be taken, and all recommendations shall be made, by a distributed simple majority vote unless otherwise provided in the Agreement.

(2) The following procedure shall apply with respect to any action by the Council which under the Agreement requires a distributed two-thirds majority vote:

(a) if a distributed two-thirds majority vote is not obtained because of the negative vote of three or less exporting or three or less importing Members, the proposal shall, if the Council so decides by a majority of the Members present and by a distributed simple majority vote, be put to a vote again within 48 hours;

(b) if a distributed two-thirds majority vote is again not obtained because of the negative vote of two or less importing or two or less exporting Members, the proposal shall, if the Council so decides by the majority of the Members present and by a distributed simple majority vote, be put to a vote again within 24 hours;

(c) if a distributed two-thirds majority vote is not obtained in the third vote because of the negative vote of one exporting Member or one importing Member, the proposal shall be considered adopted;

(d) if the Council fails to put a proposal to a further vote, it shall be considered rejected.

(3) The Members undertake to accept as binding all decisions of the Council under the provisions of the Agreement.

Article 15

Composition of the Board

(1) The Executive Board shall consist of seven exporting Members and seven importing Members, elected for each coffee year in accordance with Article 16. Members may be re-elected.

(2) Each member of the Board shall appoint one representative and one or more alternates.

(3) The Chairman of the Board shall be appointed by the Council for each coffee year and may be re-appointed. He shall not have the right to vote. If a representative is appointed Chairman, his alternate will have the right to vote in his place.

(4) The Board shall normally meet at the seat of the Organization, but may meet elsewhere.

Article 16

Election of the Board

(1) The exporting and the importing Members on the Board shall be elected in the Council by the exporting and the importing Members of the Organization respectively. The election within each category shall he held in accordance with the following paragraphs of this Article.

(2) Each Member shall cast all the votes to which it is entitled under Article 12 for a single candidate. A Member may cast for another candidate any votes which it exercises pursuant to paragraph (2) of Article 13.

(3) The seven candidates receiving the largest number of votes shall be elected; however, no candidate shall be elected on the first ballot unless it receives at least 75 votes.

(4) If under the provisions of paragraph (3) of this Article less than seven candidates are elected on the first ballot, further ballots shall be held in which only Members who did not vote for any of the candidates elected shall have the right to vote. In each further ballot, the minimum number of votes required for election shall be successively diminished by five until seven candidates are elected.

(5) Any Member who did not vote for any of the Members elected shall assign its votes to one of them, subject to paragraphs (6) and (7) of this Article.

(6) A Member shall be deemed to have received the number of votes originally cast for it when it was elected and, in addition, the number of votes assigned to it, provided that the total number of votes shall not exceed 499 for any Member elected.

(7) If the votes deemed received by an elected Member would otherwise exceed 499, Members which voted for or assigned their votes to such elected Member shall arrange among themselves for one or more of them to withdraw their votes from that Member and assign or reassign them to another elected Member so that the votes received by each elected Member shall not exceed the limit of 499.

Article 17

Competence of the Board

(1) The Board shall be responsible to and work under the general direction of the Council.

(2) The Council may, by a distributed simple majority vote, delegate to the Board the exercise of any or all of its powers, other than the following:

(a) annual distribution of votes under paragraph (5) of Article 12;

(b) approval of the administrative budget and assessment of contributions under Article 24;

(c) determination of quotas under the Agreement;

(d) imposition of enforcement measures other than those whose application is automatic;

(e) suspension of the voting rights of a Member under Article 45 or 61;

(f) determination of individual country and world production goals under Article 48;

(g) establishment of a policy relative to stocks under Article 51;

(h) waiver of the obligations of a Member under Article 60;

(i) decision of disputes under Article 61;

(j) establishment of conditions for accession under Article 65;

(k) a decision to require the withdrawal of a Member under Article 69;

(l) extension or termination of the Agreement under Article 71; and

(m) recommendation of amendments to Members under Article 73.

(3) The Council may at any time, by a distributed simple majority vote, revoke any delegation of powers to the Board.

Article 18

Voting Procedure of the Board

(1) Each member of the Board shall be entitled to cast the number of votes received by it under the provisions of paragraphs (6)

and (7) of Article 16. Voting by proxy shall not be allowed. A member may not split its votes.

(2) Any action taken by the Board shall require the same majority as such action would require if taken by the Council.

Article 19

Quorum for the Council and the Board

(1) The quorum for any meeting of the Council shall be the presence of a majority of the Members representing a distributed two-thirds majority of the total votes. If there is no quorum on the day appointed for the opening of any Council session, or if in the course of any Council session there is no quorum at three successive meetings, the Council shall be convened seven days later; at that time and throughout the remainder of that session the quorum shall be the presence of a majority of the Members representing a distributed simple majority of the votes. Representation in accordance with paragraph (2) of Article 13 shall be considered as presence.

(2) The quorum for any meeting of the Board shall be the presence of a majority of the members representing a distributed two-thirds majority of the total votes.

Article 20

The Executive Director and the Staff

(1) The Council shall appoint the Executive Director on the recommendation of the Board. The terms of appointment of the Executive Director shall be established by the Council and shall be comparable to those applying to corresponding officials of similar inter-governmental organizations.

(2) The Executive Director shall be the chief administrative officer of the Organization and shall be responsible for the performance of any duties devolving upon him in the administration of the Agreement.

(3) The Executive Director shall appoint the staff in accordance with regulations established by the Council.

(4) Neither the Executive Director nor any member of the staff shall have any financial interest in the coffee industry, coffee trade, or coffee transportation.

(5) In the performance of their duties, the Executive Director and the staff shall not seek or receive instructions from any Member or from any other authority external to the Organization. They shall refrain from any action which might reflect on their position as international officials responsible only to the Organization. Each Member undertakes to respect the exclusively international character

of the responsibilities of the Executive Director and the staff and not to seek to influence them in the discharge of their responsibilities.

Article 21

Co-operation with other Organizations

The Council may make whatever arrangements are desirable for consultation and co-operation with the United Nations and its specialized agencies and with other appropriate inter-governmental organizations. The Council may invite these organizations and any organizations concerned with coffee to send observers to its meetings.

CHAPTER V - PRIVILEGES AND IMMUNITIES

Article 22

Privileges and Immunities

(1) The Organization shall have in the territory of each Member, to the extent consistent with its laws, such legal capacity as may be necessary for the exercise of its functions under the Agreement.

(2) The Government of the United Kingdom of Great Britain and Northern Ireland shall grant exemption from taxation on the salaries paid by the Organization to its employees, except that such exemption need not apply to nationals of that country. It shall also grant exemption from taxation on the assets, income and other property of the Organization.

CHAPTER VI - FINANCE

Article 23

Finance

(1) The expenses of delegations to the Council, representatives on the Board, and representatives on any of the committees of the Council or the Board shall be met by their respective Governments.

(2) The other expenses necessary for the administration of the Agreement shall be met by annual contributions from the Members assessed in accordance with Article 24.

(3) The financial year of the Organization shall be the same as the coffee year.

Article 24

Determination of the Budget and
Assessment of Contributions

(1) During the second half of each financial year, the Council
shall approve the administrative budget of the Organization for the
following financial year, and shall assess the contribution of each
Member to that budget.

(2) The contribution of each Member to the budget for each
financial year shall be in the proportion which the number of its votes
at the time the budget for that financial year is approved bears to
the total votes of all the Members. However, if there is any change
in the distribution of votes among Members in accordance with the
provisions of paragraph (5) of Article 12 at the beginning of the
financial year for which contributions are assessed, such contributions
shall be correspondingly adjusted for that year. In determining contributions, the votes of each Member shall be calculated without
regard to the suspension of any Member's voting rights or any redistribution of votes resulting therefrom.

(3) The initial contribution of any Member joining the Organization after the entry into force of the Agreement shall be assessed
by the Council on the basis of the number of votes to be held by it
and the period remaining in the current financial year, but the assessments made upon other Members for the current financial year shall
not be altered:

(4) If the Agreement comes into force more than eight months
before the beginning of the first financial year of the Organization,
the Council shall at its first session approve an administrative budget
covering only the period up to the commencement of the first full
financial year. Otherwise the first administrative budget shall cover
both the initial period and the first full financial year.

Article 25

Payment of Contributions

(1) Contributions to the administrative budget for each financial
year shall be payable in freely convertible currency, and shall become due on the first day of that financial year.

(2) If any Member fails to pay its full contribution to the administrative budget within six months of the date on which the contribution is due, both its voting rights in the Council and its right
to have its votes cast in the Board shall be suspended until such
contribution has been paid. However, unless the Council so decides

by a distributed two-thirds majority vote, such Member shall not be deprived of any of its other rights nor relieved of any of its obligations under the Agreement.

(3) Any Member whose voting rights have been suspended, either under paragraph (2) of this Article or under Article 45 or 61, shall nevertheless remain responsible for the payment of its contribution.

Article 26

Audit and Publication of Accounts

As soon as possible after the close of each financial year, an independently audited statement of the Organization's receipts and expenditures during that financial year shall be presented to the Council for approval and publication.

CHAPTER VII - REGULATION OF EXPORTS

Article 27

General Undertakings by Members

(1) The Members undertake to conduct their trade policy so that the objectives set forth in Article 1 and, in particular, paragraph (4) of that Article, may be achieved. They agree on the desirability of operating the Agreement in a manner such that the real income derived from the export of coffee could be progressively increased so as to make it consonant with their needs for foreign exchange to support their programmes for social and economic progress.

(2) To attain these purposes through the fixing of quotas as provided for in this Chapter and in other ways carrying out the provisions of the Agreement, the Members agree on the necessity of assuring that the general level of coffee prices does not decline below the general level of such prices in 1962.

(3) The Members further agree on the desirability of assuring to consumers prices which are equitable and which will not hamper a desirable increase in consumption.

Article 28

Basic Export Quotas

(1) For the first three coffee years, beginning on 1 October 1962, the exporting countries listed in Annex A [1] shall have the basic export quotas specified in that Annex.

---

[1] Post, p. 2159.

(2) During the last six months of the coffee year ending 30
September 1965, the Council shall review the basic export quotas
specified in Annex A in order to adjust them to general market conditions. The Council may then revise such quotas by a distributed two-
thirds majority vote; if not revised, the basic export quotas specified
in Annex A shall remain in effect.

Article 29

Quota of a Member Group

Where two or more countries listed in Annex A form a Member group in accordance with Article 5, the basic export quotas
specified for those countries in Annex A shall be added together
and the combined total treated as a single quota for the purposes of
this Chapter.

Article 30

Fixing of Annual Export Quotas

(1) At least 30 days before the beginning of each coffee year
the Council shall adopt by a two-thirds majority vote an estimate of
total world imports for the following coffee year and an estimate of
probable exports from nonmember countries.

(2) In the light of these estimates the Council shall forthwith
fix annual export quotas which shall be the same percentage for all
exporting Members of the basic export quotas specified in Annex A.
For the first coffee year this percentage is fixed at 99, subject to the
provisions of Article 32.

Article 31

Fixing of Quarterly Export Quotas

(1) Immediately following the fixing of the annual export
quotas the Council shall fix quarterly export quotas for each exporting
Member for the purpose of keeping supply in reasonable balance with
estimated demand throughout the coffee year.

(2) These quotas shall be, as nearly as possible, 25 percent
of the annual export quota of each Member during the coffee year.
No Member shall be allowed to export more than 30 percent in the
first quarter, 60 percent in the first two quarters, and 80 percent
in the first three quarters of the coffee year. If exports from any
Member in one quarter are less than its quota for that quarter, the
outstanding balance shall be added to its quota for the following
quarter of that coffee year.

Article 32

Adjustment of Annual Export Quotas

If market conditions so require, the Council may review the quota situation and may vary the percentage of basic export quotas fixed under paragraph (2) of Article 30. In so doing, the Council shall have regard to any likely shortfalls by Members.

Article 33

Notification of Shortfalls

(1) Exporting Members undertake to notify the Council at the end of the eight month of the coffee year, and at such later dates as the Council may request, whether they have sufficient coffee available to export the full amount of their quota for that year.

(2) The Council shall take into account these notifications in determining whether or not to adjust the level of export quotas in accordance with Article 32.

Article 34

Adjustment of Quarterly Export Quotas

(1) The Council shall in the circumstances set out in this Article vary the quarterly export quotas fixed for each Member under paragraph (1) of Article 31.

(2) If the Council varies the annual export quotas as provided in Article 32, then the change in that annual quota shall be reflected in the quotas for the current and remaining quarters, or the remaining quarters, of the coffee year.

(3) Apart from the adjustment provided for in the preceding paragraph, the Council may, if it finds the market situation so requires, make adjustments among the current and remaining quarterly export quotas for the same coffee year, without, however, altering the annual export quotas.

(4) If on account of exceptional circumstances an exporting Member considers that the limitations provided in paragraph (2) of Article 31 would be likely to cause serious harm to its economy, the Council may, at the request of that Member, take appropriate action under Article 60. The Member concerned must furnish evidence of harm and provide adequate guarantees concerning the maintenance of price stability. The Council shall not, however, in any event, authorize a Member to export more than 35 percent of its annual export quota in the first quarter, 65 percent in the first two quarters, and 85 percent in the first three quarters of the coffee year.

(5) All Members recognize that marked price rises or falls occurring within brief periods may unduly distort underlying trends in price, cause grave concern to both producers and consumers, and jeopardize the attainment of the objectives of the Agreement. Accordingly if such movements in general price levels occur within brief periods, Members may request a meeting of the Council which, by distributed simple majority vote, may revise the total level of the quarterly export quotas in effect.

(6) If the Council finds that a sharp and unusual increase or decrease in the general level of prices is due to artificial manipulation of the coffee market through agreements among importers or exporters or both, it shall then decide by a simple majority vote on what corrective measures should be applied to readjust the total level of the quarterly export quotas in effect.

Article 35

Procedure for Adjusting Export Quotas

(1) Annual export quotas shall be fixed and adjusted by altering the basic export quota of each Member by the same percentage.

(2) General changes in all quarterly export quotas, made pursuant to paragrahs (2), (3), (5) and (6) of Article 34, shall be applied pro rata to individual quarterly export quotas in accordance with appropriate rules established by the Council. Such rules shall take account of the different percentages of annual export quotas which the different Members have exported or are entitled to export in each quarter of the coffee year.

(3) All decisions by the Council on the fixing and adjustment of annual and quarterly export quotas under Articles 30, 31, 32 and 34 shall be taken, unless otherwise provided, by a distributed two-thirds majority vote.

Article 36

Compliance with Export Quotas

(1) Exporting Members subject to quotas shall adopt the measures required to ensure full compliance with all provisions of the Agreement relating to quotas. The Council may request such Members to adopt additional measures for the effective implementation of the quota system provided for in the Agreement.

(2) Exporting Members shall not exceed the annual and quarterly export quotas allocated to them.

(3) If an exporting Member exceeds its quota for any quarter, the Council shall deduct from one or more of its future quotas a total amount equal to that excess.

(4) If an exporting Member for the second time while the Agreement remains in force exceeds its quarterly quota, the Council shall deduct from one or more of its future quotas a total amount equal to twice that excess.

(5) If an exporting Member for a third or subsequent time while the Agreement remains in force exceeds its quarterly quota, the Council shall make the same deduction as provided in paragraph (4) of this Article, and in addition the Council may take action in accordance with Article 69 to require the withdrawal of such a Member from the Organization.

(6) The deductions in quotas provided in paragraphs (3), (4) and (5) of this Article shall be made by the Council as soon as it receives the necessary information.

Article 37

Transitional Quota Provisions

(1) Exports of coffee after 1 October 1962 shall be charged against the annual export quota of the exporting country concerned at such time as the Agreement enters into force in respect of that country.

(2) If the Agreement enters into force after 1 October 1962, the Council shall, during its first session, make such modifications as may be necessary in the procedure for the fixing of annual and quarterly export quotas in respect of the coffee year in which the Agreement enters into force.

Article 38

Shipments of Coffee from Dependent Territories

(1) Subject to paragraph (2) of this Article, the shipment of coffee from any of the dependent territories of a Member to its metropolitan territory or to another of its dependent territories for domestic consumption therein or in any other of its dependent territories shall not be considered as the export of coffee, and shall not be subject to any export quota limitations, provided that the Member concerned enters into arrangements satisfactory to the Council with respect to the control of re-exports and such other matters as the Council may determine to be related to the operation of the Agreement and which arise out of the special relationship between the metropolitan territory of the Member and its dependent territories.

(2) The trade in coffee between a Member and any of its dependent territories which, in accordance with Article 4 or 5, is a separate Member of the Organization or a party to a Member group, shall however be treated, for the purposes of the Agreement, as the export of coffee.

Article 39

Exporting Members not Subject to Quotas

(1) Any exporting Member whose average annual exports of coffee for the preceding three-year period were less than 25,000 bags shall not be subject to the quota provisions of the Agreement, so long as its exports remain less than that quantity.

(2) Any Trust Territory administered under a trusteeship agreement with the United Nations whose annual exports to countries other than the Administering Authority do not exceed 100,000 bags shall not be subject to the quota provisions of the Agreement, so long as its exports do not exceed that quantity.

Article 40

Exports not Charged to Quotas

(1) In order to facilitate the increase of coffee consumption in certain areas of the world having a low per capita consumption and considerable potential for expansion, exports to countries listed in Annex B [1] shall not, subject to the provisions of sub-paragraph (f) of this paragraph, be charged to quotas. The Council, at the beginning of the second full coffee year after the Agreement enters into force, and annually thereafter, shall review the list with a view to determining whether any country or countries should be deleted from it, and may, if it so decides, delete any such country or countries. In connexion with exports to the countries listed in Annex B, the provisions of the following sub-paragraphs shall be applicable:

(a) At its first session, and thereafter whenever it deems necessary, the Council shall prepare an estimate of imports for internal consumption by the countries listed in Annex B, after reviewing the results obtained in the previous year with regard to the increase of coffee consumption in those countries and taking into account the probable effect of promotion campaigns and trade arrangements. Exporting Members shall not in the aggregate export to the countries listed in Annex B more than the quantity set by the Council, and for that purpose the Council shall keep those Members informed of current exports to such countries. Exporting Members shall inform the Council not later than thirty days after the end of each month of all exports made to each of the countries listed in Annex B during that month.
(b) Members shall supply such statistics and other information as the Council may require to assist it in controlling the flow of coffee to countries listed in Annex B and its consumption therein.

---

[1]Post, p. 2161.

(c) Exporting Members shall endeavour to renegotiate existing trade agreements as soon as possible in order to include in them provisions preventing re-exports of coffee from the countries listed in Annex B to other markets. Exporting Members shall also include such provisions in all new trade agreements and in all new sales contracts not covered by trade agreements, whether such contracts are negotiated with private traders or with government organizations.

(d) In order to maintain control at all times of exports to countries listed in Annex B, the Council may decide upon further precautionary steps, such as requiring coffee bags destined to those countries to be specially marked and requiring that the exporting Members receive from such countries banking and contractual guarantees to prevent re-exportation to countries not listed in Annex B. The Council may, whenever it deems necessary, engage the services of an internationally recognized world-wide organization to investigate irregularities in, or to verify exports to, countries listed in Annex B. The Council shall call any possible irregularity to the attention of the Members.

(e) The Council shall annually prepare a comprehensive report on the results obtained in the development of coffee markets in the countries listed in Annex B.

(f) If coffee exported by a Member to a country listed in Annex B is re-exported to any country not listed in Annex B, the Council shall charge the corresponding amount to the quota of that exporting Member. Should there again be a re-exportation from the same country listed in Annex B, the Council shall investigate the case, and unless it finds extenuating circumstances, may at any time delete that country from Annex B.

(2) Exports of coffee beans as raw material for industrial processing for any purposes other than human consumption as a beverage or foodstuff shall not be charged to quotas, provided that the Council is satisfied from information supplied by the exporting Member that the coffee beans are in fact used for such other purposes.

(3) The Council may, upon application by an exporting Member, decide that coffee exports made by that Member for humanitarian or other non-commercial purposes shall not be charged to its quota.

Article 41

Assurance of Supplies

In addition to ensuring that the total supplies of coffee are in accordance with estimated world imports, the Council shall seek to ensure that supplies of the types of coffee that consumers require are available to them. To achieve this objective, the Council may,

by a distributed two-thirds majority vote, decide to use whatever
methods it considers practicable.

Article 42

Regional and Inter-regional Price Arrangements

(1) Regional and inter-regional price arrangements among exporting Members shall be consistent with the general objectives of the
Agreement, and shall be registered with the Council. Such arrangements shall take into account the interests of both producers and consumers and the objectives of the Agreement. Any Member of the
Organization which considers that any of these arrangements are likely
to lead to results not in accordance with the objectives of the Agreement may request that the Council discuss them with the Members
concerned at its next session.

(2) In consultation with Members and with any regional organization to which they belong, the Council may recommend a scale of
price differentials for various grades and qualities of coffee which
Members should strive to achieve through their pricing policies.

(3) Should sharp price fluctuations occur within brief periods
in respect of those grades and qualities of coffee for which a scale
of price differentials has been adopted as the result of recommendations made under paragraph (2) of this Article, the Council may
recommend appropriate measures to correct the situation.

Article 43

Survey of Market Trends

The Council shall keep under constant survey the trends of the
coffee market with a view to recommending price policies, taking into
consideration the results achieved through the quota mechanism of the
Agreement.

CHAPTER VIII - CERTIFICATES OF ORIGIN
AND RE-EXPORT

Article 44

Certificates of Origin and Re-export

(1) Every export of coffee from any Member in whose territory
that coffee has been grown shall be accompanied by a certificate of
origin modelled on the form set forth in Annex C, [1] issued by a

---

[1]Post, p. 2162.

qualified agency chosen by that Member. Each such Member shall determine the number of copies of the certificate it will require and each copy shall bear a serial number. The original of the certificate shall accompany the documents of export, and a copy shall be furnished to the Organization by that Member. The Council shall, either directly or through an internationally recognized world-wide organization, verify the certificates of origin, so that at any time it will be able to ascertain the quantities of coffee which have been exported by each Member.

(2) Every re-export of coffee from a Member shall be accompanied by a certificate of re-export issued by a qualified agency chosen by that Member, in such form as the Council may determine, certifying that the coffee in question was imported in accordance with the provisions of the Agreement, and, if appropriate, containing a reference to the certificate or certificates of origin under which that coffee was imported. The original of the certificate of re-export shall accompany the documents of re-export, and a copy shall be furnished to the Organization by the re-exporting Member.

(3) Each Member shall notify the Organization of the agency or agencies designated by it to perform the functions specified in paragraphs (1) and (2) of this Article. The Council may at any time, for cause, declare certification by a particular agency unacceptable to it.

(4) Members shall render periodic reports to the Organization concerning imports of coffee, in such form and at such intervals as the Council shall determine.

(5) The provisions of paragraph (1) of this Article shall be put into effect not later than three months after the entry into force of the Agreement. The provisions of paragraph (2) shall be put into effect at such time as the Council shall decide.

(6) After the respective dates provided for under paragraph (5) of this Article, each Member shall prohibit the entry of any shipment of coffee from any other Member which is not accompanied by a certificate of origin or a certificate of re-export.

CHAPTER IX - REGULATION OF IMPORTS

Article 45

Regulation of Imports

(1) In order to prevent non-member exporting countries from increasing their exports at the expense of Members, the following provisions shall apply with respect to imports of coffee by Members from non-member countries.

(2) If three months after the Agreement enters into force, or at any time thereafter, the Members of the Organization represent less than 95 percent of world exports in the calendar year 1961, each Member shall, subject to paragraphs (4) and (5) of this Article, limit its total annual imports from non-member countries as a group to a quantity not in excess of its average annual imports from those countries as a group during the last three years prior to the entry into force of the Agreement for which statistics are available. However, if the Council so decides, the application of such limitations may be deferred.

(3) If at any time the Council, on the basis of information received, finds that exports from non-member countries as a group are disturbing the exports of Members, it may, notwithstanding the fact that the Members of the Organization represent 95 percent or more of world exports in the calendar year 1961, decide that the limitations of paragraph (2) shall be applied.

(4) If the Council's estimate of world imports adopted under Article 30 for any coffee year is less than its estimate of world imports for the first full coffee year after the Agreement enters into force, the quantity which each Member may import from non-member countries as a group under the provisions of paragraph (2) shall be reduced by the same proportion.

(5) The Council may annually recommend additional limitations on imports from non-member countries if it finds such limitations necessary in order to further the purposes of the Agreement.

(6) Within one month from the date on which limitations are applied under this Article, each Member shall inform the Council of the quantity of its permissible annual imports from non-member countries as a group.

(7) The obligations of the preceding paragraphs of this Article shall not derogate from any conflicting bilateral or multilateral obligations which importing Members have entered into with non-member countries before 1 August 1962; provided that any importing Member which has such conflicting obligations shall carry them out in such a way as to minimize the conflict with the obligations of the preceding paragraphs, take steps as soon as possible to bring its obligations into harmony with those paragraphs, and inform the Council of the details of the conflicting obligations and of the steps taken to minimize or eliminate the conflict.

(8) If an importing Member fails to comply with the provisions of this Article, the Council may, by a distributed two-thirds majority, vote, suspend both its voting rights in the Council and its right to have its votes cast in the Board.

CHAPTER X - INCREASE OF CONSUMPTION

Article 46

Promotion

(1) The Council shall sponsor a continuing programme for promoting the consumption of coffee. The size and cost of this programme shall be subject to periodic review and approval by the Council. The importing Members will have no obligation as respects the financing of this programme.

(2) If the Council after study of the question so decides, it shall establish within the framework of the Board a separate committee of the Organization, to be known as the World Coffee Promotion Committee.

(3) If the World Coffee Promotion Committee is established, the following provisions shall apply:

(a) The Committee's rules, in particular those regarding membership, organization, and financial affairs, shall be determined by the Council. Membership in the Committee shall be limited to Members which contribute to the promotional programme established in paragraph (1) of this Article.

(b) In carrying out its work, the Committee shall establish a technical committee within each country in which a promotional campaign will be conducted. Before a promotional campaign is inaugurated in any Member country, the Committee shall advise the representative of that Member in the Council of the Committee's intention to conduct such a campaign and shall obtain that Member's consent.

(c) The ordinary administrative expenses relating to the permanent staff of the Committee, other than the costs of their travel for promotion purposes, shall be charged to the administrative budget of the Organization, and shall not be charged to the promotion funds of the Committee.

Article 47

Removal of Obstacles to Consumption

(1) The Members recognize the utmost importance of achieving the greatest possible increase of coffee consumption as rapidly as possible, in particular through the progressive removal of any obstacles which may hinder such increase.

(2) The Members affirm their intention to promote full inter-national co-operation between all coffee exporting and importing countries.

(3) The Members recognize that there are presently in effect measures which may to a greater or lesser extent hinder the increase in consumption of coffee, in particular:

(a) import arrangements applicable to coffee, including prefer-ential and other tariffs, quotas, operations of Government import monopolies and official purchasing agencies, and other administrative rules and commercial practices;

(b) export arrangements as regards direct or indirect subsidies and other administrative rules and commercial practices; and

(c) internal trade conditions and domestic legal and administra-tive provisions which may affect consumption.

(4) The Members recognize that certain Members have shown their concurrence with the objectives stated above by announcing their intention to reduce tariffs on coffee or by taking other action to remove obstacles to increased consumption.

(5) The Members undertake, in the light of studies already carried out and those to be carried out under the auspices of the Council or by other competent international organizations, and of the Declaration adopted at the Ministerial Meeting in Geneva on 30 Nov-ember 1961:

(a) to investigate ways and means by which the obstacles to increased trade and consumption referred to in paragraph (3) of this Article could be progressively reduced and eventually, whenever possible, eliminated, or by which their effects could be substantially diminished;

(b) to inform the Council of the results of their investigation, so that the Council can review, within the first eighteen months after the Agreement enters into force, the informa-tion provided by Members concerning the effect of these obstacles and, if appropriate, the measures planned to reduce the obstacles or diminish their effects;

(c) to take into account the results of this review by the Council in the adoption of domestic measures and in proposals for international action; and

(d) to review at the session provided for in Article 72 the results achieved by the Agreement and to examine the

adoption of further measures for the removal of such
obstacles as may still stand in the way of expansion of
trade and consumption, taking into account the success of
the Agreement in increasing income of exporting Members
and in developing consumption.

(6) The Members undertake to study in the Council and in other
appropriate organizations any requests presented by Members whose
economies may be affected by the measures taken in accordance with
this Article.

CHAPTER XI - PRODUCTION CONTROLS

Article 48

Production Goals

(1) The producing Members undertake to adjust the production
of coffee while the Agreement remains in force to the amount needed
for domestic consumption, exports, and stocks as specified in Chapter
XII.

(2) Not later than one year after the Agreement enters into
force, the Council shall, in consultation with the producing Members,
by a distributed two-thirds majority vote, recommend production
goals for each of such Members and for the world as a whole.

(3) Each producing Member shall be entirely responsible for
the policies and procedures it applies to achieve these objectives.

Article 49

Implementation of Production-Control Programmes

(1) Each producing Member shall periodically submit written
reports to the Council on the measures it has taken or is taking to
achieve the objectives of Article 48, as well as on the concrete
results obtained. At its first session the Council shall, by a distributed two-thirds majority vote, establish a time-table and procedures for the presentation and discussion of such reports. Before
making any observations or recommendations the Council will consult
with the Members concerned.

(2) If the Council determines by a distributed two-thirds majority
vote either that any producing Member has not, within a period of
two years from the entry into force of the Agreement, adopted a
programme to adjust its production to the goals recommended by the
Council in accordance with Article 48, or that any producing Member's programme is not effective, it may by the same majority

decide that such Member shall not enjoy any quota increases which
may result from the application of the Agreement. The Council may
by the same majority establish whatever procedures it considers
appropriate for the purpose of verifying that the provisions of Article
48 have been complied with.

(3) At such time as it considers appropriate, but in any event
not later than the review session provided for in Article 72, the
Council may, by a distributed two-thirds majority vote, in the light
of the reports submitted for its consideration by the producing Members in accordance with paragraph (1) of this Article, revise the
production goals recommended in accordance with paragraph (2) of
Article 48.

(4) In applying the provisions of this Article, the Council shall
maintain close contact with international, national and private organizations which have an interest in or are responsible for financing
or, in general, assisting the development plans of the primary producing countries.

Article 50

Co-operation of Importing Members

Recognizing the paramount importance of bringing the production of coffee into reasonable balance with world demand, the
importing Members undertake, consistently with their general policies
regarding international assistance, to co-operate with the producing
Members in their plans for limiting the production of coffee. Their
assistance may be provided on a technical, financial or other basis,
and under bilateral, multilateral or regional arrangements, to producing Members implementing the provisions of this Chapter.

CHAPTER XII - REGULATION OF STOCKS

Article 51

Policy Relative to Coffee Stocks

(1) At its first session the Council shall take measures to
ascertain world coffee stocks, pursuant to systems which it shall
establish, and taking into account the following points: quantity,
countries of origin, location, quality, and condition. The Members
shall facilitate this survey.

(2) Not later than one year after the Agreement enters into
force, the Council shall, on the basis of the data thus obtained and in
consultation with the Members concerned, establish a policy relative
to such stocks in order to complement the recommendations provided

for in Article 48 and thereby to promote the attainment of the objectives of the Agreement.

(3) The producing Members shall endeavour by all means
within their power to implement the policy established by the Council.

(4) Each producing Member shall be entirely responsible for
the measures it applies to carry out the policy thus established by the
Council.

Article 52

Implementation of Programmes
for Regulation of Stocks

Each producing Member shall periodically submit written
reports to the Council on the measures it has taken or is taking to
achieve the objectives of Article 51, as well as on the concrete results
obtained. At its first session, the Council shall establish a time-
table and procedures for the presentation and discussion of such
reports. Before making any observations or recommendations, the
Council shall consult with the Members concerned.

CHAPTER XIII - MISCELLANEOUS OBLIGATIONS
OF MEMBERS

Article 53

Consultation and Co-operation with the Trade

(1) The Council shall encourage Members to seek the views of
experts in coffee matters.

(2) Members shall conduct their activities within the framework of the Agreement in a manner consonant with the established
channels of trade.

Article 54

Barter

In order to avoid jeopardizing the general price structure,
Members shall refrain from engaging in direct and individually linked
barter transactions involving the sale of coffee in the traditional
markets.

Article 55

Mixtures and Substitutes

Members shall not maintain any regulations requiring the mixing, processing or using of other products with coffee for commercial resale as coffee. Members shall endeavour to prohibit the sale and advertisement of products under the name of coffee if such products contain less than the equivalent of 90 percent green coffee as the basic raw material.

CHAPTER XIV - SEASONAL FINANCING

Article 56

Seasonal Financing

(1) The Council shall, upon the request of any Member who is also a party to any bilateral, multilateral, regional or inter-regional agreement in the field of seasonal financing, examine such agreement with a view to verifying its compatibility with the obligations of the Agreement.

(2) The Council may make recommendations to Members with a view to resolving any conflict of obligations which might arise.

(3) The Council may, on the basis of information obtained from the Members concerned, and if it deems appropriate and suitable, make general recommendations with a view to assisting Members which are in need of seasonal financing.

CHAPTER XV - INTERNATIONAL COFFEE FUND

Article 57

International Coffee Fund

(1) The Council may establish an International Coffee Fund. The Fund shall be used to further the objective of limiting the production of coffee in order to bring it into reasonable balance with demand for coffee, and to assist in the achievement of the other objectives of the Agreement.

(2) Contributions to the Fund shall be voluntary.

(3) The decision by the Council to establish the Fund and the adoption of guiding principles to govern its administration shall be taken by a distributed two-thirds majority vote.

CHAPTER XVI - INFORMATION AND STUDIES

Article 58

Information

(1) The Organization shall act as a centre for the collection, exchange and publication of:

(a) statistical information on world production, prices, exports and imports, distribution and consumption of coffee; and

(b) in so far as is considered appropriate, technical information on the cultivation, processing and utilization of coffee.

(2) The Council may require Members to furnish such information as it considers necessary for its operations, including regular statistical reports on coffee production, exports and imports, distribution, consumption, stocks and taxation, but no information shall be published which might serve to identify the operations of persons or companies producing, processing or marketing coffee. The Members shall furnish information requested in as detailed and accurate a manner as is practicable.

(3) If a Member fails to supply, or finds difficulty in supplying, within a reasonable time, statistical and other information required by the Council for the proper functioning of the Organization, the Council may require the Member concerned to explain the reasons for noncompliance. If it is found that technical assistance is needed in the matter, the Council may take any necessary measures.

Article 59

Studies

(1) The Council may promote studies in the fields of the economics of coffee production and distribution, the impact of governmental measures in producing and consuming countries on the production and consumption of coffee, the opportunities for expansion of coffee consumption for traditional and possible new uses, and the effects of the operation of the Agreement on producers and consumers of coffee, including their terms of trade.

(2) The Organization shall continue, to the extent it considers necessary, the studies and research previously undertaken by the

Coffee Study Group, and shall periodically carry out studies on trends and projections on coffee production and consumption.

(3) The Organization may study the practicability of prescribing minimum standards for exports from Members who produce coffee. Recommendations in this regard may be discussed by the Council.

CHAPTER XVII - WAIVER

Article 60

Waiver

(1) The Council may, by a two-thirds distributed majority vote, relieve a Member of an obligation which, on account of exceptional or emergency circumstances, force majeure, constitutional obligations, or international obligations under the United Nations Charter [1] for territories administered under the trusteeship system, either:

(a) constitutes a serious hardship;

(b) imposes an inequitable burden on such Member; or

(c) gives other Members an unfair or unreasonable advantage;

(2) The Council, in granting a waiver to a Member, shall state explicitly the terms and conditions on which and the period for which the Member is relieved of such obligation.

CHAPTER XVIII - DISPUTES AND COMPLAINTS

Article 61

Disputes and Complaints

(1) Any dispute concerning the interpretation or application of the Agreement which is not settled by negotiation, shall, at the request of any Member party to the dispute, be referred to the Council for decision.

(2) In any case where a dispute has been referred to the Council under paragraph (1) of this Article, a majority of Members, or Members holding not less than one-third of the total votes, may require the Council, after discussion, to seek the opinion of the advisory panel referred to in paragraph (3) of this Article on the issues in dispute before giving its decision.

(3) (a) Unless the Council unanimously agrees otherwise, the panel shall consist of:

---

[1]TS 993; 59 Stat. 1031.

    (i) two persons, one having wide experience in matters of the kind in dispute and the other having legal standing and experience, nominated by the exporting Members;

    (ii) two such persons nominated by the importing Members; and

    (iii) a chairman selected unanimously by the four persons nominated under (i) and (ii), or, if they fail to agree, by the Chairman of the Council.

    (b) Persons from countries whose Governments are Contracting Parties to this Agreement shall be eligible to serve on the advisory panel.

    (c) Persons appointed to the advisory panel shall act in their personal capacities and without instructions from any Government.

    (d) The expenses of the advisory panel shall be paid by the Council.

    (4) The opinion of the advisory panel and the reasons therefor shall be submitted to the Council which, after considering all the relevant information, shall decide the dispute.

    (5) Any complaint that any Member has failed to fulfil its obligations under the Agreement shall, at the request of the Member making the complaint, be referred to the Council, which shall make a decision on the matter.

    (6) No Member shall be found to have committed a breach of its obligations under the Agreement except by a distributed simple majority vote. Any finding that a Member is in breach of the Agreement shall specify the nature of the breach.

    (7) If the Council finds that a Member has committed a breach of the Agreement, it may, without prejudice to other enforcement measures provided for in other articles of the Agreement, by a distributed two-thirds majority vote, suspend that Member's voting right in the Council and its right to have its votes cast in the Board until it fulfils its obligations, or the Council may take action requiring compulsory withdrawal under Article 69.

CHAPTER XIX - FINAL PROVISIONS

Article 62

Signature

    The Agreement shall be open for signature at United Nations Headquarters until and including 30 November 1962 by any Government

invited to the United Nations Coffee Conference, 1962, and by the
Government of any State represented before independence as a dependent territory at that Conference.

Article 63

Ratification

The Agreement shall be subject to ratification or acceptance
by the signatory Governments in accordance with their respective
constitutional procedures. Instruments of ratification or acceptance
shall be deposited with the Secretary-General of the United Nations not
later than 31 December 1963. Each Government depositing an instrument of ratification or acceptance shall, at the time of such
deposit, indicate whether it is joining the Organization as an exporting
Member or an importing Member, as defined in paragraphs (7) and
(8) of Article 2.

Article 64

Entry into Force

(1) The Agreement shall enter into force between those Governments which have deposited instruments of ratification or acceptance
when Governments representing at least twenty exporting countries
having at least 80 percent of total exports in the year 1961, as specified in Annex D, and Governments representing at least ten importing
countries having at least 80 percent of world imports in the same
year, as specified in the same Annex, have deposited such instruments.
The Agreement shall enter into force for any Government which subsequently deposits an instrument of ratification, acceptance or accession on the date of such deposit.

(2) The Agreement may enter into force provisionally.[1] For
this purpose, a notification by a signatory Government containing
an undertaking to seek ratification or acceptance in accordance with
its constitutional procedures as rapidly as possible, which is received
by the Secretary-General of the United Nations not later than 30 December 1963, shall be regarded as equal in effect to an instrument of
ratification or acceptance. It is understood that a Government which
gives such a notification will provisionally apply the Agreement and
be provisionally regarded as a party thereto until either it deposits
its instrument of ratification or acceptance or until 31 December
1963, whichever is earlier.

---

[1]July 1, 1963, with respect to the United States of America
and certain other countries as specified in a circular communication
dated July 9, 1963, from the Secretary-General of the United Nations.

(3) The Secretary-General of the United Nations shall convene the first session of the Council, to be held in London within 30 days after the Agreement enters into force.

(4) Whether or not the Agreement has provisionally entered into force in accordance with paragraph (2) of this Article, if by 31 December 1963 it has not definitively entered into force in accordance with paragraph (1), those Governments which have by that date deposited instruments of ratification or acceptance may consult together to consider what action the situation requires, and may, by mutual consent, decide that it shall enter into force among themselves.

Article 65

Accession

The Government of any State Member of the United Nations or any of its specialized agencies and any Government invited to the United Nations Coffee Conference, 1962, may accede to this Agreement upon conditions that shall be established by the Council. In establishing such conditions the Council shall, if such country is not listed in Annex A, establish a basic export quota for it. If such country is listed in Annex A, the respective basic export quota specified therein shall be the basic export quota for that country unless the Council decides otherwise by a distributed two-thirds majority vote. Each Government depositing an instrument of accession shall, at the time of such deposit, indicate whether it is joining the Organization as an exporting Member or an importing Member, as defined in paragraphs (7) and (8) of Article 2.

Article 66

Reservations

Reservations may not be made with respect to any of the provisions of the Agreement.

Article 67

Notifications in respect of Dependent Territories

(1) Any Government may, at the time of signature or deposit of an instrument of acceptance, ratification or accession, or at any time thereafter, by notification to the Secretary-General of the United Nations, declare that the Agreement shall extend to any of the territories for whose international relations it is responsible, and the Agreement shall extend to the territories named therein from the date of such notification.

(2) Any Contracting Party which desires to exercise its rights under Article 4 in respect of any of its dependent territories, or which desires to authorize one of its dependent territories to become part of a Member group formed under Article 5 or 6, may do so by making a notification to that effect to the Secretary-General of the United Nations, either at the time of the deposit of its instrument of ratification, acceptance or accession, or at any later time.

(3) Any Contracting Party which has made a declaration under paragraph (1) of this Article may at any time thereafter, by notification to the Secretary-General of the United Nations, declare that the Agreement shall cease to extend to the territory named in the notification, and the Agreement shall cease to extend to such territory from the date of such notification.

(4) The Government of a territory to which the Agreement has been extended under paragraph (1) of this Article and which has subsequently become independent may, within 90 days after the attainment of independence, declare by notification to the Secretary-General of the United Nations that it has assumed the rights and obligations of a Contracting Party to the Agreement. It shall, as from the date of such notification, become a party to the Agreement.

Article 68

Voluntary Withdrawal

No Contracting Party may give notice of voluntary withdrawal from the Agreement before 30 September 1963. Thereafter, any Contracting Party may withdraw from the Agreement at any time by giving a written notice of withdrawal to the Secretary-General of the United Nations. Withdrawal shall become effective 90 days after the notice is received.

Article 69

Compulsory Withdrawal

If the Council determines that any Member has failed to carry out its obligations under the Agreement and that such failure significantly impairs the operations of the Agreement, it may, by a distributed two-thirds majority vote, require the withdrawal of such Member from the Organization. The Council shall immediately notify the Secretary-General of the United Nations of any such decision. Ninety days after the date of the Council's decision, that Member shall cease to be a Member of the Organization, and, if such Member is a Contracting Party, a party to the Agreement.

Article 70

Settlement of Accounts with Withdrawing Members

(1) The Council shall determine any settlement of accounts with a withdrawing Member. The Organization shall retain any amounts already paid by a withdrawing Member, and such Member shall remain bound to pay any amounts due from it to the Organization at the time the withdrawal becomes effective; provided, however, that in the case of a Contracting Party which is unable to accept an amendment and consequently either withdraws or ceases to participate in the Agreement under the provisions of paragraph (2) of Article 73, the Council may determine any settlement of accounts which it finds equitable.

(2) A Member which has withdrawn or which has ceased to participate in the Agreement shall not be entitled to any share of the proceeds of liquidation or the other assets of the Organization upon termination of the Agreement under Article 71.

Article 71

Duration and Termination

(1) The Agreement shall remain in force until the completion of the fifth full coffee year after its entry into force, unless extended under paragraph (2) of this Article, or earlier terminated under paragraph (3).

(2) The Council, during the fifth full coffee year after the Agreement enters into force, may, by vote of a majority of the Members having not less than a distributed two-thirds majority of the total votes, either decide to renegotiate the Agreement, or to extend it for such period as the Council shall determine.

(3) The Council may at any time, by vote of a majority of the Members having not less than a distributed two-thirds majority of the total votes, decide to terminate the Agreement. Such termination shall take effect on such date as the Council shall decide.

(4) Notwithstanding termination of the Agreement, the Council shall remain in being for as long as necessary to carry out the liquidation of the Organization, settlement of its accounts, and disposal of its assets, and shall have during that period such powers and functions as may be necessary for those purposes.

Article 72

Review

In order to review the Agreement, the Council shall hold a special session during the last six months of the coffee year ending 30 September 1965.

Article 73

Amendment

(1) The Council may, by a distributed two-thirds majority vote, recommend an amendment of the Agreement to the Contracting Parties. The amendment shall become effective 100 days after the Secretary-General of the United Nations has received notifications of acceptance from Contracting Parties representing at least 75 percent of the exporting countries holding at least 85 percent of the votes of the exporting Members, and from Contracting Parties representing at least 75 percent of the importing countries holding at least 80 percent of the votes of the importing Members. The Council may fix a time within which each Contracting Party shall notify the Secretary-General of the United Nations of its acceptance of the amendment, and, if the amendment has not become effective by such time, it shall be considered withdrawn. The Council shall provide the Secretary-General with the information necessary to determine whether the amendment has become effective.

(2) Any Contracting Party, or any dependent territory which is either a Member or a party to a Member group, on behalf of which notification of acceptance of an amendment has not been made by the date on which such amendment becomes effective, shall as of that date cease to participate in the Agreement.

Article 74

Notifications by the Secretary-General

The Secretary-General of the United Nations shall notify all Governments represented by delegates or observers at the United Nations Coffee Conference, 1962, and all other Governments of States Members of the United Nations or of any of its specialized agencies, of each deposit of an instrument of ratification, acceptance or accession, and of the dates on which the Agreement comes provisionally and definitively into force. The Secretary-General of the United Nations shall also notify all Contracting Parties of each notification under Article 5, 67, 68 or 69; of the date to which the Agreement is extended or on which it is terminated under Article 71; and of the date on which an amendment becomes effective under Article 73.

IN WITNESS WHEREOF the undersigned, having been duly authorized to this effect by their respective Governments, have signed this Agreement on the dates appearing opposite their signatures.

The texts of this Agreement in the English, French, Russian, Spanish and Portuguese languages shall all be equally authentic.

The originals shall be deposited in the archives of the United Nations, and the Secretary-General of the United Nations shall transmit certified copies thereof to each signatory and acceding Government.

MULTILATERAL

International Coffee Agreement, 1968

Open for signature at United Nations Headquarters March 18-31,
    1968;
Ratification advised by the Senate of the United States of America
    June 28, 1968;
Ratified by the President of the United States of America July 10,
    1968;
Ratification of the United States of America deposited with the General
    Secretariat of the United Nations November 1, 1968;
Proclaimed by the President of the United States of America November
    18, 1968;
Entered into force provisionally October 1, 1968.

BY THE PRESIDENT OF
THE UNITED STATES OF AMERICA

A PROCLAMATION

WHEREAS the International Coffee Agreement, 1968, was open
for signature at the United Nations Headquarters in New York until
and including March 31, 1968, and was signed by the respective
Plenipotentiaries of the Government of the United States of America
and the Governments of certain other countries;

WHEREAS the text of the said Agreement, in the English, French,
Portuguese, Russian, and Spanish languages as certified by the General
Secretariat of the United Nations, is word for word as follows:

INTERNATIONAL COFFEE AGREEMENT, 1968

Preamble

The Governments Parties to this Agreement,

Recognizing the exceptional importance of coffee to the economies of many countries which are largely dependent upon this commodity for their export earnings and thus for the continuation of their
development programmes in the social and economic fields;

215

Considering that close international co-operation on coffee marketing will stimulate the economic diversification and development of coffee-producing countries and thus contribute to a strengthening of the political and economic bonds between producers and consumers;

Finding reason to expect a tendency toward persistent disequilibrium between production and consumption, accumulation of burdensome stocks, and pronounced fluctuations in prices, which can be harmful both to producers and to consumers;

Believing that, in the absence of international measures, this situation cannot be corrected by normal market forces; and

Noting the renegotiation by the International Coffee Council of the International Coffee Agreement, 1962,[1]

Have agreed as follows:

CHAPTER I - OBJECTIVES

Article 1

Objectives

The objectives of the Agreement are:

(1) to achieve a reasonable balance between supply and demand on a basis which will assure adequate supplies of coffee to consumers and markets for coffee to producers at equitable prices and which will bring about long-term equilibrium between production and consumption:

(2) to alleviate the serious hardship caused by burdensome surpluses and excessive fluctuations in the prices of coffee which are harmful both to producers and to consumers;

(3) to contribute to the development of productive resources and to the promotion and maintenance of employment and income in the Member countries, thereby helping to bring about fair wages, higher living standards, and better working conditions;

(4) to assist in increasing the purchasing power of coffee-exporting countries by keeping prices at equitable levels and by increasing consumption;

---

[1]TIAS 5505; 14 UST 1911. (Footnote added by the Department of State.)

(5) to encourage the consumption of coffee by every possible means; and

(6) in general, in recognition of the relationship of the trade in coffee to the economic stability of markets for industrial products, to further international co-operation in connexion with world coffee problems.

CHAPTER II - DEFINITIONS

Article 2

Definitions

For the purposes of the Agreement:

(1) "Coffee" means the beans and berries of the coffee tree, whether parchment, green or roasted, and includes ground, decaffeinated, liquid and soluble coffee. These terms shall have the following meaning:

(a) "green coffee" means all coffee in the naked bean form before roasting;

(b) "coffee-berries" means the complete fruit of the coffee tree; to find the equivalent of coffee berries to green coffee, multiply the net weight of the dried coffee berries by 0.50;

(c) "parchment coffee" means the green coffee bean contained in the parchment skin; to find the equivalent of parchment coffee to green coffee, multiply the net weight of the parchment coffee by 0.80;

(d) "roasted coffee" means green coffee roasted to any degree and includes ground coffee; to find the equivalent of roasted coffee to green coffee, multiply the net weight of roasted coffee by 1.19;

(e) "decaffeinated coffee" means green, roasted or soluble coffee from which caffein has been extracted; to find the equivalent of decaffeinated coffee to green coffee, multiply the net weight of the decaffeinated coffee in green, roasted or soluble form by 1.00, 1.19 or 3.00 respectively;

(f) "liquid coffee" means the water-soluble solids derived from roasted coffee and put into liquid form; to find the equivalent of liquid to green coffee, multiply the net weight of the dried coffee solids contained in the liquid coffee by 3.00;

(g) "soluble coffee" means the dried water-soluble solids derived from roasted coffee; to find the equivalent of soluble coffee to green coffee, multiply the net weight of the soluble coffee by 3.00.

(2) "Bag" means 60 kilogrammes or 132.276 pounds of green coffee; "ton" means a metric ton of 1,000 kilogrammes or 2,204.6 pounds; and "pound" means 453.597 grammes.

(3) "Coffee year" means the period of one year, from 1 October through 30 September.

(4) "Export of Coffee" means, except as otherwise provided in Article 39, any shipment of coffee which leaves the territory of the country where the coffee was grown.

(5) "Organization", "Council" and "Board" mean, respectively, the International Coffee Organization, the International Coffee Council, and the Executive Board referred to in Article 7 of the Agreement.

(6) "Member" means a Contracting Party; a dependent territory or territories in respect of which separate Membership has been declared under Article 4; or two or more Contracting Parties or dependent territories, or both, which participate in the Organization as a Member group under Article 5 or 6.

(7) "Exporting Member" or "exporting country" means a Member or country, respectively, which is a net exporter of coffee; that is, whose exports exceed its imports.

(8) "Importing Member" or "importing country" means a Member or country, respectively, which is a net importer of coffee; that is, whose imports exceed its exports.

(9) "Producing Member" or "producing country" means a Member or country, respectively, which grows coffee in commercially significant quantities.

(10) "Distributed simple majority vote" means a majority of the votes cast by exporting Members present and voting, and a majority of the votes cast by importing Members present and voting, counted separately.

(11) "Distributed two-thirds majority vote" means a two-thirds majority of the votes cast by exporting Members present and voting and a two-thirds majority of the votes cast by importing Members present and voting, counted separately.

(12) "Entry into force" means, except as otherwise provided, the date on which the Agreement enters into force, whether provisionally or definitively.

(13) "Exportable production" means the total production of coffee of an exporting country in a given coffee year less the amount destined for domestic consumption in the same year.

(14) "Availability for export" means the exportable production of an exporting country in a given coffee year plus accumulated stocks from previous years.

(15) "Export entitlement" means the total quantity of coffee which a Member is authorized to export under the various provisions of the Agreement, but excluding exports which under the provisions of Article 40 are not charged to quotas.

(16) "Authorized exports" means actual exports covered by the export entitlement.

(17) "Permitted exports" means the sum of authorized exports and exports which under the provisions of Article 40 are not charged to quotas.

CHAPTER III - MEMBERSHIP

Article 3

Membership in the Organization

(1) Each Contracting Party, together with those of its dependent territories to which the Agreement is extended under paragraph (1) of Article 65, shall constitute a single Member of the Organization, except as otherwise provided under Articles 4, 5 and 6.

(2) A Member may change its category of Membership, previously declared on approval, ratification, acceptance or accession to the Agreement, on such conditions as the Council may agree.

(3) On application by two or more importing Members for a change in the form of their participation in the Agreement and/or their representation in the Organization, and notwithstanding other provisions of the Agreement, the Council may, after consultation with the Members concerned, determine the conditions which shall be applicable to such changed participation and/or representation.

Article 4

Separate Membership in respect of
Dependent Territories

Any Contracting Party which is a net importer of coffee may, at any time, by appropriate notification in accordance with paragraph (2) of Article 65, declare that it is participating in the Organization separately with respect to any of its dependent territories which are net exporters of coffee and which it designates. In such case, the metropolitan territory and its non-designated dependent territories will have a single Membership, and its designated dependent territories, either individually or collectively as the notification indicates, will have separate Membership.

Article 5

Group Membership upon Joining the Organization

(1) Two or more Contracting Parties which are net exporters of coffee may, by appropriate notification to the Secretary-General of the United Nations at the time of deposit of their respective instruments of approval, ratification, acceptance or accession and to the Council, declare that they are joining the Organization as a Member group. A dependent territory to which the Agreement has been extended under paragraph (1) of Article 65 may constitute part of such a Member group if the Government of the State responsible for its international relations has given appropriate notification thereof under paragraph (2) of Article 65. Such Contracting Parties and dependent territories must satisfy the following conditions:

(a) they shall declare their willingness to accept responsibility for group obligations in an individual as well as a group capacity;

(b) they shall subsequently provide sufficient evidence to the Council that the group has the organization necessary to implement a common coffee policy, and that they have the means of complying, together with the other parties to the group, with their obligations under the Agreement; and

(c) they shall subsequently provide evidence to the Council either:

    (i) that they have been recognized as a group in a previous international coffee agreement; or

    (ii) that they have:

(a) a common or co-ordinated commercial and economic policy in relation to coffee; and

(b) a co-ordinated monetary and financial policy, as well as the organs necessary for implementing such a policy, so that the Council is satisfied that the Member group can comply with the spirit of group membership and the group obligations involved.

(2) The Member group shall constitute a single Member of the Organization, except that each party to the group shall be treated as if it were a single Member as regards all matters arising under the following provisions:

(a) Chapters XII, XIII and XVI;

(b) Articles 10, 11 and 19 of Chapter IV; and

(c) Article 68 of Chapter XX.

(3) The Contracting Parties and dependent territories joining as a Member group shall specify the Government or organization which will represent them in the Council as regards all matters arising under the Agreement other than those specified in paragraph (2) of this Article.

(4) The Member group's voting rights shall be as follows:

(a) the Member group shall have the same number of basic votes as a single Member country joining the Organization in an individual capacity. These basic votes shall be attributed to and exercised by the Government or organization representing the group;

(b) in the event of a vote on any matters arising under provisions specified in paragraph (2) of this Article, the parties to the Member group may exercise separately the votes attributed to them by the provisions of paragraph (3) of Article 12 as if each were an individual Member of the Organization, except for the basic votes, which shall remain attributable only to the Government or organization representing the group.

(5) Any Contracting Party or dependent territory which is a party to a Member group may, by notification to the Council, withdraw from that group and become a separate Member. Such withdrawal

shall take effect upon receipt of the notification by the Council. In case of such withdrawal from a group, or in case a party to a group ceases, by withdrawal from the Organization or otherwise, to be such a party, the remaining parties to the group may apply to the Council to maintain the group, and the group shall continue to exist unless the Council disapproves the application. If the Member group is dissolved, each former party to the group will become a separate Member. A Member which has ceased to be a party to a group may not, as long as the Agreement remains in force, again become a party to a group.

Article 6

Subsequent Group Membership

Two or more exporting Members may, at any time after the Agreement has entered into force with respect to them, apply to the Council to form a Member group. The Council shall approve the application if it finds that the Members have made a declaration, and have provided evidence, satisfying the requirements of paragraph (1) of Article 5. Upon such approval, the Member group shall be subject to the provisions of paragraphs (2), (3), (4) and (5) of that Article.

CHAPTER IV - ORGANIZATION AND ADMINISTRATION

Article 7

Seat and Structure of the International Coffee Organization

(1) The International Coffee Organization established under the 1962 Agreement shall continue in being to administer the provisions and supervise the operation of the Agreement.

(2) The seat of the Organization shall be in London unless the Council by a distributed two-thirds majority vote decides otherwise.

(3) The Organization shall function through the International Coffee Council, its Executive Board, its Executive Director and its staff.

Article 8

Composition of the International Coffee Council

(1) The highest authority of the Organization shall be the International Coffee Council, which shall consist of all the Members of the Organization.

(2) Each Member shall be represented on the Council by a representative and one or more alternates. A Member may also designate one or more advisers to accompany its representative or alternates.

Article 9

Powers and Functions of the Council

(1) All powers specifically conferred by the Agreement shall be vested in the Council, which shall have the powers and perform the functions necessary to carry out the provisions of the Agreement.

(2) The Council shall, by a distributed two-thirds majority vote, establish such rules and regulations, including its own rules of procedure and the financial and staff regulations of the Organization, as are necessary to carry out the provisions of the Agreement and are consistent therewith. The Council may, in its rules of procedure, provide a procedure whereby it may, without meeting, decide specific questions.

(3) The Council shall also keep such records as are required to perform its functions under the Agreement and such other records as it considers desirable. The Council shall publish an annual report.

Article 10

Election of the Chairman and Vice-Chairmen of the Council

(1) The Council shall elect, for each coffee year, a Chairman and a first, a second and a third Vice-Chairman.

(2) As a general rule, the Chairman and the first Vice-Chairman shall both be elected either from among the representatives of exporting

Members, or from among the representatives of importing Members, and the second and the third Vice-Chairmen, shall be elected from representatives of the other category of Members. These offices shall alternate each coffee year between the two categories of Members.

(3) Neither the Chairman nor any Vice-Chairman acting as Chairman shall have the right to vote. His alternate will in such case exercise the Member's voting rights.

Article 11

Sessions of the Council

As a general rule, the Council shall hold regular sessions twice a year. It may hold special sessions if it so decides. Special sessions shall also be held when either the Executive Board, or any five Members, or a Member or Members having at least 200 votes so request. Notice of sessions shall be given at least thirty days in advance, except in cases of emergency. Sessions shall be held at the seat of the Organization, unless the Council decides otherwise.

Article 12

Votes

(1) The Exporting Members shall together hold 1,000 votes and the importing Members shall together hold 1,000 votes, distributed within each category of Members—that is, exporting and importing Members, respectively—as provided in the following paragraphs of this Article.

(2) Each Member shall have five basic votes, provided that the total number of basic votes within each category of Members does not exceed 150. Should there be more than thirty exporting Members or more than thirty importing Members, the number of basic votes for each Member within that category of Members shall be adjusted so as to keep the number of basic votes for each category of Members within the maximum of 150.

(3) The remaining votes of exporting Members shall be divided among those Members in proportion to their respective basic export quotas, except that in the event of a vote on any matter arising under the provisions specified in paragraph (2) of Article 5, the remaining votes of a Member group shall be divided among the parties to that group in proportion to their respective participation in the basic export quota of the Member group. Any exporting Member to which

a basic quota has not been allotted shall receive no share of these remaining votes.

(4) The remaining votes of importing Members shall be divided among those Members in proportion to the average volume of their respective coffee imports in the preceding three-year period.

(5) The distribution of votes shall be determined by the Council at the beginning of each coffee year and shall remain in effect during that year, except as provided in paragraph (6) of this Article.

(6) The Council shall provide for the redistribution of votes in accordance with this Article whenever there is a change in the Membership of the Organization, or if the voting rights of a Member are suspended or regained under the provisions of Articles 25, 38, 45, 48, 54 or 59.

(7) No Member shall hold more than 400 votes.

(8) There shall be no fractional votes.

Article 13

Voting Procedure of the Council

(1) Each representative shall be entitled to cast the number of votes held by the Member represented by him, and cannot divide its votes. He may, however, cast differently any votes which he exercises pursuant to paragraph (2) of this Article.

(2) Any exporting Member may authorize any other exporting Member, and any importing Member may authorize any other importing Member, to represent its interests and to exercise its right to vote at any meeting or meetings of the Council. The limitation provided for in paragraph (7) of Article 12 shall not apply in this case.

Article 14

Decisions of the Council

(1) All decisions of the Council shall be taken, and all recommendations shall be made, by a distributed simple majority vote unless otherwise provided in the Agreement.

(2) The following procedure shall apply with respect to any action by the Council which under the Agreement requires a distributed two-thirds majority vote:

(a) if a distributed two-thirds majority vote is not obtained because of the negative vote of three or less exporting or three or less importing Members, the proposal shall, if the Council so decides by a majority of the Members present and by a distributed simple majority vote, be put to a vote again within 48 hours;

(b) if a distributed two-thirds majority vote is again not obtained because of the negative vote of two or less importing or two or less exporting Members, the proposal shall, if the Council so decides by a majority of the Members present and by a distributed simple majority vote, be put to a vote again within 24 hours;

(c) if a distributed two-thirds majority vote is not obtained in the third vote because of the negative vote of one exporting Member or one importing Member, the proposal shall be considered adopted;

(d) if the Council fails to put a proposal to a further vote, it shall be considered rejected.

(3) The Members undertake to accept as binding all decisions of the Council under the provisions of the Agreement.

Article 15

Composition of the Board

(1) The Executive Board shall consist of eight exporting Members and eight importing Members, elected for each coffee year in accordance with Article 16. Members may be re-elected.

(2) Each member of the Board shall appoint one representative and one or more alternates.

(3) The Chairman of the Board shall be appointed by the Council for each coffee year and may be re-appointed. He shall not have the right to vote. If a representative is appointed Chairman, his alternate will have the right to vote in his place.

(4) The Board shall normally meet at the seat of the Organization, but may meet elsewhere.

Article 16

Election of the Board

(1) The exporting and the importing Members on the Board shall be elected in the Council by the exporting and the importing Members of the Organization respectively. The election within each category shall be held in accordance with the following paragraphs of this Article.

(2) Each Member shall cast all the votes to which it is entitled under Article 12 for a single candidate. A Member may cast for another candidate any votes which it exercises pursuant to paragraph (2) of Article 13.

(3) The eight candidates receiving the largest number of votes shall be elected; however, no candidate shall be elected on the first ballot unless it receives at least 75 votes.

(4) If under the provisions of paragraph (3) of this Article less than eight candidates are elected on the first ballot, further ballots shall be held in which only Members which did not vote for any of the candidates elected shall have the right to vote. In each further ballot, the minimum number of votes required for election shall be successively diminished by five until eight candidates are elected.

(5) Any Member who did not vote for any of the Members elected shall assign its votes to one of them, subject to paragraphs (6) and (7) of this Article.

(6) A Member shall be deemed to have received the number of votes originally cast for it when it was elected and, in addition, the number of votes assigned to it, provided that the total number of votes shall not exceed 499 for any Member elected.

(7) If the votes deemed received by an elected Member would otherwise exceed 499, Members which voted for or assigned their votes to such elected Member shall arrange among themselves for one or more of them to withdraw their votes from that Member and assign or reassign them to another elected Member so that the votes received by each elected Member shall not exceed the limit of 499.

Article 17

Competence of the Board

(1) The Board shall be responsible to and work under the general direction of the Council.

(2) The Council by a distributed simple majority vote may delegate to the Board the exercise of any or all of its powers, other than the following:

(a) approval of the administrative budget and assessment of contributions under Article 24;

(b) determination of quotas under the Agreement with the exception of adjustments made under the provisions of Article 35 paragraph (3) and of Article 37;

(c) suspension of the voting rights of a Member under Articles 45 or 59;

(d) establishment or revision of individual country and world production goals under Article 48;

(e) establishment of a policy relative to stocks under Article 49;

(f) waiver of the obligations of a Member under Article 57;

(g) decision of disputes under Article 59;

(h) establishment of conditions for accession under Article 63;

(i) a decision to require the withdrawal of a Member under Article 67;

(j) extension or termination of the Agreement under Article 69; and

(k) recommendation of amendments to Members under Article 70.

(3) The Council by a distributed simple majority vote may at any time revoke any delegation of powers to the Board.

Article 18

Voting Procedure of the Board

(1) Each member of the Board shall be entitled to cast the number of votes received by it under the provisions of paragraphs (6) and (7) of Article 16. Voting by proxy shall not be allowed. A member may not split its votes.

(2) Any action taken by the Board shall require the same majority as such action would require if taken by the Council.

Article 19

Quorum for the Council and the Board

(1) The quorum for any meeting of the Council shall be the presence of a majority of the Members representing a distributed two-thirds majority of the total votes. If there is no quorum on the day appointed for the opening of any Council session, or if in the course of any Council session there is no quorum at three successive meetings, the Council shall be convened seven days later; at that time and throughout the remainder of that session the quorum shall be the presence of a majority of the Members representing a distributed simple majority of the votes. Representation in accordance with paragraph (2) of Article 13 shall be considered as presence.

(2) The quorum for any meeting of the Board shall be the presence of a majority of the members representing a distributed two-thirds majority of the total votes.

Article 20

The Executive Director and the Staff

(1) The Council shall appoint the Executive Director on the recommendation of the Board. The terms of appointment of the Executive Director shall be established by the Council and shall be comparable to those applying to corresponding officials of similar inter-governmental organizations.

(2) The Executive Director shall be the chief administrative officer of the Organization and shall be responsible for the performance of any duties devolving upon him in the administration of the Agreement.

(3) The Executive Director shall appoint the staff in accordance with regulations established by the Council.

(4) Neither the Executive Director nor any member of the staff shall have any financial interest in the coffee industry, coffee trade, or coffee transportation.

(5) In the performance of their duties, the Executive Director and the staff shall not seek or receive instructions from any Member or from any other authority external to the Organization. They shall refrain from any action which might reflect on their position as international officials responsible only to the Organization. Each Member undertakes to respect the exclusively international character of the responsibilities of the Executive Director and the staff and not to seek to influence them in the discharge of their responsibilities.

Article 21

Co-operation with other Organizations

The Council may make whatever arrangements are desirable for consultation and co-operation with the United Nations and its specialized agencies and with other appropriate inter-governmental organizations. The Council may invite these organizations and any organizations concerned with coffee to send observers to its meetings.

CHAPTER V - PRIVILEGES AND IMMUNITIES

Article 22

Privileges and Immunities

(1) The Organization shall have legal personality. It shall in particular have the capacity to contract, acquire and dispose of movable and immovable property and to institute legal proceedings.

(2) The Government of the country in which the headquarters of the Organization is situated (hereinafter referred to as "the host Government") shall conclude with the Organization as soon as possible an agreement to be approved by the Council relating to the status, privileges and immunities of the Organization, of its Executive Director and its staff and of representatives of Members while in the territory of the host Government for the purpose of exercising their functions.

(3) The agreement envisaged in paragraph (2) of this Article shall be independent of the present Agreement and shall prescribe the conditions for its termination.

(4) Unless any other taxation arrangements are implemented under the agreement envisaged in paragraph (2) of this Article the host Government:

> (a) shall grant exemption from taxation on the remuneration paid by the Organization to its employees, except that such exemption need not apply to nationals of that country; and

> (b) shall grant exemption from taxation on the assets, income and other property of the Organization.

(5) Following the approval of the agreement envisaged in paragraph (2) of this Article, the Organization may conclude with one or more other Members agreements to be approved by the Council relating to such privileges and immunities as may be necessary for the proper functioning of the International Coffee Agreement.

CHAPTER VI - FINANCE

Article 23

Finance

(1) The expenses of delegations to the Council, representatives on the Board, and representatives on any of the committees of the Council or the Board shall be met by their respective Governments.

(2) The other expenses necessary for the administration of the Agreement shall be met by annual contributions from the Members assessed in accordance with Article 24. However, the Council may levy fees for specific services.

(3) The financial year of the Organization shall be the same as the coffee year.

Article 24

Determination of the Budget and Assessment of Contributions

(1) During the second half of each financial year the Council shall approve the administrative budget of the Organization for the following financial year and shall assess the contribution of each Member to that budget.

(2) The contribution of each Member to the budget for each financial year shall be in the proportion which the number of its votes

at the time the budget for that financial year is approved bears to the total votes of all the Members. However, if there is any change in the distribution of votes among Members in accordance with the provisions of paragraph (5) of Article 12 at the beginning of the financial year for which contributions are assessed, such contributions shall be correspondingly adjusted for that year. In determining contributions, the votes of each Member shall be calculated without regard to the suspension of any Member's voting rights or any redistribution of votes resulting therefrom.

(3) The initial contribution of any Member joining the Organization after the entry into force of the Agreement shall be assessed by the Council on the basis of the number of votes to be held by it and the period remaining in the current financial year, but the assessments made upon other Members for the current financial year shall not be altered.

Article 25

Payment of Contributions

(1) Contributions to the administrative budget for each financial year shall be payable in freely convertible currency, and shall become due on the first day of that financial year.

(2) If any Member fails to pay its full contribution to the administrative budget within six months of the date on which the contribution is due, both its voting rights in the Council and its right to have its votes cast in the Board shall be suspended until such contribution has been paid. However, unless the Council by a distributed two-thirds majority vote so decides, such Member shall not be deprived of any of its other rights nor relieved of any of its obligations under the Agreement.

(3) Any Member whose voting rights have been suspended, either under paragraph (2) of this Article or under Articles 38, 45, 48, 54 or 59 shall nevertheless remain responsible for the payment of its contribution.

Article 26

Audit and Publication of Accounts

As soon as possible after the close of each financial year an independently audited statement of the Organization's receipts and expenditures during that financial year shall be presented to the Council for approval and publication.

CHAPTER VII - REGULATION OF EXPORTS

Article 27

General Undertakings by Members

(1) The Members undertake to conduct their trade policy so that the objectives set forth in Article 1, and in particular paragraph (4) of that Article, may be achieved. They agree on the desirability of operating the Agreement in a manner such that the real income derived from the export of coffee could be progressively increased so as to make it consonant with their needs for foreign exchange to support their programmes for social and economic progress.

(2) To attain these purposes through the fixing of quotas as provided for in this Chapter and in other ways carrying out the provisions of the Agreement, the Members agree on the necessity of assuring that the general level of coffee prices does not decline below the general level of such prices in 1962.

(3) The Members further agree on the desirability of assuring to consumers prices which are equitable and which will not hamper a desirable increase in consumption.

Article 28

Basic Export Quotas

Beginning on 1 October 1968 the exporting countries shall have the basic export quotas specified in Annex A.

Article 29

Basic Export Quota of a Member Group

Where two or more countries listed in Annex A form a Member group in accordance with Article 5, the basic export quotas specified for those countries in Annex A shall be added together and the combined total treated as a single basic quota for the purposes of this Chapter.

Article 30

Fixing of Annual Export Quotas

(1) At least 30 days before the beginning of each coffee year

the Council by a two-thirds majority vote shall adopt an estimate of total world imports and exports for the following coffee year and an estimate of probable exports from non-member countries.

(2) In the light of these estimates the Council shall forthwith fix annual export quotas for all exporting Members. Such annual export quotas shall be the same percentage of the basic export quotas specified in Annex A, save for those exporting Members whose annual quotas are subject to the provisions of paragraph (2) of Article 31.

Article 31

Additional Provisions Concerning
Basic and Annual Export Quotas

(1) A basic quota shall not be allotted to an exporting Member whose average annual authorized exports of coffee for the preceding three year period were less than 100,000 bags and its annual export quota shall be calculated in accordance with paragraph (2) of this Article. When the annual export quota of any such Member reaches 100,000 bags the Council shall establish a basic quota for the exporting Member concerned.

(2) Without prejudice to the provisions of footnote[2] of Annex A to the Agreement each exporting Member to which a basic quota has not been allotted shall have in the coffee year 1968-69 the quota indicated in footnote[1] of Annex A to the Agreement. In each of the subsequent years the quota, subject to the provisions of paragraph (3) of this Article, shall be increased by 10 percent of that initial quota until the maximum of 100,000 bags mentioned in paragraph (1) of this Article is reached.

(3) Not later than 31 July of each year, each Member concerned shall notify the Executive Director, for the information of the Council, of the amount of coffee likely to be available for export under quota during the next coffee year. The quota for the next coffee year shall be the amount thus indicated by the exporting Member provided that such amount is within the permissible limit defined in paragraph (2) Article.

(4) Exporting Members to which basic quotas have not been allotted shall be subject to the provisions of Articles 27, 29, 32, 34, 35, 38 and 40.

(5) Any Trust Territory, administered under a trusteeship agreement with the United Nations, whose annual exports to countries other than the Administering Authority do not exceed 100,000 bags

shall not be subject to the quota provisions of the Agreement so long
as its exports do not exceed that quantity.

Article 32

Fixing of Quarterly Export Quotas

(1) Immediately following the fixing of the annual export
quotas the Council shall fix quarterly export quotas for each exporting
Member for the purpose of keeping supply in reasonable balance
with estimated demand throughout the coffee year.

(2) These quotas shall be, as nearly as possible, 25 percent
of the annual export quota of each Member during the coffee year.
No Member shall be allowed to export more than 30 percent in the
first quarter, 60 percent in the first two quarters, and 80 percent in
the first three quarters of the coffee year. If exports by any Member
in one quarter are less than its quota for that quarter, the outstanding
balance shall be added to its quota for the following quarter of that
coffee year.

Article 33

Adjustment of Annual Export Quotas

If market conditions so require, the Council may review the
quota situation and may vary the percentage of basic export quotas
fixed under paragraph (2) of Article 30. In so doing, the Council
shall have regard to any likely shortfalls by Members.

Article 34

Notification of Shortfalls

(1) Exporting Members undertake to notify the Council as
early in the coffee year as possible but not later than the end of the
eighth month thereof, as well as at such later dates as the Council
may require, whether they have sufficient coffee available to export
the full amount of their quota for that year.

(2) The Council shall take into account these notifications in
determining whether or not to adjust the level of export quotas in
accordance with Article 33.

Article 35

Adjustment of Quarterly Export Quotas

(1) The Council shall in the circumstances set out in this Article vary the quarterly export quotas fixed for each Member under paragraph (1) of Article 32.

(2) If the Council varies the annual export quotas as provided in Article 33, then that change shall be reflected in the quotas for the current quarter, current and remaining quarters, or the remaining quarters of the coffee year.

(3) Apart from the adjustment provided for in the preceding paragraph, the Council may, if it finds the market situation so requires, make adjustments among the current and remaining quarterly export quotas for the same coffee year, without, however, altering the annual export quotas.

(4) If on account of exceptional circumstances an exporting Member considers that the limitations provided in paragraph (2) of Article 32 would be likely to cause serious harm to its economy, the Council may, at the request of that Member, take appropriate action under Article 57. The Member concerned must furnish evidence of harm and provide adequate guarantees concerning the maintenance of price stability. The Council shall not, however, in any event, authorize a Member to export more than 35 percent of its annual export quota in the first quarter, 65 percent in the first two quarters, and 85 percent in the first three quarters of the coffee year.

(5) All Members recognize that marked price rises or falls occurring within brief periods may unduly distort underlying trends in price, cause grave concern to both producers and consumers, and jeopardize the attainment of the objectives of the Agreement. Accordingly, if such movements in general price levels occur within brief periods, Members may request a meeting of the Council which, by a distributed simple majority vote, may revise the total level of the quarterly export quotas in effect.

(6) If the Council finds that a sharp and unusual increase or decrease in the general level of prices is due to artificial manipulation of the coffee market through agreements among importers or exporters or both, it shall then by a simple majority vote decide on what corrective measures should be applied to readjust the total level of the quarterly export quotas in effect.

Article 36

Procedure for Adjusting Export Quotas

(1) Except as provided for in Articles 31 and 37 annual export quotas shall be fixed and adjusted by altering the basic export quota of each Member by the same percentage.

(2) General changes in all quarterly export quotas, made pursuant to paragraphs (2), (3), (5) and (6) of Article 35, shall be applied pro rata to individual quarterly export quotas in accordance with appropriate rules established by the Council. Such rules shall take account of the different percentages of annual export quotas which the different Members have exported or are entitled to export in each quarter of the coffee year.

(3) All decisions by the Council on the fixing and adjustment of annual and quarterly export quotas under Articles 30, 32, 33 and 35 shall be taken, unless otherwise provided, by a distributed two-thirds majority vote.

Article 37

Additional Provisions for Adjusting Export Quotas

(1) In addition to fixing annual export quotas in accordance with estimated total world imports and exports as required by Article 30, the Council shall seek to ensure that:

   (a) supplies of the types of coffee that consumers require are available to them;

   (b) the prices for the different types of coffee are equitable; and

   (c) sharp price fluctuations within brief periods do not occur.

(2) To achieve these objectives the Council may, notwithstanding the provisions of Article 36, adopt a system for the adjustment of annual and quarterly quotas in relation to the movement of the prices of the principal types of coffee. The Council shall annually set a limit not exceeding five percent by which annual quotas may be reduced under any system so established. For the purposes of such a system the Council may establish price differentials and price brackets for

the various types of coffee. In so doing the Council shall take into consideration, among other things, price trends.

(3) Decisions of the Council under the provisions of paragraph (2) of this Article shall be taken by a distributed two-thirds majority vote.

Article 38

Compliance with Export Quotas

(1) Exporting Members subject to quotas shall adopt the measures required to ensure full compliance with all provisions of the Agreement relating to quotas. In addition to any measures it may itself take, the Council by a distributed two-thirds majority vote may require such Members to adopt additional measures for the effective implementation of the quota system provided for in the Agreement.

(2) Exporting Members shall not exceed the annual and quarterly export quotas allocated to them.

(3) If an exporting Member exceeds its quota for any quarter, the Council shall deduct from one or more of its subsequent quotas a quantity equal to 110 percent of that excess.

(4) If an exporting Member for the second time while the Agreement remains in force exceeds its quarterly quota, the Council shall deduct from one or more of its subsequent quotas a total amount equal to twice that excess.

(5) If an exporting Member for a third or subsequent time while the Agreement remains in force exceeds its quarterly quota, the Council shall make the same deduction as provided in paragraph (4) of this Article and the voting rights of the Member shall be suspended until such time as the Council decides whether to take action in accordance with Article 67 to require the withdrawal of such a Member from the Organization.

(6) In accordance with rules established by the Council the deductions in quotas provided for in paragraphs (3), (4) and (5) of this Article and the additional action required by paragraph (5) shall be effected by the Council as soon as the necessary information is received.

Article 39

Shipments of Coffee from Dependent Territories

(1) Subject to paragraph (2) of this Article, the shipment of coffee from any of the dependent territories of a Member to its metropolitan territory or to another of its dependent territories for domestic consumption therein or in any other of its dependent territories shall not be considered as the export of coffee, and shall not be subject to any export quota limitations, provided that the Member concerned enters into arrangements satisfactory to the Council with respect to the control of re-exports and such other matters as the Council may determine to be related to the operation of the Agreement and which arise out of the special relationship between the metropolitan territory of the Member and its dependent territories.

(2) The trade in coffee between a Member and any of its dependent territories which, in accordance with Article 4 or 5, is a separate Member of the Organization or a party to a Member group, shall however be treated, for the purposes of the Agreement, as the export of coffee.

Article 40

Exports not Charged to Quotas

(1) To facilitate the increase of coffee consumption in certain areas of the world having a low per capita consumption and considerable potential for expansion, exports to countries listed in Annex B shall not, subject to the provisions of sub-paragraph 2 (f) of this Article, be charged to quotas. The Council shall review Annex B annually to determine whether any country or countries should be deleted or added, and may, if it so decides, take action accordingly.

(2) The provisions of the following sub-paragraphs shall be applicable to exports to the countries listed in Annex B:

(a) The Council shall prepare annually an estimate of imports for internal consumption by the countries listed in Annex B after reviewing the results obtained in the previous year with regard to the increase of coffee consumption in those countries and taking into account the probable effect of promotion campaigns and trade arrangements. The Council may revise this estimate in the course of the year. Exporting Members shall not in the aggregate export to the countries listed in Annex B more than the quantity set by the Council and for that purpose the Organization shall keep Members informed of current exports to such countries. Exporting Members shall inform the Organization not later than thirty days after the end of each month of all exports made to each of the countries listed in Annex B during that month.

(b) Members shall supply such statistics and other information as the Organization may require to assist it in controlling the flow of coffee to countries listed in Annex B and to ensure that it is consumed in such countries.

(c) Exporting Members shall endeavour to renegotiate existing trade agreements as soon as possible in order to include in them provisions designed to prevent re-exports of coffee from the countries listed in Annex B to traditional markets. Exporting Members shall also include such provisions in all new trade agreements and in all new sales contracts not covered by trade agreements, whether such contracts are negotiated with private traders or with government organizations.

(d) To maintain control at all times of exports to countries listed in Annex B, exporting Members shall clearly mark all coffee bags destined to those countries with the words "New Market" and shall require adequate guarantees to prevent re-exportation or diversion to countries not listed in Annex B. The Council may establish appropriate rules for this purpose. All Members other than those listed in Annex B, shall prohibit, without exception, the entry of all shipments of coffee consigned directly from, or diverted from, any country listed in Annex B, or which bear evidence on the bags or the export documents of having been originally destined to a country listed in Annex B, or which are accompanied by a Certificate showing a destination in a country listed in Annex B or marked "New Market."

(e) The Council shall annually prepare a comprehensive report on the results obtained in the development of coffee markets in the countries listed in Annex B.

(f) If coffee exported by a Member to a country listed in Annex B is re-exported, or diverted to any country not listed in Annex B, the Council shall charge the corresponding amount to the quota of that exporting Member and in addition may, in accordance with rules established by the Council, apply the provisions of paragraph (4) of Article 38. Should there again be a re-exportation from the same country listed in Annex B, the Council shall investigate the case and, if it deems necessary, may at any time delete that country from Annex B.

(3) Exports of coffee beans as raw material for industrial processing for any purposes other than human consumption as a beverage or foodstuff shall not be charged to quotas, provided that the Council is satisfied from information supplied by the exporting Member that the coffee beans are in fact used for such other purposes.

(4) The Council may, upon application by an exporting Member, decide that coffee exports made by that Member for humanitarian or other non-commercial purposes shall not be charged to its quota.

Article 41

Regional and Inter-regional Price Arrangements

(1) Regional and inter-regional price arrangements among exporting Members shall be consistent with the general objectives of the Agreement and shall be registered with the Council. Such arrangements shall take into account the interests of both producers and consumers and the objectives of the Agreement. Any Member of the Organization which considers that any of these arrangements are likely to lead to results not in accordance with the objectives of the Agreement may request that the Council discuss them with the Members concerned at its next session.

(2) In consultation with Members and with any regional organization to which they belong, the Council may recommend a scale of price differentials for various grades and qualities of coffee which Members should strive to achieve through their pricing policies.

(3) Should sharp price fluctuations occur within brief periods in respect of those grades and qualities of coffee for which a scale of price differentials has been adopted as the result of recommendations made under paragraph (2) of this Article, the Council may recommend appropriate measures to correct the situation.

Article 42

Survey of Market Trends

The Council shall keep under constant survey the trends of the coffee market with a view to recommending price policies, taking into consideration the results achieved through the quota mechanism of the Agreement.

CHAPTER VIII - CERTIFICATES OF ORIGIN AND RE-EXPORT

Article 43

Certificates of Origin and Re-export

(1) Every export of coffee from any Member in whose territory that coffee has been grown shall be accompanied by a valid Certificate of Origin in accordance with rules established by the Council and issued by a qualified agency chosen by that Member and approved by the Organization. Each Member shall determine the number of copies of the Certificate it will require and each original Certificate and all copies thereof shall bear a serial number. Unless the Council decides otherwise the original of the Certificate shall accompany the documents of export and a copy shall be furnished immediately to the Organization by that Member, except that original Certificates issued to cover exports of coffee to non-member countries shall be despatched directly to the Organization by that Member.

(2) Every re-export of coffee from a Member shall be accompanied by a valid Certificate of Re-export, in accordance with the rules established by the Council, issued by a qualified agency chosen by that Member and approved by the Organization, certifying that the coffee in question was imported in accordance with the provisions of the Agreement. Each Member shall determine the number of copies of the Certificate it will require and each original Certificate and all copies thereof shall bear a serial number. Unless the Council decides otherwise, the original of the Certificate of Re-export shall accompany the documents of re-export and a copy shall be furnished immediately to the Organization by the re-exporting Member, except that original Certificates of Re-export issued to cover re-exports of coffee to a non-member country shall be despatched directly to the Organization.

(3) Each Member shall notify the Organization of the government or non-government agency which is to administer and perform the functions specified in paragraphs (1) and (2) of this Article. The

Organization shall specifically approve any such non-government agency upon submission of satisfactory evidence by the Member country of the agency's ability and willingness to fulfil the Member's responsibilities in accordance with the rules and regulations established under the provisions of this Agreement. The Council may at any time, for cause, declare a particular non-government agency to be no longer acceptable to it. The Council shall, either directly or through an internationally recognized world-wide organization, take all necessary steps so that at any time it will be able to satisfy itself that Certificates of Origin and Certificates of Re-export are being issued and used correctly and to ascertain the quantities of coffee which have been exported by each Member.

(4) A non-government agency approved as a certifying agency under the provisions of paragraph (3) of this Article shall keep records of the Certificates issued and the basis for their issue, for a period of not less than two years. In order to obtain approval as a certifying agency under the provisions of paragraph (3) of this Article a non-government agency must previously agree to make the above records available for examination by the Organization.

(5) Members shall prohibit the entry of any shipment of coffee from any other Member, whether imported direct or via a non-member, which is not accompanied by a valid Certificate of Origin or of Re-export issued in accordance with the rules established by the Council.

(6) Small quantities of coffee in such forms as the Council may determine, or coffee for direct consumption on ships, aircraft and other international carriers, shall be exempt from the provisons of paragraphs (1) and (2) of this Article.

CHAPTER IX - PROCESSED COFFEE

Article 44

Measures relating to Processed Coffee

(1) No Member shall apply governmental measures affecting its exports and re-exports of coffee to another Member which, when taken as a whole in relation to that other Member, amount to discriminatory treatment in favour of processed coffee as compared with green coffee. In the application of this provision, Members may have due regard to:

> (a) the special situation of markets listed in Annex B of the Agreement;

(b) differential treatment in an importing Member as far as imports or re-exports of the various forms of coffee are concerned;

(2) (a) If a Member considers that the provisions of paragraph (1) of this Article are not being complied with, it may notify the Executive Director in writing of its complaint with a detailed report of the reasons for its opinion together with a description of the measures it considers should be taken. The Executive Director shall forthwith inform the Member against which the complaint has been made and seek its views. He shall encourage the Members to reach a mutually satisfactory solution and as soon as possible make a full report to the Council including the measures the complaining Member considers should be taken and the views of the other party.

(b) If a solution has not been found within 30 days after receipt of the notification by the Executive Director, he shall not later than 40 days after the receipt of the notification establish an arbitration panel. The panel shall consist of:

   (i) one person designated by the complaining Member;

   (ii) one person designated by the Member against which the complaint has been made; and

   (iii) a chairman mutually agreed upon by the Members involved or, failing such agreement, by the two persons designated under (i) and (ii).

(c) If the panel is not fully constituted within 45 days after the receipt of the notification by the Executive Director, the remaining arbitrators shall be appointed within 10 further days by the Chairman of the Council after consultation with the Members involved.

(d) None of the arbitrators shall be officials of any Government involved in the case or have any interest in its outcome.

(e) The Members concerned shall facilitate the work of the panel and make available all relevant information.

(f) The arbitration panel shall, on the basis of all the information at its disposal, determine, within three weeks after its establishment whether, and if so to what extent, there exists discriminatory treatment.

(g) Decisions of the panel on all questions, whether of substance or procedure, shall if necessary be by majority vote.

(h) The Executive Director shall forthwith notify the Members concerned and inform the Council of the panel's conclusions.

(i) The costs of the arbitration panel shall be charged to the administrative budget of the Organization.

(3) (a) If discriminatory treatment is found to exist the Member concerned will be given a period of 30 days after it has been notified of the conclusions of the arbitration panel, to correct the situation in accordance with the panel's conclusions. The Member shall inform the Council of the measures it intends to take.

(b) If after this period, the complaining Member considers that the situation has not been corrected it may, after informing the Council, take counter measures which shall not go beyond what is necessary to counteract the discriminatory treatment determined by the arbitration panel and shall last no longer than the discriminatory treatment exists.

(c) The Members concerned shall keep the Council informed of the measures being taken by them.

(4) In applying the counter measures Members undertake to have due regard to the need of developing countries to practice policies designed to broaden the base of their economies through, inter alia, industrialization and the export of manufactured products and to do what is necessary to ensure that the provisions of this Article are applied equitably to all Members in a like situation.

(5) None of the provisions of this Article shall be deemed to prevent a Member from raising in the Council an issue under this Article or having recourse to Article 58 or 59, provided that any such action shall not interrupt any procedure that has been started under this Article without the consent of the Members concerned, nor prevent such procedure from being initiated unless a procedure under Article 59 in regard to the same issue has been completed.

(6) Any time limit in this Article may be varied by agreement of the Members concerned.

CHAPTER X - REGULATION OF IMPORTS

Article 45

Regulation of Imports

(1) To prevent non-member exporting countries from increasing their exports at the expense of Members, each Member shall limit its annual imports of coffee produced in non-member exporting countries to a quantity not in excess of its average annual imports of coffee from those countries during the calendar years 1960, 1961 and 1962.

(2) The Council by a distributed two-thirds majority may suspend or vary these quantitative limitations if it finds such action necessary to further the purposes of the Agreement.

(3) The Council shall prepare annual reports of the quantity of permissible imports of coffee of non-member origin and quarterly reports of imports by each importing Member under the provisions of paragraph (1) of this Article.

(4) The obligations of the preceding paragraphs of this Article shall not deregate from any conflicting bilateral or multilateral obligations which importing Members entered into with non-member countries before 1 August 1962 provided that any importing Member which has such conflicting obligations shall carry them out in such a way as to minimize the conflict with the obligations of the preceding paragraphs, take steps as soon as possible to bring its obligations into harmony with those paragraphs, and inform the Council of the details of the conflicting obligations and of the steps taken to minimize or eliminate the conflict.

(5) If an importing Member fails to comply with the provisions of this Article the Council by a distributed two-thirds majority may suspend both its voting rights in the Council and its right to have its votes cast in the Board.

CHAPTER XI - INCREASE OF CONSUMPTION

Article 46

Promotion

(1) The Council shall sponsor the promotion of coffee consumption. To achieve this purpose it may maintain a separate committee with the objective of promoting consumption in importing countries by all appropriate means without regard to origin, type or brand of coffee and of striving to achieve and maintain the highest quality and purity of the beverage.

(2) The following provisions shall apply to such committee:

  (a) The cost of the promotion programme shall be met by contributions from exporting Members.

  (b) Importing Members may also contribute financially to the promotion programme.

  (c) Membership in the committee shall be limited to Members contributing to the promotion programme.

  (d) The size and cost of the promotion programme shall be reviewed by the Council.

  (e) The bye-laws of the committee shall be approved by the Council.

  (f) The committee shall obtain the approval of a Member before conducting a campaign in that Member's country.

  (g) The committee shall control all resources of promotion and approve all accounts related thereto.

(3) The ordinary administrative expenses relating to the permanent staff of the Organization employed directly on promotion activities, other than the costs of their travel for promotion purposes, shall be charged to the administrative budget of the Organization.

Article 47

Removal of Obstacles to Consumption

(1) The Members recognize the utmost importance of achieving the greatest possible increase of coffee consumption as rapidly as possible, in particular through the progressive removal of any obstacles which may hinder such increase.

(2) The Members recognize that there are presently in effect measures which may to a greater or lesser extent hinder the increase in consumption of coffee, in particular:

(a) import arrangements applicable to coffee, including preferential and other tariffs, quotas, operations of Government import monopolies and official purchasing agencies, and other administrative rules and commercial practices;

(b) export arrangements as regards direct or indirect subsidies and other administrative rules and commercial practices; and

(c) internal trade conditions and domestic legal and administrative provisions which may affect consumption.

(3) Having regard to the objectives stated above and to the provisions of paragraph (4) of this Article, the Members shall endeavour to pursue tariff reductions on coffee or to take other action to remove obstacles to increased consumption.

(4) Taking into account their mutual interest and in the spirit of Annex A. II.1 of the Final Act of the First United Nations Conference on Trade and Development, [1] the Members undertake to seek ways and means by which the obstacles to increased trade and consumption referred to in paragraph (2) of this Article could be progressively reduced and eventually wherever possible eliminated, or by which their effects could be substantially diminished.

(5) Members shall inform the Council of all measures adopted with a view to implementing the provisions of this Article.

---

[1] UN doc. E/CONF. 46/139, E/CONF. 46/141, Vol. 1, p. 26. (Footnote added by the Department of State.)

(6) The Council may, in order to further the purposes of this Article, make any recommendations to Members, and shall examine the results achieved at the first session of the coffee year 1969-70.

CHAPTER XII - PRODUCTION POLICY AND CONTROLS

Article 48

Production Policy and Controls

(1) Each producing Member undertakes to adjust its production of coffee to a level not exceeding that needed for domestic consumption, permitted exports and stocks as referred to in Article 49.

(2) Prior to 31 December 1968 each exporting Member shall submit to the Executive Board its proposed production goal for coffee year 1972-73, based on the elements set forth in paragraph (1) of this Article. Unless rejected by the Executive Board by a distributed simple majority vote prior to the first session of the Council after 31 December 1968 such goal shall be considered as approved. The Executive Board shall inform the Council of the production goals which have been approved in this manner. If the production goal proposed by an exporting Member is rejected by the Executive Board, the Board shall recommend a production goal for that exporting Member. At its first session after 31 December 1968, which shall be not later than 31 March 1969, the Council by a distributed two-thirds majority vote and in the light of the Board's recommendations shall establish individual production goals for exporting Members whose own proposed goals have been rejected by the Board or who have not submitted proposed production goals.

(3) Until its production goal has been approved by the Organization or established by the Council, in accordance with paragraph (2) of this Article, no exporting Member shall enjoy any increase in its annual export entitlement above the level of its annual export entitlement in effect on 1 April 1969.

(4) The Council shall establish production goals for exporting Members acceding to the Agreement and may establish production goals for producing Members which are not exporting Members.

(5) The Council shall keep the production goals, established or approved under the terms of this Article, under constant review

and shall revise them to the extent necessary to ensure that the agreed aggregate of the individual goals is consistent with estimated world requirements.

(6) Members undertake to conform with the individual production goals established or approved under the terms of this Article and each producing Member shall apply whatever policies and procedures it deems necessary for this purpose. Individual production goals established or approved under the terms of this Article are not binding minima nor do they confer any entitlement to specific levels of exports.

(7) Producing Members shall submit to this Organization, in such form and at such times as the Council shall determine, periodic reports on the measures taken to control production and to conform with their individual production goals established or approved under the terms of this Article. In the light of its appraisal of this and other relevant information the Council shall take such action, general or particular, as it deems necessary or appropriate.

(8) If the Council determines that any producing Member is not taking adequate steps to comply with the provisions of this Article such Member shall not enjoy any subsequent increase in its annual export entitlement and may have its voting rights suspended under the terms of paragraph (7) of Article 59 until the Council is satisfied that the Member is fulfilling its obligations in respect of this Article. If, however, after the elapse of such additional period as the Council shall determine it is established that the Member concerned has still not taken the steps necessary to implement a policy to conform with the objectives of this Article, the Council may require the withdrawal of such Member from the Organization under the terms of Article 67.

(9) The Organization shall, under such conditions as may be determined by the Council, extend to those Members so requesting it all possible assistance within its powers to further the purposes of this Article.

(10) Importing Members undertake to co-operate with exporting Members in their plans for adjusting the production of coffee in accordance with paragraph (1) above. In particular, Members shall refrain from offering directly financial or technical assistance or from supporting proposals for such assistance by any international body to which they belong, for the pursuit of production policies which are contrary to the objectives of this Article, whether the recipient country is a Member of the International Coffee Organization

or not.   The Organization shall maintain close contact with the international bodies concerned, with a view to securing their maximum co-operation in the implementation of this Article.

(11) Except as specified in paragraph (2) hereof, all decisions provided for in this Article shall be taken by a distributed two-thirds majority vote.

CHAPTER XIII - REGULATION OF STOCKS

Article 49

Policy Relative to Coffee Stocks

(1) To complement the provisions of Article 48 the Council by a distributed two-thirds majority may establish a policy relating to coffee stocks in producing Member countries.

(2) The Council shall take measures to ascertain annually the volume of coffee stocks in the hands of individual exporting Members in accordance with procedures which it shall establish.   Members concerned shall facilitate this annual survey.

(3) Producing Members shall ensure that adequate facilities exist in their respective countries for the proper storage of coffee stocks.

CHAPTER XIV - MISCELLANEOUS
OBLIGATIONS OF MEMBERS

Article 50

Consultation and Co-operation with the Trade

(1) The Organization shall maintain close liaison with appropriate non-governmental organizations concerned with international commerce in coffee and with experts in coffee matters.

(2) Members shall conduct their activities within the framework of the Agreement in a manner consonant with established trade channels.   In carrying out these activities they shall endeavour to take due account of the legitimate interests of the coffee trade.

Article 51

Barter

In order to avoid jeopardizing the general price structure, Members shall refrain from engaging in direct and individually linked barter transactions involving the sale of coffee in the traditional markets.

Article 52

Mixtures and Substitutes

(1) Members shall not maintain any regulations requiring the mixing, processing or using of other products with coffee for commercial resale as coffee. Members shall endeavour to prohibit the sale and advertisement of products under the name of coffee if such products contain less than the equivalent of 90 percent green coffee as the basic raw material.

(2) The Executive Director shall submit to the Council an annual report on compliance with the provisions of this Article.

(3) The Council may recommend to any Member that it take the necessary steps to ensure observance of the provisions of this Article.

CHAPTER XV - SEASONAL FINANCING

Article 53

Seasonal Financing

(1) The Council shall, upon the request of any Member who is also a party to any bilateral, multilateral, regional or inter-regional agreement in the field of seasonal financing, examine such agreement with a view to verifying its compatibility with the obligations of the Agreement.

(2) The Council may make recommendations to Members with a view to resolving any conflict of obligations which might arise.

(3) The Council may, on the basis of information obtained from the Members concerned, and if it deems appropriate and suitable, make general recommendations with a view to assisting Members which are in need of seasonal financing.

CHAPTER XVI - DIVERSIFICATION FUND

Article 54

Diversification Fund

(1) There is hereby established the Diversification Fund of the International Coffee Organization to further the objectives of limiting the production of coffee in order to bring supply into reasonable balance with world demand. The Fund shall be governed by Statutes to be approved by the Council not later than 31 December 1968.

(2) Participation in the Fund shall be compulsory for each Contracting Party that is not an importing Member and has an export entitlement of over 100, 000 bags. Voluntary participation in the Fund by Contracting Parties to which this provision does not apply, and contributions from other sources, shall be under such conditions as may be agreed between the Fund and the parties concerned.

(3) An exporting Participant liable to compulsory participation shall contribute to the Fund in quarterly instalments an amount equivalent to US$0. 60 times the number of bags it actually exports in excess of 100, 000 bags each coffee year to quota markets. Contributions shall be made for five consecutive years commencing with coffee year 1968-69. The Fund by a two-thirds majority vote may increase the rate of contribution to a level not exceeding US$1. 00 per bag. The annual contribution of each exporting Participant shall be assessed initially on the basis of its export entitlement for the year of assessment as at 1 October. This initial assessment shall be revised on the basis of the actual quantity of coffee exported to quota markets by the Participant during the year of assessment and any necessary adjustment in contribution shall be effected during the ensuing coffee year. The first quarterly instalment of the annual contribution for coffee year 1968-69 becomes due on 1 January 1969 and shall be paid not later than 28 February 1969.

(4) The contribution of each exporting Participant shall be utilized for programmes or projects approved by the Fund carried out inside its territory, but in any case twenty percent of the contribution shall be payable in freely convertible currency for use in any programmes or projects approved by the Fund. In addition a percentage of the contribution within limits to be established in the Statutes shall be payable in freely convertible currency for the administrative expenses of the Fund.

(5) The percentage of the contribution to be made in freely convertible currency in accordance with paragraph (4) may be increased by mutual agreement between the Fund and the exporting Participant concerned.

(6) At the commencement of the third year of operation of the Fund the Council shall review the results obtained in the first two years and may then revise the provisions of this Article with a view to improving them.

(7) The Statutes of the Fund shall provide for:

    (a) the suspension of contributions in relation to stipulated changes in the level of coffee prices;

    (b) the payment to the Fund in freely convertible currency of any part of the contribution which has not been utilized by the Participant concerned;

    (c) arrangements that would permit the delegation of appropriate functions and activities of the Fund to one or more international financial institutions.

(8) Unless the Council decides otherwise, an exporting Participant which fails to meet its obligations under this Article shall have its voting rights in the Council suspended and shall not enjoy any increase in its export entitlement. If the exporting Participant fails to meet the obligations for a continuous period of one year, it shall cease to be a Party to the Agreement ninety days thereafter, unless the Council decides otherwise.

(9) Decisions of the Council under the provisions of this Article shall be taken by a distributed two-thirds majority vote.

CHAPTER XVII - INFORMATION AND STUDIES

Article 55

Information

(1) The Organization shall act as a centre for the collection, exchange and publication of:

    (a) statistical information on world production, prices, exports and imports, distribution and consumption of coffee; and

(b) in so far as is considered appropriate, technical information on the cultivation, processing and utilization of coffee.

(2) The Council may require Members to furnish such information as it considers necessary for its operations, including regular statistical reports on coffee production, exports and imports, distribution, consumption, stocks and taxation, but no information shall be published which might serve to identify the operations of persons or companies producing, processing or marketing coffee. The Members shall furnish information requested in as detailed and accurate a manner as is practicable.

(3) If a Member fails to supply, or finds difficulty in supplying, within a reasonable time, statistical and other information required by the Council for the proper functioning of the Organization, the Council may require the Member concerned to explain the reasons for non-compliance. If it is found that technical assistance is needed in the matter, the Council may take any necessary measures.

Article 56

Studies

(1) The Council may promote studies in the fields of the economics of coffee production and distribution, the impact of governmental measures in producing and consuming countries on the production and consumption of coffee, the opportunities for expansion of coffee consumption for traditional and possible new uses, and the effects of the operation of the Agreement on producers and consumers of coffee, including their terms of trade.

(2) The Organization may study the practicability of establishing minimum standards for exports of coffee from producing Members. Recommendations in this regard may be discussed by the Council.

CHAPTER XVIII - WAIVER

Article 57

Waiver

(1) The Council by a distributed two-thirds majority vote may relieve a Member of an obligation, on account of exceptional or emergency circumstances, force majeure, constitutional obligations,

or international obligations under the United Nations Charter [1] for territories administered under the trusteeship system.

(2) The Council, in granting a waiver to a Member, shall state explicitly the terms and conditions on which and the period for which the Member is relieved of such obligation.

(3) The Council shall not consider a request for a waiver of quota obligations on the basis of the existence in a Member country, in one or more years, of an exportable production in excess of its permitted exports, or which is the consequence of the Member having failed to comply with the provisions of Articles 48 and 49.

CHAPTER XIX - CONSULTATIONS, DISPUTES AND COMPLAINTS

Article 58

Consultations

Each Member shall accord sympathetic consideration to, and shall afford adequate opportunity for, consultation regarding such representations as may be made by another Member with respect to any matter relating to the Agreement. In the course of such consultation, on request by either party and with the consent of the other, the Executive Director shall establish an independent panel which shall use its good offices with a view to conciliating the parties. The costs of the panel shall not be chargeable to the Organization. If a party does not agree to the establishment of a panel by the Executive Director, or if the consultation does not lead to a solution, the matter may be referred to the Council in accordance with Article 59. If the consultation does lead to a solution, it shall be reported to the Executive Director who shall distribute the report to all Members.

Article 59

Disputes and Complaints

(1) Any dispute concerning the interpretation or application of the Agreement which is not settled by negotiation shall, at the request of any Member party to the dispute, be referred to the Council for decision.

---

[1]TS 993; 59 Stat. 1031. (Footnote added by the Department of State.)

(2) In any case where a dispute has been referred to the Council under paragraph (1) of this Article, a majority of Members, or Members holding not less than one-third of the total votes, may require the Council, after discussion, to seek the opinion of the advisory panel referred to in paragraph (3) of this Article on the issue in dispute before giving its decision.

(3) (a) Unless the Council unanimously agrees otherwise, the panel shall consist of:

   (i) two persons, one having wide experience in matters of the kind in dispute and the other having legal standing and experience, nominated by the exporting Members;

   (ii) two such persons nominated by the importing Members; and

   (iii) a chairman selected unanimously by the four persons nominated under (i) and (ii) or, if they fail to agree, by the Chairman of the Council.

   (b) Persons from countries whose Governments are Contracting Parties to this Agreement shall be eligible to serve on the advisory panel.

   (c) Persons appointed to the advisory panel shall act in their personal capacities and without instructions from any Government.

   (d) The expenses of the advisory panel shall be paid by the Organization.

(4) The opinion of the advisory panel and the reasons therefor shall be submitted to the Council which, after considering all the relevant information, shall decide the dispute.

(5) Any complaint that any Member has failed to fulfil its obligations under the Agreement shall, at the request of the Member making the complaint, be referred to the Council, which shall make a decision on the matter.

(6) No Member shall be found to have committed a breach of its obligations under the Agreement except by a distributed simple majority vote. Any finding that a Member is in breach of the Agreement shall specify the nature of the breach.

(7) If the Council finds that a Member has committed a breach of the Agreement, it may, without prejudice to other enforcement measures provided for in other Articles of the Agreement, by a distributed two-thirds majority vote, suspend that Member's voting rights in the Council and its right to have its votes cast in the Board until it fulfils its obligations, or the Council may take action requiring compulsory withdrawal under Article 67.

(8) A Member may seek the prior opinion of the Executive Board in a matter of dispute or complaint before the matter is discussed by the Council.

CHAPTER XX - FINAL PROVISIONS

Article 60

Signature

The Agreement shall be open for signature at the United Nations Headquarters until and including 31 March 1968 by any Government which is a Contracting Party to the International Coffee Agreement, 1962.

Article 61

Ratification

The Agreement shall be subject to approval, ratification or acceptance by the signatory Governments or by any other Contracting Party to the International Coffee Agreement, 1962, in accordance with their respective constitutional procedures. Except as provided in paragraph (2) of Article 62 instruments of approval, ratification or acceptance shall be deposited with the Secretary-General of the United Nations not later than 30 September 1968.

Article 62

Entry into Force

(1) The Agreement shall enter into force definitively on 1 October 1968 among those Governments that have deposited instruments of approval, ratification or acceptance if, on that date, such Governments represent at least twenty exporting Members holding at least 80 percent of the votes of the exporting Members and at least ten importing Members holding at least 80 percent of the votes of the importing Members. The votes for this purpose shall be as

distributed in Annex C. Alternatively, it shall enter into force definitively at any time after it is provisionally in force and the aforesaid requirements of this paragraph are satisfied. The Agreement shall enter into force definitively for any Government that deposits an instrument of approval, ratification, acceptance or accession subsequent to the definitive entry into force of the Agreement for other Governments on the date of such deposit.

(2) The Agreement may enter into force provisionally on 1 October 1968. For this purpose a notification by a signatory Government or by any other Contracting Party to the International Coffee Agreement, 1962, containing an undertaking to apply the Agreement provisionally and to seek approval, ratification or acceptance in accordance with its constitutional procedures, as rapidly as possible, that is received by the Secretary-General of the United Nations not later than 30 September 1968, shall be regarded as equal in effect to an instrument of approval, ratification or acceptance. A Government that undertakes to apply the Agreement provisionally will be permitted to deposit an instrument of approval, notification or acceptance and shall be provisionally regarded as a party thereto until either it deposits its instrument of approval, ratification or acceptance or up to and including 31 December 1968, whichever is the earlier.

(3) If the Agreement has not entered into force definitively or provisionally by 1 October 1968, those Governments that have deposited instruments of approval, ratification or acceptance or notifications containing an undertaking to apply the Agreement provisionally and to seek approval, ratification or acceptance may immediately after that date consult together to consider what action the situation requires and may, by mutual consent, decide that it shall enter into force among themselves. Likewise, if the Agreement has entered into force provisionally but has not entered into force definitively by 31 December 1968, those Governments that have deposited instruments of approval, ratification, acceptance or accession may consult together to consider what action the situation requires and may, by mutual consent, decide that it shall continue in force provisionally or enter into force definitively among themselves.

Article 63

Accession

(1) The Government of any State Member of the United Nations or of any of its specialized agencies may accede to this Agreement upon conditions that shall be established by the Council. In establishing such conditions the Council shall, if such country is an exporting country and is not named in Annex A, establish quota

provisions for it. If such exporting country is named in Annex A, the respective quota provisions specified therein shall be applied to that country unless the Council by a distributed two-thirds majority vote decides otherwise. Not later than 31 March 1969 or such other date as may be determined by the Council, any importing Member of the International Coffee Agreement, 1962, may accede to the Agreement on the same conditions under which it could have approved, ratified or accepted the Agreement and, if it applies the Agreement provisionally, it shall provisionally be regarded as a party thereto until either it deposits its instrument of accession or up to and including the above date, whichever is the earlier.

(2) Each Government depositing an instrument of accession shall, at the time of such deposit, indicate whether it is joining the Organization as an exporting Member or an importing Member, as defined in paragraphs (7) and (8) of Article 2.

Article 64

Reservations

Reservations may not be made with respect to any of the provisions of the Agreement.

Article 65

Notifications in respect of Dependent Territories

(1) Any Government may, at the time of signature or deposit of an instrument of approval, ratification, acceptance or accession, or at any time thereafter, by notification to the Secretary-General of the United Nations, declare that the Agreement shall extend to any of the territories for whose international relations it is responsible and the Agreement shall extend to the territories named therein from the date of such notification.

(2) Any Contracting Party which desires to exercise its rights under Article 4 in respect of any of its dependent territories, or which desires to authorize one of its dependent territories to become part of a Member group formed under Article 5 or 6, may do so by making a notification to that effect to the Secretary-General of the United Nations, either at the time of the deposit of its instrument of approval, ratification, acceptance or accession, or at any later time.

(3) Any Contracting Party which has made a declaration under paragraph (1) of this Article may at any time thereafter, by notification

to the Secretary-General of the United Nations, declare that the Agreement shall cease to extend to the territory named in the notification and the Agreement shall cease to extend to such territory from the date of such notification.

(4) The Government of a territory to which the Agreement has been extended under paragraph (1) of this Article and which has subsequently become independent may, within 90 days after the attainment of independence, declare by notification to the Secretary-General of the United Nations that it has assumed the rights and obligations of a Contracting Party to the Agreement. It shall, as from the date of such notification, become a party to the Agreement.

Article 66

Voluntary Withdrawal

Any Contracting Party may withdraw from the Agreement at any time by giving a written notice of withdrawal to the Secretary-General of the United Nations. Withdrawal shall become effective 90 days after the notice is received.

Article 67

Compulsory Withdrawal

If the Council determines that any Member has failed to carry out its obligations under the Agreement and that such failure significantly impairs the operations of the Agreement, it may by distributed two-thirds majority vote require the withdrawal of such Member from the Organization. The Council shall immediately notify the Secretary-General of the United Nations of any such decision. Ninety days after the date of the Council's decision that Member shall cease to be a Member of the Organization and, if such Member is a Contracting Party, a party to the Agreement.

Article 68

Settlement of Accounts with Withdrawing Members

(1) The Council shall determine any settlement of accounts with a withdrawing Member. The Organization shall retain any amounts already paid by a withdrawing Member and such Member shall remain bound to pay any amounts due from it to the Organization at the time the withdrawal becomes effective; provided, however, that in the case of a Contracting Party which is unable to accept an amendment and consequently either withdraws or ceases to participate

in the Agreement under the provisions of paragraph (2) of Article 70, the Council may determine any settlement of accounts which it finds equitable.

(2) A Member which has withdrawn or which has ceased to participate in the Agreement shall not be entitled to any share of the proceeds of liquidation or the other assets of the Organization upon termination of the Agreement under Article 69.

Article 69

Duration and Termination

(1) The Agreement shall remain in force until 30 September 1973 unless extended under paragraph (2) of this Article, or terminated earlier under paragraph (3).

(2) The Council after 30 September 1972 may, by a vote of a majority of the Members having not less than a distributed two-thirds majority of the total votes, either renegotiate the Agreement or extend it, with or without modification, for such period as the Council shall determine. Any Contracting Party, or any dependent territory which is either a Member or a party to a Member group, on behalf of which notification of acceptance of such a renegotiated or extended Agreement has not been made by the date on which such renegotiated or extended Agreement becomes effective, shall as of that date cease to participate in the Agreement.

(3) The Council may at any time, by vote of a majority of the Members having not less than a distributed two-thirds majority of the total votes, decide to terminate the Agreement. Such termination shall take effect on such date as the Council shall decide.

(4) Notwithstanding termination of the Agreement, the Council shall remain in being for as long as necessary to carry out the liquidation of the Organization, settlement of its accounts and disposal of its assets, and shall have during that period such powers and functions as may be necessary for those purposes.

Article 70

Amendment

(1) The Council by a distributed two-thirds majority vote may recommend an amendment of the Agreement to the Contracting Parties. The amendment shall become effective 100 days after the Secretary-General of the United Nations has received notifications of acceptance

from Contracting Parties representing at least 75 percent of the
exporting countries holding at least 85 percent of the votes of the
exporting Members, and from Contracting Parties representing at
least 75 percent of the importing countries holding at least 80 percent
of the votes of the importing Members. The Council may fix a time
within which each Contracting Party shall notify the Secretary-General
of the United Nations of its acceptance of the amendment and if the
amendment has not become effective by such time, it shall be considered withdrawn. The Council shall provide the Secretary-General
with the information necessary to determine whether the amendment
has become effective.

(2) Any Contracting Party, or any dependent territory which is
either a Member or a party to a Member group, on behalf of which
notification of acceptance of an amendment has not been made by the
date on which such amendment becomes effective, shall as of that
date cease to participate in the Agreement.

Article 71

Notifications by the Secretary-General

The Secretary-General of the United Nations shall notify all
Contracting Parties to the International Coffee Agreement, 1962,
and all other Governments of States Members of the United Nations
or of any of its specialized agencies, of each deposit of an instrument
of approval, ratification, acceptance or accession and of the dates on
which the Agreement comes provisionally and definitively into force.
The Secretary-General of the United Nations shall also notify all
Contracting Parties of each notification under Articles 5, 62 paragraph (2), 65, 66 or 67; of the date to which the Agreement is
extended or on which it is terminated under Article 69; and of the
date on which an amendment becomes effective under Article 70.

Article 72

Supplementary and Transitional Provisions

(1) The present Agreement shall be considered as a continuation
of the International Coffee Agreement, 1962.

(2) In order to facilitate the uninterrupted continuation of the
1962 Agreement:

> (a) All acts by or on behalf of the Organization or any of
> its organs under the 1962 Agreement, in effect on
> 30 September 1968 and whose terms do not provide

for expiry on that date, shall remain in effect unless
changed under the provisions of the present Agreement.

(2) All decisions required to be taken by the Council
during coffee year 1967-68 for application in coffee
year 1968-69 shall be taken during the last regular
session of the Council in coffee year 1967-68 and
applied on a provisional basis as if the present Agreement had already entered into force.

IN WITNESS WHEREOF the undersigned, having been duly
authorized to this effect by their respective Governments, have signed
this Agreement on the dates appearing opposite their signatures.

The texts of this Agreement in the English, French, Portuguese,
Russian and Spanish languages shall all be equally authentic. The
originals shall be deposited in the archives of the United Nations
and the Secretary-General of the United Nations shall transmit
certified copies thereof to each signatory and acceding Government.

ANNEX A

Basic Export Quotas [1]

(thousands of 60-kilo bags)

Brazil	20,926
Burundi [2]	233
Cameroon	1,000
Central African Republic	200
Colombia	7,000
Congo (Democratic Republic) [2]	1,000
Costa Rica	1,100
Dominican Republic	520
Ecuador	750
El Salvador	1,900
Ethiopia	1,494
Guatemala	1,800
Guinea (basic export quota to be established by the Council)	
Haiti	490
Honduras	425
India	423
Indonesia	1,357
Ivory Coast	3,073

Kenya	860
Malagasy Republic	910
Mexico	1,760
Nicaragua	550
Peru	740
Portugal	2,776
Rwanda [2]	150
Tanzania	700
Togo	200
Uganda	2,379
Venezuela [2]	325
Grand Total	55,041

---

[1]   According to the provisions of Article 31 (1), the following exporting countries do not have a basic export quota and shall receive in coffee year 1968-69 export quotas of: Bolivia 50,000 bags; Congo (Brazzaville) 25,000 bags; Cuba 50,000 bags; Dahomey 33,000 bags; Gabon 25,000 bags; Ghana 51,000 bags; Jamaica 25,000 bags; Liberia 60,000 bags; Nigeria 52,000 bags; Panama 25,000 bags; Paraguay 70,000 bags; Sierra Leone 82,000 bags; Trinidad and Tobago 69,000 bags.

[2]   Burundi, Congo (Democratic Republic), Cuba, Rwanda and Venezuela, after presentation to the Executive Board of acceptable evidence of an exportable production larger than 233,000; 1,000,000; 50,000; 150,000 and 325,000 bags respectively shall each be granted an annual export entitlement not exceeding the annual export entitlement it would receive with a basic quota of 350,000; 1,300,000; 200,000; 260,000 and 475,000 bags respectively. In no event, however, shall the increases allowed to these countries be taken into account for the purpose of calculating the distribution of votes.

ANNEX B

Non-quota countries of destination referred to in Article 40, Chapter VII

The geographical areas which are non-quota countries for the purposes of this Agreement are:

Bahrain
Botswana

Ceylon
China (Taiwan)
China (mainland)
Hungary
Iran
Iraq
Japan
Korea, Republic of
Kuwait
Lesotho
Malawi
Muscat and Oman
North Korea
Poland
Qatar
Romania
Saudi Arabia
Somalia
South-Africa, Republic of
Southern Rhodesia
South-West Africa
Sudan
Swaziland
Thailand
Trucial Oman
Union of Soviet Socialist Republics
Zambia

Note: The abbreviated names above are intended to be of
purely geographical significance and to convey no political implications
whatsoever.

DISTRIBUTION OF VOTES   ANNEX C

COUNTRY	EXPORTING	IMPORTING
Argentina	–	16
Australia	–	9
Austria	–	11
Belgium*	–	28
Bolivia	4	–
Brazil	332	–
Burundi	8	–
Canada	–	32
Colombia	114	–
Congo (Democratic Republic of)	20	–
Costa Rica	21	–
Cuba	4	–
Cyprus	–	5
Czechoslovakia	–	9
Denmark	–	23
Dominican Republic	12	–
Ecuador	16	–
El Salvador	34	–
Ethiopia	27	–
Federal Republic of Germany	–	101
Finland	–	21
France	–	84
Ghana	4	–
Guatemala	32	–
Guinea	4	–
Haiti	12	–
Honduras	11	–
India	11	–
Indonesia	25	–
Israel	–	7
Italy	–	47
Jamaica	4	–
Japan	–	18
Kenya	17	–
Liberia	4	–
Mexico	32	–

COUNTRY	EXPORTING	IMPORTING
Netherlands	-	35
New Zealand	-	6
Nicaragua	13	-
Nigeria	4	-
Norway	-	16
OAMCAF	(86)	-
OAMCAF	(4) [1]	-
Cameroon	15	-
Central African Republic	3	-
Congo (Brazzaville)	1	-
Dahomey	1	-
Gabon	1	-
Ivory Coast	47	-
Malagasy Republic	13	-
Togo	3	-
Panama	4	-
Peru	16	-
Portugal	48	-
Rwanda	6	-
Sierra Leone	4	-
Spain	-	21
Sweden	-	38
Switzerland	-	19
Tanzania	15	-
Trinidad & Tobago	4	-
Tunisia	-	6
Uganda	41	-
U.S.S.R.	-	16
United Kingdom	-	32
United States of America	-	400
Venezuela	9	-
TOTAL	996	1,000

*Includes Luxembourg.
[1]Basic votes not attributable to individual contracting parties under Article 5 (4) (b)

SELECTED BIBLIOGRAPHY

BOOKS

Alexandrowicz, Charles Henry. World Economic Agencies: Law and Practice. New York: Frederick A. Praeger, 1962.

Bain, Joe S. Price Theory. New York: John Wiley & Sons, 1967.

Bauer, Raymond A., Ithiel de Sola Pool, and Lewis Anthony Dexter. American Business and Public Policy. New York: Atherton Press, 1963.

Chayes, Abram, Thomas Ehrlich, and Andreas F. Lowenfeld. The International Legal Process. Boston: Little, Brown and Company, 1968.

Eisenhower, Milton. The Wine Is Bitter. New York: Doubleday and Company, 1963.

Fenwick, Charles G. International Law. New York: Appleton-Century-Crofts, 1965.

Galbraith, John K. American Capitalism: The Concept of Countervailing Power. Boston: Houghton Mifflin Company, 1952.

Haarer, A. E. Modern Coffee Production. London: Leonard Hill (Books) Limited, 1962.

Haas, Ernst B. Beyond the Nation-State. Stanford, Calif.: Stanford University Press, 1964.

Johnson, Harry G. Economic Policies Toward Less Developed Countries. New York: Frederick A. Praeger, 1967.

Ikle, Fred Charles. How Nations Negotiate. New York: Harper & Row, 1964.

Leff, Nathaniel H. Economic Policy-Making and Development in Brazil, 1947-1964. New York: John Wiley & Sons, 1968.

Liska, George. International Equilibrium. Cambridge, Mass.: Harvard University Press, 1957.

MacBean, Alisdair I. Export Instability and Economic Development. Cambridge, Mass.: Harvard University Press, 1966.

271

Nierenberg, Gerard I. The Art of Negotiating. New York: Hawthorne
    Books, 1968.

Olson, Mancur. The Logic of Collective Action. Cambridge, Mass.:
    Harvard University Press, 1965.

Parsons, Talcott. The Social System. New York: The Free Press,
    1951.

Perkins, Dexter. The United States and Latin America. Baton
    Rouge: Louisiana State University Press, 1961.

Pincus, John A. Economic Aid and International Cost-Sharing.
    Baltimore: Johns Hopkins University Press, 1965.

_____. Trade, Aid, and Development: The Rich and Poor Nations.
    New York: McGraw-Hill Book Company, 1967.

Rowe, J. W. F. Primary Commodities in International Trade.
    Cambridge: Cambridge University Press, 1965.

_____. The World's Coffee. London: H.M. Stationery Office,
    1963.

Schlesinger, Arthur M. A Thousand Days: John F. Kennedy in the
    White House. Boston: Houghton Mifflin Company, 1965.

Shubik, Martin. Strategy and Market Structure. New York: John
    Wiley & Sons, 1959.

Stigler, George J. The Theory of Price. New York: The Macmillan
    Company, 1963.

Ukers, William H. All About Coffee. New York: The Tea and Coffee
    Trade Journal Company, 1935.

Wickizer, Vernon D. Coffee, Tea, and Cocoa, An Economic and
    Political Analysis. Stanford, Calif.: Food Research Institute,
    Stanford University, 1951.

_____. The World Coffee Economy. Stanford, Calif.: Food
    Research Institute, Stanford University, 1943.

ARTICLES

Bilder, Richard B. "The International Coffee Agreement: A Case
    History in Negotiation," Law and Contemporary Problems,
    XXVIII (Spring, 1963), 328-91.

Borio, Leonidas Lopes. "Brazil's Coffee Policy, " Coffee Annual, 1965. New York: George Gordon Paton and Company, 1966. Pp. 53-55.

Cordell, Arthur J. "The Brazilian Soluble Problem: A Review, " The Quarterly Review of Economics and Business, IX (Spring, 1969), 29-38.

Economic Bulletin for Latin America (1960-64).

Economist (1963-68).

Escalante, Manuel G. "Latin American Coffee Agreement, " Coffee Annual, 1958. New York: George Gordon Paton and Company, 1959. Pp. 67 and 68.

Flores, Arturo Morales. "The Mexican Agreement, " Coffee Annual, 1958. New York: George Gordon Paton and Company, 1959. Pp. 61 and 63.

Frank, Isaiah. "Aid, Trade and Economic Development: Issues before the U.N. Conference, " Foreign Affairs, XLII (January, 1964), 210-26.

_____. "New Perspectives on Trade and Development, " Foreign Affairs, XLV (April, 1967), 520-40.

Fried, Edward R. "1966-A Year for Emerging Solutions, " Coffee Annual, 1966. New York: George Gordon Paton and Company, 1967. Pp. 57 and 58.

Griffin, Keith B. "Coffee and the Economic Development of Colombia, " Bulletin, Oxford University Institute of Economics and Statistics, XXX (May, 1968), 105-29.

Haley, Bernard F. "The Relation between Cartel Policy and Commodity Agreement Policy, " American Economic Review, Papers and Proceedings of the Fifth-Eighth Annual Meeting, American Economic Association, XXXVI (May, 1946), 717-34.

Jacobson, Jerome. "The Agreement and the United States, " Coffee Annual, 1964. New York: George Gordon Paton and Company, 1965. Pp. 45-47.

_____. "Difficulties in Framing Effective Commodity Agreements, " International Development Review, X (June, 1968), 10-15.

_____. "The U.S. and the Agreement, " Coffee Annual, 1963. New York: George Gordon Paton and Company, 1964. Pp. 43-45.

Jaramillo, Arturo Gomez. "Colombia and the Agreement, " Coffee
    Annual, 1965. New York: George Gordon Paton and Company,
    1966. Pp. 67, 68.

_____. "Colombia's Point of View, " Coffee Annual, 1964. New
    York: George Gordon Paton and Company, 1965. Pp. 61 and 62.

_____. "ICA Quotas Must Not Exceed World Demand, " Coffee
    Annual, 1963. New York: George Gordon Paton and Company,
    1964. Pp. 55, 56.

Kravis, Irving B. "International Commodity Agreements to Promote
    Aid and Efficiency: the Case of Coffee, " Canadian Journal of
    Economics, I (May, 1968) 295-318.

Krumme, Robert D. "International Commodity Agreements: Purpose,
    Policy, and Procedure, " in Robert L. Tontz, ed., Foreign Agri-
    cultural Trade, Selected Readings. Ames: Iowa State Univer-
    sity Press, 1966. Pp. 380-407.

Lovasy, Gertrude. "The International Coffee Market: a Note, " Inter-
    national Monetary Fund Staff Papers, IX (July, 1962), 226-42.

_____, and Lorette Boissonneault. "The International Coffee
    Market, " International Monetary Fund Staff Papers, XI (Novem-
    ber, 1964), 367-89.

Lowenfeld, Andreas F. "International Coffee Controls-Some Lessons
    from the Coffee Agreement, " The American Journal of Inter-
    national Law, LXI (July, 1967), 785-89.

McKiernan, John F. "The Role of the N. C. A. " Coffee Annual, 1961.
    New York: George Gordon Paton and Company, 1962. Pp. 41
    and 42.

Pincus, John A. "What Policy for Commodities?, " Foreign Affairs,
    XLII (January, 1964), 227-41.

Robbins, George V. "The Meetings in London, " Coffee Annual, 1963.
    New York: George Gordon Paton and Company, 1964. Pp. 59
    and 62.

Santos, Joao Oliveira. "ICO Developments During 1966, " Coffee
    Annual, 1966. New York: George Gordon Paton and Company,
    1967. Pp. 45-47.

_____. "The ICO-An Inventory of Achievement, " Coffee Annual,
    1965. New York: George Gordon Paton and Company, 1966.
    Pp. 45-47.

_____. "A Short-Term Solution, " Coffee Annual, 1958. New
York: George Gordon Paton and Company, 1959. Pp. 70-72.

Schmidt, Wilson E. "The Case Against Commodity Agreements, "
Law and Contemporary Problems, XXVIII (Spring, 1963), 313-27.

Walker, Herman. "The International Law of Commodity Agreements, "
Law and Contemporary Problems, XXVIII (Spring, 1963), 392-
416.

Wickizer, Vernon D. "International Collaboration in the World Coffee
Market, " Food Research Institute Studies, Stanford University,
Vol. IV, No. 3 (1964).

ICO DOCUMENTS

These documents are not available to the general public. They
may be requested, however, on an individual basis, from the ICO in
London.

Executive Director

Findings of Arbitration Panel Established Under the Provisions of
Article 44. ED-397/69, March 3, 1969.

Executive Board

Draft Comprehensive Plan for the Consideration of Pending Questions.
EB-403/66, August 17, 1966.

Estimate of Imports for Consumption by Countries Listed in Annex
B in 1965/66. EB-297/65, July 12, 1965.

Legal Considerations on the Question of Certificates of Origin. EB-
326/65, September 6, 1965.

Proposals and Comments on the Extension, Renegotiation and/or
Amendment of the Agreement. EB-468/67 Rev. 1 and Add. 1,
May 30, 1967.

Proposals for Amendment of the Agreement Submitted during the
Tenth Session of the Council. EB-577/67, October 16, 1967.

Report of the Conclusions of the Board of Directors of the Inter-
African Coffee Organization on the Draft Comprehensive Plan
for the Consideration of Pending Questions Prepared by the
Executive Director. EB-404/66, August 17, 1966.

Report on Requests of Certain Members for Revisions of Quotas and Quarterly Percentages. EB-28/63, November 8, 1963.

Statistical and Other Background Information to the Report of the Executive Board on Basic Quotas, Production Goals, and Stocks. Vols. I and II. EB-349/65 Revs. 1, 2, November 16, 1965.

Statutes of the Diversification Fund of the International Coffee Organization. EB-717/68 Rev. 2, January 16, 1969.

ICC

Background Paper on the Issue Related to Sharp Price Rises and Remedial Action. ICC-3-1, February 3, 1964.

History of Recent International Coffee Agreements: Their Background, Provisions, Operations and Related Developments, 1954-1963. ICC-1-1, 1963.

Proposals Submitted by the Brazilian Delegation for Improvement of the System of Stabilization in the International Coffee Agreement. ICC-4-1, April 27, 1964.

Report of the Executive Director. ICC-6-3, March 10, 1965.

Report of the Advisory Panel on the Legality of a System for the Selective Adjustment of Quotas.

Resolutions of the ICC. Note that all resolutions cited in the text are those passed by the ICC. Decisions of the Executive Board and the Executive Director are marked accordingly.

OTHER INTERNATIONAL ORGANIZATION DOCUMENTS

International Monetary Fund and International Bank for Reconstruction and Development Staff Study. The Problem of Stabilization of Prices of Primary Products, Part I. Washington D.C.: IMF IBRD, 1968.

Pan American Coffee Bureau. Annual Coffee Statistics. New York, Pan American Coffee Bureau, 1958-68.

Pan American Union. Measures to Relieve Seasonal Pressures on the Prices of Central American Coffee. Washington, D.C.: Pan American Union, 1962.

Singh, Shamsher. International Coffee Agreement, 1968. Washington,
    D.C.: International Bank for Reconstruction and Development,
    1968.

U.N. United Nations Coffee Conference, 1962. New York: UN,
    E/Conf. 42/8, 1962.

_____. Records of the 1962 UNCC (these are unavailable to the
    general public).
        Provisional Summary Records, Economic Committee 1
        Provisional Summary Records, Administrative and Legal
            Committee
        Provisional Summary Records, Executive Committee

PUBLIC DOCUMENTS

Brazil. Survey of the Brazilian Economy. Brazilian Embassy,
    Washington, D.C. 1966.

U.S. Congress. First Annual Report of the President of the United
    States on the International Coffee Agreement. January 14, 1966.

U.S. Congress. President Johnson's Third Annual Report to the
    United States Congress on the International Coffee Agreement.
    January, 1968.

U.S. Congress. Senate. Committee on Foreign Relations. Inter-
    national Coffee Agreement, 1968. Hearing. —Cong., 2d Sess.
    Washington, D.C. U.S. Government Printing Office, 1968.

U.S. Congress. Senate. Committee on Foreign Relations. Survey
    of the Alliance for Progress, Foreign Trade Policies. Wash-
    ington, D.C.: U.S. Government Printing Office, 1967.

UNPUBLISHED MATERIAL

Cia. Iguacu de Cafe Soluval. "The Soluble Coffee Industry in Brazil."
    Mimeographed.

Geer, Thomas. The World Coffee Economy and Stabilization Schemes
    since 1945. Bachelor of Arts dissertation, Oxford University,
    1966.

Gordon, Lincoln. "Memorandum for Mr. Richard J. Goodwin, White
    House: Key Issues for Presidential Address on the Inter-Amer-
    ican Alliance for Progress," Memorandum, March 6, 1961.

International Bank for Reconstruction and Development, The Coffee
Papers: An Inquiry into the Economics of Commodity Markets.
Washington, D.C.: IBRD, 1969.

Knight, Peter. "The Critical Coffee Sector in Brazil: Potential
Export Earnings from a Diversification Scheme." Paper for
U.S. AID, September 7, 1966.

Rourke, Blair. "Causes and Predictability of Annual Changes in
Supplies and Prices of Coffee." Ph.D. dissertation, Food
Research Institute, Stanford University, 1968.

Shapleigh, Alexander W. "Soluble Coffee and the International Coffee
Agreement, 1968." Paper for Johns Hopkins School of Advanced
International Studies, May 22, 1968.

Vanderslice, Lane. "The International Coffee Agreement and Control
of Coffee Overproduction." Ph.D. dissertation, University of
Michigan, Department of Economics, in process.

INTERVIEWS

Morton Abramowitz. U.S. Department of State. November 15, 1968.

Benito Castinada Aguilar. Instituto Mexicano del Cafe. August 15,
1968.

Richard F. Balzac. Balzac Brothers & Company, Inc. June 26, 1969.

Abba Bayer. James W. Phyfe & Co. Inc. June 26, 1969.

Kenworth V. Bohlmar. Administrative Secretary, New York Coffee
and Sugar Exchange, Inc. June 26, 1969.

J. A. C. Brown. Bristol University. September 10, 1968.

D. H. Burns. Department of Food and Commerce, Canadian Federal
Government. September 7, 1968.

Harry Bryan. Agricultural Attache to Guatemala, Foreign Agricultural
Service, U.S. Department of Agricultural. August 6, 1968.

Paul Callanan. Office of Tropical Products, U.S. Department of
State. December 20, 1968.

John G. Cargill. Executive Secretary, Green Coffee Association of
New York City, Inc. June 26, 1969.

Compania Salvadoreña de Café, S.A. San Salvador, El Salvador. Interviews with department heads. August 2, 1968.

Miguel Angel Cordera. President, Instituto Mexicano del Cafe. August 13, 1969.

Oscar Diaz Echeverria. Assistant Manager, Asociacion Nacional del Café (Guatemala). August 12, 1968.

Arturo Falla. Owner of finca in Department of Sacatepequez, Guatemala. August 7, 1968.

J. H. W. Fietelaars. Second Secretary of Royal Netherlands Embassy in London. September 13, 1968.

J. M. Figuerero-Antequeda. Counsellor, Embassy of Argentina in London. September 11, 1968.

M. Fisher. East African Marketing Association. September 3, 1968.

Edward Fried. Senior staff member, The Brookings Institution. May 2, 1968.

Thomas Geer. Commodities Section, The International Bank for Reconstruction and Development. October 28, 1968.

Alvin Gilbert. Tropical Products Division, U.S. Department of Agriculture. July 25, 1968.

Sheldon Hochberg. Office of the Legal Advisor, U.S. Department of State. May 27, 1969.

Julio R. Herrera. Director, Asociacion Nacional del Cafe (Guatemala). September 9, 1968.

Jerome Jacobson. Robert R. Nathan and Associates. June 16, 1969.

Hector Jaramillo. Secretariat, ICO. September 10, 1968.

W. M. G. Kazuka. Statistician, ICO. September 3, 1968.

George McEvoy. J. Aron and Company. June 26, 1969.

Juan R. Molina. Oficina del Cafe, Banco Nacional de Fumento (Honduras). August 29, 1968.

Carlos L. Nottebohm. Cia. Agro-Comercial, S.A. (Guatemala). August 6, 1968.

Mario Pasquale. Assistant Secretary, Green Coffee Association of New York City, Inc. June 26, 1969.

Kenneth Paton. George Gordon Paton, Inc. June 24, 1969.

Ignacio Pichardo. Member, Mexican House of Representatives. September 2, 1968.

Arthur L. Ransohoff. Arthur L. Ransohoff, Inc. June 27, 1969.

Nicolas Rivero, IV. Economist, Pan American Union. August 28, 1968.

John D. Robison. Assistant Director, Division of Appraisement and Collections, U.S. Bureau of Customs. June 11, 1969.

William Rodman. U.S. Agricultural Attache to Mexico, Foreign Agricultural Service, U.S. Department of Agriculture. August 13, 1968.

Antonio Rodriguez. Export Control Department, ICO. September 3, 1968.

Ronaldo Sandenberg. Second Secretary, Brazilian Embassy, Washington, D.C. November 5, 1969.

James Schutz. Manager, Incasa, Cafetenango, Industria de Cafe, S.A. (Guatemala City, Guatemala). August 7, 1968.

Mauricio Schwartz. Owner of finca at San Antonio, El Salvador. August 4, 1968.

David Stoner. Office of the Legal Advisor, U.S. Department of State. May 27, 1969.

William Struning. Director of Statistics, Pan American Coffee Bureau. September 3, 1968.

Richard Ware. Anderson, Clayton and Company. June 26, 1969.

John Wohlfart. S. A. Schonbrunn and Company, Inc., June 26, 1969.

Charles York. Tropical Products Division, U.S. Department of State. September 2, 1968.

OTHER

Speech by Joao O. Santos. Georgetown University. November 23, 1968.

Newsletter (New York: National Coffee Association, year of 1969).

Complete Coffee Coverage (New York: George Gordon Paton and Company, years of 1963-68). This is a daily coffee trade newsletter.

Coffee Annual (1958-68). New York: George Gordon Paton and Company. This is a valuable annual covering the events of the coffee year. It is referred to in the text as George Gordon Paton and Co. Coffee Annual, with the proper year.

The Green Coffee Association of New York City, "Annual Summary of Imports into U.S. Atlantic Ports, January to December 31, 1966." 1966.

BART S. FISHER is a candidate for the J.D. degree from the
Law School of Harvard University in 1972. During the academic year
1968-69, he was a Fellow of the Foreign Policy Studies Program of
The Brookings Institution.

Dr. Fisher received his M.A. and Ph. D. degrees in international
relations from the Johns Hopkins School of Advanced International
Studies. He is the author of "Enforcing Export Quota Commodity
Agreements: The Case of Coffee, " which appeared in the 1971 Harvard
Journal of International Law.